4

MEASURING THE PERFORMANCE OF THE PUBLIC POSTAL SERVICE PROVIDER IN GERMANY

Heinz Hofmann

1. Introduction

Measurement of service quality in the reserved section of postal services has become a major topic of the debate on postal policies. Some of the origins of this subject can be related to the fact that quality measurement is (i) a political postulate (most prominently formulated in the EC-Greenbook on postal policies) *and* (ii) a practical activity taking place in a number of countries. Some of its appeal might also lie in the fact that as a task practical *and* technical-scientific challenges are implied: It is neither non trivial practically to organize and manage a measurement system nor to do so on solid scientific grounds.

Compared to other, more innovative countries, Germany was relatively late in introducing quality measurements in postal services. In early 1993, however, Germany joined the group of countries running independent measurement systems, and, just like its predecessors, *end-to-end delivery time* is taken as single indicator of quality in the reserved section of postal services. There are certainly other, and perhaps even more indicative, quality measures. (See section 5 below.) A common feature of the systems presently established, however, is the more or less exclusive measurement of service quality in terms of delivery time. While the new German system is no exception to this rule, there are also some distinguishing features. One is lying in the status of the executing institution: The system which will be presented in the following is *not* directly or indirectly run by the national postal service or a contracted enterprise- it is a system established for and by the *regulator*. This setup leaves it unavoidable to shed some light on the institutional background of the measurement system.

2. Institutional Background

With the postal reform of 1989, the operational and regulatory functions of Posts and Telecommunications have been separated, leaving operations to three government-owned enterprises, DBP Telekom, DBP Postdienst, and DBP Postbank. [1] The regulatory functions are being observed by the Federal Ministry of Posts and Telecommunications. For the execution of a number of regulatory tasks, the Federal Ministry makes use of two subordinate institutions, (i) the Federal Approvals Office for Telecommunications and (ii) the Federal Office for Posts and Telecommunications (BAPT). The latter institution carries out postal quality measurements on behalf of the Federal Ministry.

The BAPT is a relatively large institution with headquarters in Mainz and 55 regional offices distributed over the entire area of the Federal Republic, according to the existing infrastructure and population density. The responsibilities of BAPT, which are largely related to the telecommunications sector, include: (i) licensing (and monitoring) of trunked mobile radio networks and of countrywide paging networks; (ii) licensing of wired telecommunication installations, radio installations, and certain types of electrical appliances; (iii) standardization, definition of type approval requirements (on the basis of technical specifications, standards, test procedures, and administrative provisions), technical regulations (definition of transmission parameters, emmission, and immunity limits, etc.), accreditation of test laboratories; (iv) frequency management and monitoring of radio frequencies (routine monitoring of transmitters, localization of sources of interference, detection of stations operated illegally).

These mainstream responsibilities of BAPT are predominantly technical in character. There are also, however, some organizational units entrustred with tasks of the economic-statistical type. In order to provide the regulator (i.e., the Federal Ministry) with information and data describing the structures and developments of postal and telecommunication markets, sections have been established within BAPT responsible for the observation of the telecommunication markets, as well as the postal and postal banking markets. It is the market observation section of BAPT (postal and postal banking) where the regulator's quality monitoring system has been conceptualized and where the system's central operational functions are being carried out.

3. The Structure of the System

3.1. What Is Being Measured and What Is Not ?

The fact that it is a regulator's system with central functions being allocated to a relatively small organizational unit (which is also entrusted with a number of other tasks and projects in the field of market observation) is not without effect on the dimension and the organization of the system. The first consequence is that the measurements are *not* aiming at producing operational and management information, for instance in the sense of identifying local/regional or organizational weak points and subsequent operational improvements. Briefly: we want to know *how*

1 ""DBP" stands for "Deutsche Bundespost" (German Federal Posts). The postal service provider is DBP Postdienst."

well the postal service is working, not *how*. This approach should correspond to the views and interests of the customer. Secondly, the system is being built up in a stepwise process, with restrictions to be gradually lifted and with exchangeable test modules. If, for instance, one test item, say, handwritten versus machine-typed adresses on the envelopes, should show no significant differences in test results, the test item can be dropped for a certain period of time and another one included. Another effect (of very limited personal and financial resources) is that sacrifices have to be made with respect to (i) the regional breakdown of results and (ii) the overall scope of test items included in the measurement procedures.

Having these basic conditions in mind, the principles and main features of the regulator's quality measurement system in Germany can be summarized as follows:

- based on test mail;
- carried out by an independent institution;
- end-to-end measurement;
- publication of results;
- continuity and permanence of measurements;
- full area coverage;
- consolidation of results in terms of
  - (i) percent rates of delivery in one, two, three....etc. days after mailings (D+1 and "tail");
  - (ii) mean delivery time in days;
  - (iii) maximum delivery time in days (letters reach receivers with a probability of 99 % within x days).

While these features meanwhile have become well accepted criteria for an adequate measurement of delivery performance, there is also a number of restrictions most of which are going to be lifted as the extension of the system proceeds. One temporary limitation is that, for the time being, measurements of delivery time are restricted to *"Standard Letters"* with a weight limit of 20 g. This means that testing relates to roughly three quarters of the total real mail volume within the core section of reserved services. Inclusion of other weights and formats according to the new tariff structure of the DBP Postdienst is planned for the second half of 1994 as a stable distribution pattern of real mail flows has emerged.[2]

Another temporary restriction is that so far measurements relate to *private Mail* only. For our test purposes, we define private mail as mail which carries a *stamp* and which is either dropped into a mail box or delivered to a post office. It is either destined for another (private) delivery address or for a P.O.Box address, the latter representing "business" on the receiving end. The BAPT system includes tests of

2 "The new structure of fully tariffed letter services (valid since April 1st, 1993) includes four weight/format related "basic products": (i) "Standard Letter" - weight: up to 20 g; format: up to 235x125x5 mm; (ii) "Compact Letter" - up to 50 g; up to 235x125x10 mm; (iii) "Large Letter" - up to 500g; up to 353x250x20 mm; (iv) "Maxi Letter" - up to 1000g; up to 353x250x50 mm."

differences in delivery time between delivery and P.O.Box addresses. Business mail, in contrast is often *metered* and generally delivered to a post office in the afternoon/early evening hours and, of course, also destined for house delivery or P.O.Box addresses. The type of *receiving address* (house delivery address or P.O.Box) seems to be of secondary importance for the definition of both types of mail. Differences in delivery time- if any -tend to be caused by procedures and habits at the front end of the service chain and not—as our investigations suggest—on the receiving end.

Our definition of private and business mail draws from a survey of the "mailing habits and practices" of public institutions and private enterprises which a market research consultant carried out for BAPT in 1993. According to the survey results, the majority of businesses follow private mailing patterns: They stamp their letters and drop them into a mail box or at the post office. In that respect, the test design also includes business mail elements. The greater part of the mail *volume*, however, is metered and delivered to a post office in the afternoon/early evening hours. Computer metering (as mode of franking) and collection by the Postal Service (as mode of delivery) still are of minor importance.

Inclusion of business mail according to the above definition and mailing pattern is also scheduled for 1994. So far, however, we have no convincing indication with respect to statistically significant differences in delivery time between both types of mail. A first test of 1000 private and business letter pairs gave no indication of delivery time differences. BAPT is presently conducting a second paired test on a larger scale and with modified procedures. Results are being expected for the end of June.

While the concept provides for a stepwise extension of the system and a gradual removal of limitations, there certainly are permanent restrictions as well. One is that the system will confine itself to the investigation into the delivery time of *domestic* mail only. International mail is and will remain excluded. Another permanent limitation will be the concentration on the *core section of the postal monopoly*. In other words, direct mail, a potential candidate for liberalization of the postal service markets, is not going to be part of the system. These limitations should also be applicable to most of the end-to-end measurement systems so far established within the European Union. A difference, however, between the conceptually leading and well established systems on the one hand and the BAPT system on the other, lies in the approach and detail of the regionalization of the test results, an aspect which might be interpreted as a limitation of the latter system and which deserves some elaboration.

3.2. Regionalization

The pattern of regionalization of the established end-to-end measurement systems reflects the regional organization and structures of postal operations. Results published by regional categories, therefore, are for instance classified by "postal districts, areas, or zones" or other regional units denominated in postal terms. One can assume that the classification of results according to postal categories is related to the (triple) function of providing information to customer, regulator, *and* management. The level of regional detail of the results made available to the public may vary from country to country. Internal management information, however, e.g., for the purpose of identifying operational weak points at the local/regional level, requires a high degree of regional disaggregation. In order to produce statistically valid information in a deep regional/local breakdown of postal organization, high volumes of test mail are indispensable.

BAPT's regionalization pattern does not follow the organization and structures of postal operations. There is no need to do so because the system is not required to produce management information for operational improvement, nor do we -as an outside institution- dispose of in depth knowledge of the details of postal organization. More importantly, however, test mail in the order of magnitude of, say, 700,000 to one million or more letters is not compatible with our limited resources. Thus, a regionalization pattern had to be found which, as far as test volumes are concerned, can be accommodated by the given resources and which, at the same time, still produces useful information to both customer and regulator.

The starting point of BAPT's regionalization approach is the notion (and the customer's perception) that mail is being sent and received in *communities,* the local units of residence, business headquarters, etc. of postal customers. Communities, of course, vary in size and structural characteristics, and mail being sent between them has to travel a wide range of distances. It can be assumed that the time it takes for a letter to reach its addressee is to a great extent determined by the respective types of communities at the starting and the receiving end, and by the distance the letter has to travel. The 16,132 communities, for instance, of the Federal Republic of Germany are being classified by the Federal Research Institute for Regional Geography and Regional Planning into 19 spatial-structural types. The matrix of distances between them produces values between less than one and 900 km. Measurements of postal delivery times obviously cannot cover all single communities, nor all spatial-structural community types nor a detailed classification of distances. Reduction is indispensable to make the system operational.

In the regional concept of our measurements, a formalized "if..then"-procedure is applied to reduce the 19 community types to three: big cities, medium sized towns, and rural communities. Similarly, distances are being classified into short (up to 100 km), medium (100 to 300 km), and long (more than 300). The combination of these community types and ranges of distances constitutes the skeleton of the regional concept: Three types of mailing communities (start end) and three types of communities at the receiving end result in nine strata of mail each of which can travel a short, medium, or long distance so that there are 27 basic strata by which delivery times (in terms of D+1-rates and differences thereof) are being evaluated. Two additional strata provide for information on delivery times of intra-mail within big cities and medium sized towns. Provisions are also made to investigate possible differences in delivery times of letters (i) having a hand-written versus a machine typed address; (ii) going to a delivery address versus a P.O.Box, and (iii) being dropped into a mail box versus delivery to a Post Office.

The type of information the customer and the regulator are getting according to this regionalization pattern is the expectation (in terms of percent probability) that a postal customer can have for a letter to reach its destination within one day when, for example,

(i) the mailing community (start end) is a rural community, and
(ii) the destination is an address in a big city, and
(iii) the letter has to travel over a long distance.

This level of detail is established separately for both the Old and the New Federal States.

On the aggregate level, as a consequence of the peculiarity of the German unification, apart from the grand total for Germany, results are shown for mail flows (i) within the Old Federal States (ex FRG), (ii) from Old to New Federal States (ex GDR), (iii) from New to Old Federal States, and (vi) within New Federal States. The detailed and aggregate classification of results can be produced with adequate statistical accuracy by an overall test volume of 250,000 to 300,000 letters. The key words "statistical accuracy" and "test volume" connect to another important topic of any measurement system of postal delivery performance: the sampling procedure.

3.3. Sampling

BAPT's measurement system includes more than 1400 (private) house delivery and P.O.Box addresses in about 770 destination communities, being classified by big cities, medium sized towns, and rural communities. Mailing (on the front end of the postal service chain) takes place in 660 communities (classified by the same categories). Mailings are based on a complex routing plan being designed to serve the information interests of the system (29 strata; aggregate results) and to provide the statistical accuracy desired. As far as the latter task is concerned, statistical accuracy for the 29 individual strata can relatively easy be established by making sure that each cell is furnished with an adequate number of samples (test letters). This number is determined by (i) the degree of accuracy desired and (ii) the relationship between "p" and "q", i.e., respective coefficients for letters complying with delivery in one day ($D+1=p$), and those not complying with it ($D+>1=q$). For a confidence level of 95 % and an accuracy of ± 0.025, the required sample size (n) can approximatively be determined by the formula

$$n \geq \frac{1.96^2 \times p \times q}{0.025^2}.$$

If, for instance, $D + 1$ (p) in a certain stratum or cell is or is expected to be at least 75 % (q=25%), the minimum number of test letters required to establish the statistical accuracy postulated is $n \geq 1153$. Having established quarterly evaluation and publication intervals, BAPT in its test organization is making sure that each individual stratum is furnished with 1000 to 1200 samples quarterly. This volume ensures in most cases that the desired statistical accuracy is exceeded. In strata of low $D + 1$ (p) rates, an extension of the confidence interval has to be accepted.

Things are getting more difficult when it comes to determining aggregate results of the postal delivery performance tests. It has become a well accepted postulate of the methodological discussion of quality measurements that test mail flows have to proportionally reflect real main streams. The basis for practically complying to this requirement is that regionalization of the established systems follow postal operational structures and denominations, which are also the fundament of statistical inquiry into mail flows in the framework postal statistics. BAPT's approach of regionalization is different, having established the community level as the basic local unit. Postal statistics, however, are not available by communities, at least not in any classification by type of community. In order to break this statistical data deadlock, the assumption has been made that there is a proportional relationship between the volumes of mail flows and the volumes of (potential) postal customers, i.e., the population, in the mailing (front end) *and* the destination communities.

Taking proportionality between population and the generation of mail as a basic model assumption and disposing of the required data base (population, distances), each and every individual pair of possible mail flows between the 16,132 communities of Germany ($16{,}132^2$ flows from source to target community) can be allocated to 27 strata of inter-community and two strata of intra-community mail flows (intra big cities and intra medium sized towns; intra-rural community mail has been excluded). In each stratum, the product of population in the source community and population in the target community is cumulated over each community pair falling into the respective stratum. Division by the square of Germany's total population results in a probability distribution for a real letter to fall into one of the 29 strata. These probabilities which had to be established for the four aggregate mailstreams mentioned above (West-West; West-East; East-West; East-East), constitute the *weights* to be applied to each individual measurement result per stratum in order to arrive at aggregate results. For the time being, a test volume in the order of magnitude of 250,000 letters annually is sufficient to serve the information requirements with adequate statistical accuracy.

3.4. Organization and Practical Procedures

BAPT includes of 55 regional branch offices all of which are included in the measurement system. The high degree of regional presence is a pre-condition for the existence of a regulator's system and a crucial cost saving element. Each branch office- average staff number is about 40 -is looking after its responsibilities within certain, defined district boundaries. The 55 branch office districts cover the entire area of the Federal Republic. Thus, there is no problem in allocating the 660 mailing (source) communities which had been drawn at random, to a respective branch office.

The generation of the test mail is taking place in the branch offices. Each branch office has a detailed plan, defining the daily mailing task in terms of

- how many letters have to be sent,

- from which source community (type of source community) within the district,
- to which target communities.

The plan also includes directions (i) to drop the test mail into a mail box or deliver it to a Post Office, (ii) to provide which envelopes with a machine typed and which with a hand-written address, and (iii) to send which letters to house delivery addresses and which to P.O.Boxes. Upon delivery of the test mail into a mail box or to a Post Office, the date, time and other data are registered on a separate form; these data are later entered into a branch office computer. Test mailings are taking place every work day (five days per week) over the entire year, including holiday periods.

Each mailing branch office "corresponds" with a number of selected target branch offices. Of course, only a small portion of the test letters is directed to the (P.O.Box) addresses of the target branch offices themselves. The majority of the test mail is going to the private (house delivery) addresses of the branch office staff. At present, we have more than 1400 voluntary BAPT participants in 770 communities. The relatively high number of target communities shows that the community of work place and the community of residence are not the same for a great portion of BAPT staff. In fact, target communities are scattered in short and large distances around 56 regional centers (55 branch offices plus headquarters in Mainz), so that, with respect to both source and target communities, a high degree of area coverage is obtained. Also, there is no correlation between the principle of selection of source communities (random) and of target communities (voluntary participation with a given address) on the one hand and the objective of the sample measurements on the other: finding out about postal service performance.

Upon receipt of a test letter, the envelope is opened and the date of receipt as well as the date of the postmark is entered on the test form. On the next work day, the test letter is handed over in the respective branch office for data entry. The system includes both manual and a large number of program consistency checks to assure maximum of accuracy of data entry. In the course of a month, the data entered from the mailing forms and those entered from the test letters, accumulate to files which we call "Monthly Data File Mailings" and "Monthly Data File Receipts." On the 20th day of each month, the branch offices transfer the monthly files of the preceeding month to BAPT headquarters in Mainz. Here, the merging of the data, manual and automatic data editing, as well as the subsequent evaluation, take place.

Evaluations are based on customized software, allowing for great flexibility of data screening and of defining the conditions and characteristics of aggregation. The fundament of aggregation by whatever charcteristic or classification is the delivery time of the letters in days, which is being calculated as the difference between the date of mailing and the date of receipt of the test letter. The program first calculates a "D+x original," which corresponds to the aforementioned difference without any further considerations. Should the period "D+x original" be greater than one day and include a Sunday or a public holiday, the result is corrected correspondingly, i.e., in most cases "D+x original" is reduced by one, resulting in

"D+x corrected." Should "D+x corrected" be greater than one, this provisional result goes through two more checks, before "D+x final" is reached, which is the delivery time result, which the aggregations are based on. To begin with the second (and final) check, "D+x manual" was introduced just to provide at least the theoretical possibility of manual corrections in very individual peculiar cases. Given the enormous number of data to be dealt with, so far no use has been made of this feature. The stage after "D+x corrected" (and before "D+x manual") relates to checks taking care of "unfair" mailing conditions, e.g., hours of mailing too late to expect and demand next day delivery. A brief description of what we call "postal day checks" concludes this section on organization and procedures.

The program feature "Postal Day" opens a screen with a sequence of criteria describing mailing circumstances that might or might not be considered unfair to expect next day delivery of the letter to the addressee. (See table 1.) Ticking the answer boxes defines a set of conditions that result in automatic reduction of "D+x corrected" (by one day) should a record (test letter) comply with the conditions set. The feature is designed flexibly so that "scenarios" can be created, opening the possibility of carrying out evaluation runs under various "postal day scenarios." The criteria relate to the following mailing circumstances:

Table 1

Mail Box Delivery	Post Office Delivery
End of Postal Day .... hrs	End of Postal Day .... hrs
Mailing after end of postal day No further collection this day	Mailing after end of postal day
Mailing after postal day Further collection this day	Mailing before end of postal day
Mailing before end of postal day No further collection this day	Next collection after end of postal day
Mailing before end of postal day Next collection after end of postal day	
Date of next collection is after date of mailing	
No information on next collection Mailing before end of postal day	
No information on next collection Mailing after end of postal day	

Each criterion has response boxes allowing for positive or negative answers as to whether or not to (i) correct and/or (ii) evaluate the record in question.

The most appropriate procedure would be to establish a consensus postal day-scenario that has been agreed upon between regulator, customer organizations, and the postal service. So far, however, a consensus scenario is non existant.

4. Measurement Results

BAPT started the operation of its measurement system in March 1993. The publication of results a couple of months later is the first of its kind in Germany, being based on external, independent, end-to end test mail measurements. End-to-end measurements starting in this period of time have to take two German peculiarities into consideration: One is the still existing differences in the circumstances of life in the Old and in the New Federal States (West and East Germany) which also relate to postal structures. A second aspect is that as of July 1, 1993, a new system of postal area codes has become effective. Instead of having a 4-digit postal code for each community, the new 5-digit numbering system exhibits a considerably deeper regional/local breakdown of postal areas, in some cases covering just one street or parts of a street in a big city. Also there are separate postal codes for house delivery addresses, P.O.Box addresses, and for "large customers" of the DBP Postdienst. Thus, one large customer can have up to three postal codes and a customer having both a house delivery address and a P.O.Box has two postal codes.

The DBP Postdienst used to claim that 90 % of the fully tariffed letters in Germany reach their addressee one day after mailing of the letter. As was the experience in other countries, delivery results based on end-to-end measurements, however, show that delivery performance has not yet reached the standard that had been previously assumed.

Table 2 shows average D+1 rates, mean delivery time, and maximum delivery time for the first quarter 1994 and for the four month-period preceeding and following the date of validity of the new postal area code system. The results

Table 2. Average Measurement Results of Selected Periods of 1993 and 1994

Period Category	Unit	Germany Gr. Total	Intra West G.	From West to East G.	From East to West G.	Intra East G.
March to June 1993						
D+1	%	76.9	84.5	65.4	64.1	59.2
Mean Del.Time	days	1.29	1.18	1.47	1.47	1.57
Max.Del.Time	days	3	3	4	5	5
July to November 1993						
D+1	%	79.7	83.6	75.0	71.9	69.9
Mean Del.Time	days	1.25	1.20	1.31	1.36	1.37
Max.Del.Time	days	3	3	3	4	3
January to March 1994						
D+1	%	81.7	84.7	80.9	74.0	71.6
Mean Del.Time	days	1.22	1.18	1.24	1.31	1.32
Max.Del.Time	days	3	3	3	3	3

indicate performance differences of mail delivery within West Germany and postal streams within East Germany, as well as between East and West Germany. It is also obvious, however, that the gap is getting narrower.

5. Outlook

Quality measurement systems are supposed to constitute an information basis for the customer and for political *quality regulation.* The "raison d'être" of quality regulation and quality measurement is that the prohibition of market entry calls for a substitute of the "regulatory" functions of competition. The substitute function of quality measurement and regulation becomes even more valid as postal service quality, in contrast to most other services, is not particularly *transparent* to the customer. Much of this lack of transparency is due to the fact that there are two "customers" involved, one at the front and one at the receiving end of the service chain, and that in most cases there is no communication between them about if, when, and how a letter sent has reached its addressee.

Making postal service quality transparent through quality measurement has to take into account that quality is *multi-dimensional.* Thus, it is certainly not exhaustive to have service quality be represented by the single indicator timeliness of delivery. Surveys conducted among postal customers in Germany, for instance, showed as a result that the non occurrence of losses and of damages to letters rank higher in customer's values than speediness. While these facets of service quality relate to the service production chain, there are other aspects related to the "interface" of postal service and customer which can also show various degrees of quality or lack of quality. Interface related aspects are represented by indicators of (i) access to services (pre sales), (ii) counter services,and (iii) after sales services (services in case of complaints, losses etc.).

It is in front of this background that BAPT has entrusted a research consultant with a survey on the scope of postal quality measurement in the member states of the European Union. The results of this research project are supposed to provide a basis for further discussion and consideration of extending the current measurement system.

The project, which also covered measurement systems in the United States and Sweden, has just been completed and the conceptual framework as well as the empirical survey of practical measurement activities in the countries included resulted in a number of useful quality indicators related to both the service production chain and the various facets of the customer/postal service interface. The discussion process of which conclusions to draw from the project and to extend quality measurement by which indicators has just begun so that no concrete statement can be made at this point.

An extension of the present measurement system will, of course, only be materialized as far as limited resources will permit to do so. In any case, multi dimensional measurement systems are expensive, and the more refined and facetted measurements are, the higher the costs. Thus, the relation of costs and benefits has to be strictly observed. Public administrations using taxpayer's money are under increasingly critical observation; and the costs of postal service quality measurements become more likely to be exposed to criticism and be confronted with the costs of tackling other important topics and tasks the more expensive and elaborate a monitoring system is. Given these constraints, it is helpful that some infrastructural indicators of access to postal services (e.g., collection frequencies of mail boxes; inhabitants per Post Office, mail box, counter; average distances, etc.) do not require cost intensive measurements, but the collection and evaluation of available statistical data.

Another guideline of future discussions and decisions will be the exclusion of *subjective quality indicators*, which are not the kind of data quality regulation should be based on. The survey results have shown that indicators of customer satisfaction are often inconsistent and in contradiction to objective performance data. Subjective indicators re-introduce the substitution of fact with feeling, which was tried to overcome by establishing the present measurement systems.

5

MEASURING QUALITY OF SERVICE OF INTERNATIONAL MAIL[1]

Thomas Grzesiak
Thomas Reenberg

1. Introduction

Global economic and regulatory forces in the message market are creating an environment where the customer has an increasing amount of leverage. Direct competition from private sector firms and indirect competition from electronic communications are enabling the customer to substitute away from traditional postal services to other products. A corresponding push for greater deregulation of the marketplace around much of the world is increasing customer flexibility still further. As a result, today's customer is placing pressure on all market suppliers by requiring constant improvement in quality of service, increased tailoring of service, and greater cost effectiveness.

Posts are responding to the pressure, recognizing that customer-oriented innovations have become a requirement, without being a guarantee, for successful business operations at both the domestic and international levels. Posts are committed to providing greater levels of efficiency, reliability, and accountability than ever before. At the international level, posts realize that as borders become increasingly porous, the focus on achieving even shorter and even more consistent delivery times between nations will be heightened. Posts around the world are rallying in an attempt to improve service performance while containing, and in many instances cutting, operational costs. An important first step toward improving quality of service for the customer is measuring quality of service. Only then can the relative strengths and weaknesses of an entire system be understood, problem areas identified, and remedial actions properly taken.

This paper describes the requirements of an effective quality of service measurement system and the Price Waterhouse methodology that currently is being used

1 The authors would like to thank Mike DeMarco and Elisabeth Lansner of Price Waterhouse for their creativity and assistance in preparing this paper.

for the first externally conducted, large-scale international mail measurement system: The IPC Unipost Quality of Service External Monitoring Study. The methodology also has been used effectively in several Price Waterhouse domestic mail measurement systems.

2. Quality of Service Measurement

2.1. Requirements for Quality of Service Measurement

EC Commission officials took note of the increasing needs of the postal customer in the 1992 "Green Paper on the Development of the Single Market for Postal Services." According to the authors of the Green Paper, "...customer needs are evolving, probably more rapidly than in the past." These customers need an efficient, affordable, and universally accessible postal service that will not generate market distortions. For example, if large mailers in sectors such as publishing, financial services, mail order, and advertising can not reach certain regions of the market effectively because of poor postal service, opportunities are lost. The would-be recipients and potential consumers of these goods and services miss opportunities as well, while suffering a disadvantage relative to consumers in high performance areas.

To ensure a viable postal sector that provides equal service to all customers within the Union, the Commission proposes evolutionary steps toward:

- Increased market liberalization;
- Increased harmonization of the independently developed regulatory and operational rules of the post, particularly with regard to widely varying universal service definitions; and
- Development of common quality of service benchmarks.

Liberalization and harmonization are expected to increase the efficiency and reliability of postal cross-border service that the Commission currently rates as inadequate for the desired growth of the Union by increasing both choice and consistency for the customer. However, eventual improvements can only be quantified through quality of service measurements that monitor customer experience with postal service over time and as changes are made. Quality of service measurement using common benchmarks will ultimately benefit both the customers and posts of the Union by pinpointing problem areas that can then be addressed by the posts to improve customer service and overall postal operations.

Although no formal, large-scale system for performance measurement existed at the international level until this year, several surveys assessing the quality of cross-border service suggest that the average performance of the posts is inadequate. At the same time, significant variability in performance by the posts is perceived.

Based upon these shortfalls in service performance and the need for improved customer focus, EC officials concluded in the Green Paper that, "The most important harmonization actions for quality of service are the settings of Community standards and the implementation of a single community measuring system."

The Commission identified requirements for quality of service measurement that include:

- A single, uniform, and reliable system for monitoring delivery service performance within the union;
- A focus on cross-border delivery service performance; and
- End-to-end measurement capabilities.

2.2. Response of Posts to Customers

In 1993, IPC Unipost, a corporation formed by 20 of the largest postal administrations in the world, began to take measures to improve cross-border delivery patterns. As part of its "Plan 93," IPC Unipost awarded Price Waterhouse a contract to perform the largest ever, continuous international postal quality of service monitoring system for its members. IPC Unipost envisioned a cooperative system with a common, universal methodology that would permit comparison of actual performances across borders. The system meets the proposed requirements of the Commission for cross-border quality of service.

Price Waterhouse designed and tested the end-to-end external monitoring system for IPC Unipost during the second half of 1993, and actual operations began on January 1 of this year. Currently the system is monitoring only first-class international mail between the 20 IPC Unipost countries. However, the flexible system design allows for the addition of both more products and more countries.

In quality of service measurement for posts in both North America and Price Waterhouse Europe, Price Waterhouse operates five other major quality of service measurement systems. In this paper, we discuss the fundamental underpinnings of quality of service measurement that form the basis for our international and domestic mail measurement systems.

2.3. Benefits of Quality of Service Measurement

At the domestic level, many posts already use outside consultants to operate domestic mail measurement systems. These systems reflect the growing commitment to quality among the posts by allowing for outside, independent contractors to measure performance and report those results to their customers. As noted in the Green Paper, "Customers may have more confidence in measurement schemes carried out independently."

Quality of service measurement systems are much more than cleverly orchestrated public relations devices. A properly executed quality of service measurement system benefits postal administrations and customers in a number of ways

- Management can replace feeling with fact;
- Management can pinpoint specific areas for quality of service improvement;
- Management can measure the results of subsequent quality of service improvement-based actions; and
- Customers have more faith in service and improvement efforts.

3. Quality of Service Measurement Fundamental Approach

The description of the Price Waterhouse fundamental approach to quality of service measurement is divided into nine sections, described below. Each of the sections describes a group of activities and decisions in the development and operation of a quality of service measurement system.

3.1. System Overview

The international mail measurement system designed, installed, and now being operated by Price Waterhouse for IPC Unipost is an end-to-end measurement system. The system measures mail from the time it is posted by the customer until the time that it arrives at its final destination. Only an end-to-end system can generate results that represent actual customer experience and therefore is superior to any other type of system. As the Green Paper notes, "It seems to be generally acknowledged that end-to-end measurement is the only effective system."

Price Waterhouse developed a statistical design using real-world mail characteristics as the basis for the study. Local Price Waterhouse offices manage a network of trained mail droppers to induct a representative sample of letters into the international mail flow at approved times. The test letters are received by a statistically representative group of business and private receivers. The droppers and receivers record information pertaining to their activities and relay the data back to their local Price Waterhouse offices. The local Price Waterhouse offices then use our state-of-the-art global electronic communications and data transfer system to relay this information to the Price Waterhouse Control Centre. At the Control Centre, the data is extensively checked and validated and then summarized for reporting.

The Price Waterhouse system is illustrated in figure 1.

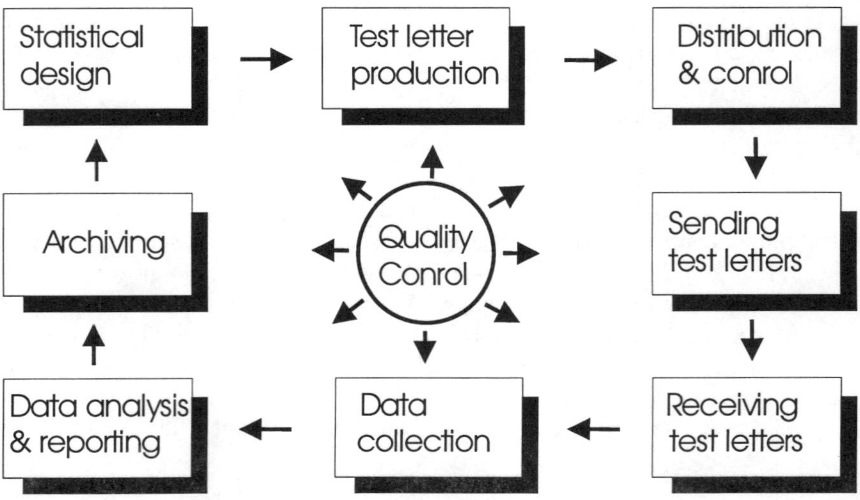

Figure 1

At the center of the Price Waterhouse mail measurement methodology is Quality Control. Effective quality control is the key to successful mail measurement. We apply quality control procedures throughout all activities in our system, using the international standard for quality programmes, EN 29001, as a guideline.

The overall system, including all computer systems and procedural elements is created based on the Price Waterhouse Systems Management Methodology/Systems Development Process. The approach identifies a controlled methodology for analysis, design, building, testing, and implementing the system. Well-defined steps and checkpoints throughout ensure the quality of the final system.

3.2. Statistical Design

The statistical design is the theoretical underpinning of any quality of service system and evolves around the requirements of the posts, or in the case of our current international system, IPC Unipost and its member posts.

3.2.1. Study Requirements

Posts must determine the value that will be added from measuring particular mail streams and particular mail products, as well as the amount of statistical precision that will be needed for the measurements. The study characteristics initially decided on during system development include: products to be measured; frequency of testing; type of test product to be used; time duration of measurement; and methodology for collecting design information from postal administrations.

Posts must decide what mail products will be tested and for how many days, months, or years the products will be tested. For example, in our study for IPC Unipost, only first-class mail currently is being measured. However, any other mail product can be measured, as best evidenced by our work for the U.S. Postal Service where we now measure first-class, second-class, and third-class mail.

Regardless of the product being measured, we believe that the best quality of service measurement systems test mail continuously. First, it is well understood that seasonal trends exist in both international and domestic mail flow. A system that monitors service across the entire year will generate a better representation of the quality and consistency of the service the customer receives. At the same time, our experience conducting mail measurement systems has shown that continuous monitoring throughout the year not only provides the most representative results for the posts, but also generates greater cost efficiencies through better control of the network of mail droppers and receivers.

Another important decision involves what type of test product will be inducted into the quality of service measurement system. Pieces can be actual mail or fabricated test mail. Although it has been argued that actual mail pieces will more closely represent reality than fabricated pieces, problems exist that make the sampling of actual mail pieces inappropriate, especially at the international level, but also at the domestic level.

First, for an international study, forming a representative sample is difficult because of the low proportion of international mail relative to domestic mail that exists in the actual mail stream. Second, testing actual mail pieces sacrifices the total end-to-end control of the system that can be generated through the joint usage of test piece production and a dropper network, because the recording of actual piece induction can only be measured feasibly upon postmarking. If pick-up service at homes, neighborhood boxes, or within individual post offices is inconsistent, the measurement results will be distorted, and actual customer experience will not be represented.

Based on the needs of our clients, the test mail sampling technique guaranteed the best possible results. To ensure that test pieces are indistinguishable from actual mail in the international mail stream, it is necessary to understand the characteristics of actual mail and reproduce these characteristics in the test mail.

The overall statistical design of a particular study must satisfy two goals necessary for mail measurement. First, through Sample Design Requirements, we determine what the mail analyzed in the system will look like by identifying important characteristics of the actual mail flow that can then be duplicated for testing. Second, through Precision and Volume Determination, we generate and distribute enough mail pieces to ensure that precision requirements of the post are met and the validity of the system results are ensured. We discuss achieving each of these goals in detail below.

3.2.2. Sample Design Requirements

A sample that accurately represents the population of mail being measured is an essential element of an effective quality of service measurement system. In order to design a proper sample set, the mail population being observed must be well understood both qualitatively and quantitatively. A quality of service measurement system analyzing sample mail pieces in the international stream that are not representative of the actual stream will clearly create problems for the posts. Customer perceptions of postal services, as well as their subsequent choices in the use of postal services, may be altered by inaccurate estimates generated by an inaccurate system.

In the case of an international quality of service measurement system, the sample must accurately mirror the matrix of international mail streams existing between the posts taking part in the study and be large enough to ensure statistical validity. The accuracy of the sample is determined by reflecting real mail characteristics and measuring a sufficient volume of mail to produce precise performance estimates.

The total array of sample design requirements determines what the test mail will look like, how it will be inducted into the mail stream, and who will receive the mail. In each instance, the mail must be created, inducted, and received in proportion to the actual flow of international mail.

3.2.2.1. Mail Characteristics. A decision must be made to determine how the test mail will appear, specifically for the following characteristics: weight categories; formats (length and height of envelope, parcel, etc.); addressing style (by hand or machine); franking methods (stamped or metered); labelling method; and combining the previous five combinations proportionately. Price Waterhouse worked with IPC Unipost and the postal administrations to identify the most prevalent formats used in international mail and the proportions for each weight category, format, addressing style, franking method, and labelling method.

3.2.2.2. User Segments. The mail must be inducted and received in realistic fashion. Considerations include: induction methods (mail box, pick-up, post office); permissible collection days of the week by country; number, location, and type of droppers; number and location of receivers; receiver type (business or private); and permissible delivery days of the week by country. Each receiver in the network is classified as a business or a household. In a destination country, business and household receivers are recruited in proportion to the real mail volume provided by the postal administration.

Rules on dropping and receiving days must be identified as well. In the case of an international quality of service measurement study, these rules are particularly important as variations in Saturday and Sunday delivery and public holidays exist and must be accounted for in the system methodology.

It is vital to know when mail collection and delivery is scheduled in a country. Dropping can only be done on mail collection days, usually excluding Sundays and postal holidays. For mailbox drops, the mail must be inducted before the last pick-up time. At the same time, receivers should not report having received test pieces on non-delivery days such as Sundays or postal holidays.

3.2.2.3. Geographical Coverage. Inherent in these decisions is the determination of geographical coverage that a given system will encompass. A system that is both cost effective and statistically valid will not be able to measure every mail flow existing within a particular nation or group of nations. Therefore, depending on the objective of the measurement system, combinations of origin and destination countries, regions, cities, and rural communities of interest must be chosen. Again, as long as the flow of the sample mail remains proportional to real international mail flow between the different geographical combinations, the results will be valuable.

The study is designed to accomodate two complementary geographical summarizations: regions within a country and size of city within a country.

We begin at the country-to-country level. For each country-to-country mail stream, the origin and destination countries are divided into regions, with each region being served by one exchange office. If a country-to-country mail stream has only one outbound exchange office, the origin country will consist of only one region: the entire country. The same logic applies for single inbound exchange offices. For countries with many exchange offices, the division into regions depends on which exchanges office processes mail to or from the other country. By determining the actual percentages of incoming and outgoing mail volumes for each exchange office, we are able to design a proportionate sample set.

Test mail is sent to and from cities in proportion to real mail volumes. For example, cities with the largest number of businesses and the largest populations tend to both send and receive more mail than rural areas with small business and private populations.

Thus, our test mail is representative of actual mail distribution in all of our countries of origin and destination, postal regions of origin and destination, cities of origin and destination, and rural areas of origin and destination.

3.2.3. Precision and Volume Determination

Once a post has established what, when, and how the mail will be measured, it must define the characteristics of service performance that will be measured and the precision required for these measurements. We can then determine the volume of test letters to use in each mail stream of our study and how to prepare these test letters for release to our "dropper" network. The post must determine: quality of service characteristics to be measured such as percent on-time and average delivery days; assumptions about characteristics - distribution of delivery days and the actual percent on-time; confidence level of measurements - usually 95 percent; confidence range around estimates; time period for reporting - monthly, quarterly, or annually.

Price Waterhouse uses a comprehensive set of software applications to assign droppers and receivers to test letters. The applications store all sample design and sample size parameters in a control table. Test letters are created based on these control table parameters and assigned to droppers and receivers to best utilize these resources.

3.3. Test Letter Production

Test letters are produced most cost effectively by single, centrally controlled printing subcontractors. We have substantial experience working with subcontractors who produce test letters on our behalf and find that the approach can be efficiently managed and generates maximum economies of scale. Price Waterhouse prepares detailed production specifications for the test letter producer to assure the quality of the test letters.

The test letter production process is divided into three phases: (1) defining requirements for test letter inserts and distribution packages; (2) quality control procedures for fabricated test letters; and (3) transportation to scheduled originations.

The test letter producer receives computer discs from Price Waterhouse each week containing all specifications necessary for the production of test letters. Thus, changes in the network of droppers and receivers can be corrected and reflected in the test letters. Inserts are prepared for each test letter. In our international systems, these inserts are printed in the local language of the receiver. The inserts are enclosed in the appropriate envelopes to reflect the required characteristics of the test letter.

Information about the characteristics of each test letter is printed on the corresponding test letter insert. The information enables the test letter producer to cross-check to master lists during the production process and minimize mistakes. Cross-checking is performed in conformity with the internationally accepted standard MIL.STD 105D, and Price Waterhouse requires that the test letter producer provides us with weekly quality control reports. We also conduct random audits and inspections of the test letter production facility.

The test letters are then packaged for our droppers with appropriate documentation of the materials for both the local Price Waterhouse office and the droppers. The documentation for the local office includes a summary of droppers and necessary control data on each dropper. Each dropper receives instructions on entering the mail into the mail stream and mail package and piece identification required for control purposes.

Price Waterhouse and the subcontractor establish a schedule for producing the mail and shipping it to the local Price Waterhouse office. The pick-up and delivery of each package is confirmed and documented.

3.4. Distribution and Control

The local Price Waterhouse offices play a central role in mail distribution and control. The local office is involved in the verification process before the test mail is dispatched to individual droppers. Our system has been designed to ensure both simplicity for the local offices and maximum quality control.

Each local Price Waterhouse office receives a country package every week from the test letter producer. Each country package contains all dropper packages for the following week. The local office verifies the contents of the country package against a copy of a packing list to ensure that all dropper packages have been received.

The same control procedure is repeated at subsequent levels with slight variation to accommodate for large volume. A random sample of dropper packages and test letters are opened and checked against specifications. Discrepancies are immediately reported to the Control Centre.

Only after these controls have been taken can the dropper packages be distributed to the droppers. Following distribution, all dropper package and individual piece specifications are archived at the local office.

3.5. Sending Test Letters

Price Waterhouse frequently uses a centrally coordinated approach that utilizes charitable organizations as a base for our dropper network. In this approach, Price Waterhouse pays the charitable organizations to induct the test mail. When necessary, individual droppers are recruited and paid for their efforts. Each local office uses customized questionnaires to control recruiting and instruction manuals for dropper training.

In the case of the international measurement system, droppers are recruited at the country, region, and city level, again maintaining proportions reflecting real mail flow. Our domestic systems utilize the same general strategy, with all recruiting occurring, of course, within the borders of that country. Droppers are recruited by entry method such as at a post office, mail box, or collection at a business according to real mail flow proportions.

Precise rules must be maintained to ensure the validity of the system. Price Waterhouse must be able to determine when a mailing has occurred and if the mailing has occurred according to plan. Droppers must report induction results to the local Price Waterhouse office. The information then is forwarded electronically to our Control Centre for processing and analysis.

3.6. Receiving Test Letters

Receivers are also recruited, approved through screening, and trained using customized instruction materials. Receivers are recruited to ensure that the distribution of the test mail conforms to actual mail flow proportions. The international system maintains an appropriate number of receivers by destination country, region, and city size. These receivers are divided appropriately among businesses and private citizens.

Precise rules are maintained in the receipt of letters. For example, if a business operates in a country where the post delivers six times a week, including Saturday, that business must be able to receive mail on Saturday and distinguish this mail from that received on Monday.

Receivers document and report receipt results to the local Price Waterhouse operator. The information then is forwarded electronically to our Control Centre for processing and analysis.

3.7. Data Collection

The data collection procedures developed by Price Waterhouse ensure the timely, accurate reporting of induction and receipt information, through a common data collection procedure installed at each local office. Droppers send induction documentation and receivers send received test letters to the local office for data collection and archiving. Data is key entered and then transferred electronically to the Control Centre daily.

Each local office uses the same methodology to screen documentation for completeness and to key enter data. Discrepancies are investigated and reconciled by Price Waterhouse utilizing both manual and computer validation as means of quality control. All collected data is transmitted to the Control Centre.

The central database of test letter information is updated daily with the locally collected data. Automated validation procedures are used to ensure the consistency of the database.

3.8. Data Analysis and Reporting

Through our efforts on domestic and international mail measurement systems, Price Waterhouse has gained extensive experience in analyzing mail measurement data and providing the posts with valuable, high quality reports.

3.8.1. Data Analysis

Price Waterhouse has developed an information management database to analyze the quality of the study in the following areas: test letter production; recruitment of droppers and receivers; performance of droppers and receivers; and data cleaning.

Test letter production is analyzed to ensure that it satisfies the requirements of the statistical design. Whenever necessary, the production is adjusted to conform with requirements.

We perform data analyses measuring both the need for and the performance of droppers and receivers. Dropper compliance with the instruction manual is measured to determine if the dropper inducts the mail in the planned geographic area on the planned date. New droppers are recruited to replace those droppers that fail to comply with instructions.

Receiver performance is measured by the response rate and the proportion of mail received on-time, early, and late. We identify distortions such as "batching," when a reporter receives test letters across a time period but reports receiving all the mail on the same day. Receiver performance reports analyze the percentage of mail each receiver reports. They also summarize the number of pieces receivers report with an unknown receipt date or report as on-time, early, or late according to the defined service standards.

Comparisons of the percentage of mail on-time, early, and late for all receivers in the same local area enable us to gauge receiver performance and eliminate non-performing receivers and their test mail from the study.

Extensive data screening and cleaning procedures are performed prior to report generation. The screening identifies errors and questionable data reported by droppers and receivers. Errors are corrected, and questionable data is removed from the report calculations. A typical screening find might indicate that all pieces in a certain dropper package were received exceptionally early or late or that a given receiver consistently reports a high proportion of early or late mail. If there is any question about the validity of a test letter, it is removed from the study prior to report generation. Reports only include valid, reliable data.

3.8.2. Reporting

In all Price Waterhouse quality of service measurement systems, reports are generated to summarize two key performance figures: the number of days required to deliver test letters, and the number of test letters delivered on-time. In the case of our international system, common methodologies had to be established to develop computation rules for the two figures. Holidays, non-collection, and non-delivery days are not the same across all countries. Service standards vary across and even within particular countries. These and other variations between the countries had to be considered when establishing a system that would be acceptable and valuable to all participating posts.

Price Waterhouse produces reports that provide different levels of information to satisfy different users of the data. Reports for high-level users present a more general overview of the results than reports designed to satisfy the needs of operations managers.

An example of the data Price Waterhouse reports is shown in figure 2.

Route	On-time percen-tage	J+										
		1	2	3	4	5	6	7	8	9	10	Average delivery days
X-Y	40.0±0,9	1.6	17.3	40,0	49.4	64.6	76.4	85.6	92.3	97.0	99.4	5.0

Figure 2

The report line displays the following information:

- Route, or the geographical coverage, such as the inbound and outbound country;
- On-time percentage compared to a service standard and the precision of the estimate;
- Average delivery days based on the computation rule; and
- J+, or the distribution of the percent of test letters delivered within 1,2,...10 days of induction.

3.9. Archiving

Test letters are returned by receivers and archived by local Price Waterhouse offices. The letters are stored for six months and are available for client audits. The letters also help Price Waterhouse correct errors and solve problems at the individual test letter level. For example, proof of cancellation is available on most test letters and can be used to resolve conflicting data in the information management database.

4. Conclusion

Posts around the world realize that a focus on customer needs is the key to success in the message market today. Therefore, continual improvement in quality of service is the key to maintaining and gaining market share in the rapidly changing market of the 1990s and beyond.

Postal customers competing in the fast-paced global economy of today and tomorrow will continually demand shorter and more consistent delivery times of messages. Private competitors in the physical message market and indirect competitors from the rapidly changing and developing telephone, cable television, telefax, and computer markets all pose a threat to the survival of the posts. However, with quality of service measurement as a first step toward better delivery, many posts are showing a readiness and willingness to meet the needs of the customer.

A properly executed quality of service measurement system provides management with precise indicators of problem areas and bottlenecks in the delivery stream and a benchmark to gauge the success of subsequent improvement efforts. At the same time, the results enhance the reputation of the post with customers, the public, and regulators when provided by a reputable, independent and external contractor.

6

POST-APPOINTMENT PREFERENCE SHAPING AND ITS INFLUENCE ON JUDICIAL ANALYSIS OF ECONOMIC REGULATION ISSUES[1]

William E. Kovacic

1. Introduction

1994 marks the 20th anniversary of a formative event in the modern development of law and economics. In 1974, Henry Manne established the Law and Economics Center (LEC) at the University of Miami and laid an important foundation for the ascent of economic analysis as a tool for evaluating and structuring legal rules. The LEC was designed to change the way law schools and economics departments did business, but its intended audience reached beyond the walls of the academy.

Since 1976, the LEC has offered a variety of courses in economics for federal judges in the United States. Resident at the George Mason University School of Law since 1986, the LEC has provided economics courses to over 400 federal judges, including members of the courts of appeals, district courts, bankruptcy courts, and the Court of International Trade. The LEC's basic offerings have included short courses in microeconomics, quantitative methods, antitrust economics, corporate governance, risk, and science and health. Judges who have taken one or more of these courses currently include two members of the United States Supreme Court (Ruth Ginsburg and Clarence Thomas).

From the time of its first courses for federal judges, the LEC's program of instruction for the judiciary has aroused periodic controversy.[2] Critics of the LEC's

---

1 The author is grateful to William Adams, James Campbell,Michael Crew, Nicholas Crew, Andrew Dick, Mario Dunn, Kathryn Fenton, Bruce Kobayashi, John Lott, and Donald O'Hara for many useful discussions, and to Neil Graham for outstanding research assistance. The John M. Olin Foundation and the Sarah Scaife Foundation provided generous financial support for the research for this paper.

2 See Fred Barbash, "Big Corporations Bankroll Seminars For U.S. Judges," *Washington Post*, Jan. 20, 1980, at A1; Fred Barbash, "Judges' Seminars in Fla. Faulted," *Washington Post*, Oct. 4, 1980, at A-7; David Beckwith, "Judges Study Free Market Economics," *Legal Times*, Feb.

judicial instruction programs have argued that the Center seeks to imbue attendees with the policy biases of large corporations and pro-business foundations that provide most of the LEC's operating funds (Alliance for Justice 1993; Mueller 1987; Mueller 1990; Mueller et al. 1988). In a representative statement of this view, Nan Aron, the Executive Director of the Alliance for Justice, has observed that the "funding campaign for legal change" undertaken by sponsors of the LEC and similar programs "has created a legal system where justice is bought and sold just like any other commodity." Aron added that sponsorship of activities such as courses in economics for judges "is not, as its proponents claim, simply about making the law more efficient and fair. Rather, it is designed to make protecting corporate profits and private wealth the cornerstones of our legal system."[3]

This line of criticism commonly assumes that exposure to LEC programs in fact influences attendees to adopt pro-business positions in deciding subsequent cases. If LEC programs significantly influenced judicial preferences concerning economic regulation, such programs would have important implications for judicial decisionmaking. In varying degrees, all legal rules—whether "judge-made" through common law adjudication, or created by statute or administrative regulation—give judges discretion to affect litigation outcomes through their interpretation and application of the rules' key operative terms. Any post-appointment instructional program that materially affected the way in which judges exercised the omnipresent element of discretion would be important. Indeed, the fact of discretion makes the selection of federal judges a closely-watched (and sometimes contentious) process.

The assumption that LEC programs help generate pro-business litigation outcomes rests heavily on anonymous quotations from selected letters that the LEC receives from past judicial participants and excerpts in its promotional literature (Mueller et al. 1988, 5-7). Such comments give little insight into how LEC programs actually affect post-attendance decisionmaking.[4] Relying on a few letters

5, 1979, at 1; Walter Guzzardi, Jr., "Judges Discover the World of Economics," *Fortune* 58 (May 21, 1979).

3 Jay Mathews, "Business Tries to Shape Legal System, Report Says," *Washington Post*, May 19, 1993, at F4.

4 One much-quoted testimonial from a judge who attended an LEC program states that "[a]s a result of my better understanding of the concept of marginal cost, I have recently set aside a $15 million anti-trust verdict." See Mueller et al. (1989, 5). Few quotations in the LEC's promotional literature suggest so direct a causal relationship between the courses and outcomes in later cases. Most correspondents give flattering assessments of LEC courses but do not indicate how such programs influenced future decisionmaking. One LEC brochure quotes a "U.S. District Judge" as saying "I am a great fan of your programs. I have urged all of our new judges to apply. Indeed, these courses have been most helpful to me in a number of cases that I have tried." Another "U.S. District Judge" writes that "I know that all of the judges who attended benefitted tremendously. . . . All too often, federal judges tend to be 'jacks-of-all-trades' and 'masters-of-none.' The opportunity to spend two intense weeks studying law and economics under the outstanding faculty you assembled was marvelous." See Office of Public Affairs and Development, Law and Economics Center, George Mason

screened by the LEC (which presumably omits mention of letters that denigrate its courses) falls short of the systematic review of pre- and post-attendance decision-making behavior of program attendees that would be needed to determine actual effects.[5]

This paper examines the hypothesis that the LEC's post-appointment training programs for federal judges induce attendees to endorse pro-business views in deciding economic regulation cases. It does so by considering the impact of LEC programs on judicial analysis in antitrust cases decided by judges who have taken LEC courses relating to industrial organization economics. The paper focuses on antitrust cases because the federal antitrust statutes give federal judges more discretion than any other system of federal economic regulation (Kovacic 1991; 1993). The meaning of the Sherman Antitrust Act, for example, hinges on the construction of general phrases such as "conspiracy in restraint of trade" and "monopolization."[6] In casting the critical operative provisions of the antitrust statutes in broad, openended terms, Congress deliberately delegated to the judiciary a crucial role in elaborating general standards of business conduct and specific operational criteria for applying them. In effect, Congress authorized the courts to create a federal common law of competition principles (Freyer 1989; Sklar 1988, 117-54).

This expansive delegation of decisionmaking authority gives federal judges considerable power to determine litigation outcomes through the manner in which they interpret and apply the general commands of the antitrust statutes. This elevates the importance of the judge's policy preferences. To the extent that LEC programs seek to encourage judges to focus on the efficiency implications of legal rules (as opposed to "fairness" effects) and apply "Chicago School" economics, the payoff from post-appointment preference shaping activities would appear to be larger in antitrust than in most other areas of federal economic regulation, where statutes or regulations impose comparatively greater limits on the judge's discretion to use economic analysis in formulating business conduct standards.

This paper approaches the subject as follows. The second section more fully describes the hypothesis that LEC programs succeed in indoctrinating judges to exculpate corporate defendants. The third section presents conceptual problems raised by the assumption that exposure to LEC programs necessarily predisposes judges to adopt pro-business positions more frequently or emphatically in post-at-

---

University School of Law, *Law and Economics Center* (undated promotional brochure) (on file with the author).

5 Organizations that sponsor continuing professional education programs frequently recite testimonials from past program attendees in their promotional literature. In the past fifteen years, I have read hundreds of promotional brochures that trumpet past successes or tout new programs. I recall seeing no testimonials that criticized the sponsor's previous programs, nor do I anticipate seeing a conference announcement that quotes a past attendee as saying something along the lines of "This program wasted my time and money."

6 15 U.S.C. §§ 1 and 2.

tendance cases. The fourth section describes qualitative evidence from court of appeals antitrust decisions that suggests caution in readily accepting the hypothesis that LEC programs generate pro-business judicial decisions. The paper concludes by describing possible empirical approaches for evaluating more precisely the capacity of post-appointment training programs to mold judicial preferences concerning economic regulation and alter litigation outcomes.

2. The "Justice Bought and Sold" Hypothesis

The LEC's donor pool consists mainly of Fortune 500 companies and not-for-profit foundations ordinarily associated with conservative economic policy preferences. As commonly used in debates about LEC programs, the term "conservative" denotes a strong taste for the recognition and protection of private property rights and limited government regulatory intervention in the economy.[7] The conservative preference-shaping hypothesis posits that corporate and foundation donors who contribute to LEC judicial instruction programs do so to induce judges to embrace their policy views and render decisions that favor their interests in litigated disputes. In antitrust cases, the conservative preference shaping hypothesis assumes that LEC donors want judges to issue decisions that disfavor plaintiffs (i.e., public enforcement agencies and private plaintiffs) and minimize exposure for corporate defendants.[8] Means to this end in antitrust litigation would include adopting permissive

---

7 For example, the LEC's 1991 contributor list includes the following entities: Abbott Laboratories, Adria Laboratories, Aetna Foundation, Alcoa Foundation, American Cyanamid, Amoco Foundation, Atlantic Richfield, Bell Atlantic, BellSouth, Bethlehem Steel, BFGoodrich, BP America, Bradley Foundation, Chevron, Coca-Cola Foundation, CPC International, Dana Corporation Foundation, R.R. Donnelley & Sons, du Pont, Eastman Kodak Charitable Trust, Ethyl, Exxon, Ford Motor Company Fund, General Electric Foundation, General Mills, General Motors, General Reinsurance, Gilder Foundation, Glaxo, H.J. Heinz Company Foundation, Honeywell, ITT, Kraft General Foods Foundation, Kreible Foundation, Eli Lilly, Thomas J. Lipton Foundation, Philip M. McKenna Foundation, Merck Company Foundation, 3M, Mobil Foundation, Monsanto Fund, Montgomery Ward, NYNEX, Olin Foundation, PepsiCo, Pfizer, PPG Industries Foundation, Proctor & Gamble Fund, Reynolds Metals Company Foundation, Rockwell, Rohm and Haas, Sara Lee, Scaife Foundation, Schering-Plough Foundation, Sears, Roebuck & Co., Starr Foundation, Sunmark Foundation, Textron Charitable Trust, Union Carbide Foundation, USX Foundation, West Publishing, and Xerox. George Mason University School of Law, *Law & Economics Center 1991 Annual Report* 9 (1991).

8 The assumption that large corporations always want judges to apply the antitrust laws narrowly (thus reducing antitrust exposure for corporate defendants) is not always realistic. Large businesses sometimes use the antitrust laws to accomplish various commercial objectives. These include defeating attempted takeovers, avoiding enforcement of disfavored contracts, and recovering overcharges imposed by a cartel of input suppliers. See, e.g., Chicago Professional Sports Ltd. Partnership v. National Basketball Ass'n, 961 F.2d 667 (7th Cir.) (successful effort by the Chicago Bulls professional basketball franchise to use the antitrust laws to challenge the validity of NBA limits on the number of games that may be televised by broadcast superstations) cert. denied, 113 S. Ct. 409 (1992); Marathon Oil Co. v.

liability standards, imposing stringent evidentiary tests, applying rigorous standing and injury screens, and using restrictive formulas to minimize awards of damages and attorneys fees (Kovacic 1991, 59-71).

To analyze the conservative preference-shaping hypothesis, this paper assumes that corporate donors and foundations invest in LEC programs mainly to predispose judges to implement a favored policy agenda. Success in preference shaping could take at least two basic paths. The first is to imbue judges with narrower tastes for government intervention, including more limited antitrust preferences. For example, one could attempt to persuade judges with strong tastes for intervention to accept economic efficiency as the central criterion for deciding antitrust cases and to abandon reliance on nonefficiency social and political considerations.

A second basic approach is to give judges with essentially non-interventionist instincts a better set of tools for analyzing specific cases, persuading colleagues in appellate deliberations, and writing opinions that move doctrine in non-interventionist directions. It is one thing to vote to reject liability in a predatory pricing dispute; it is another to write powerfully reasoned opinions that articulate permissive standards and induce other courts to adopt identical or similar decision-making principles. Many high-impact antitrust opinions of the past fifteen years have been authored by law and economics scholars such as Stephen Breyer, Frank Easterbrook, Richard Posner, and Ralph Winter, whose writing strongly reflects Chicago School views.[9]

3. Conceptual Limitations of the Conservative Preference-Shaping Hypothesis

For this paper, I assume that an overriding objective of LEC donors is to predispose judges to reach pro-defendant litigation outcomes in antitrust cases. This raises the intriguing question of whether donors are likely to get, or do receive, what they pay for. There are a number of reasons to doubt ex ante that such an investment strategy would necessarily be effective.

Mobil Co., 669 F.2d 384 (6th Cir.) (successful effort by Marathon to use antitrust laws to repulse takeover attempt by Mobil), cert. denied, 455 U.S. 982 (1982); Grumman Corp. v. LTV Corp., 665 F.2d 10 (2d Cir. 1981) (successful effort by Grumman to use the antitrust laws to resist takeover by LTV).

9 See, e.g., A.A. Poultry Farms, Inc. v. Rose Acre Farms, Inc., 881 F.2d 1396 (7th Cir. 1989) (opinion by Judge Easterbrook), cert denied, 494 U.S. 1019 (1990); Olympia Equipment Leasing Co.v. Western Union Tel. Co., 797 F.2d 370 (7th Cir. 1986) (opinion by Judge Posner), cert. denied, 480 U.S. 934 (1987); United States v. Waste Management, Inc., 743 F.2d 976 (2d Cir. 1984) (opinion by Judge Winter); Barry Wright Corp. v. ITT Grinnell Corp., 724 F.2d 227 (1st Cir. 1983) (opinion by Judge Breyer).

3.1. Self-Selection

Participation in LEC programs is by self-selection; judges attend LEC programs by choice, not compulsion.[10] Self-selection has important implications for efforts to shape preferences through post-appointment education programs. Among the most important is that most attendees may be relatively impervious to efforts by LEC program instructors to alter their behavior. The pool of attendees may consist substantially of (a) judges who already are skeptical toward antitrust intervention and do not need to be converted to embrace a conservative agenda, and (b) judges who have entrenched tastes that favor expansive government intervention but are intellectually curious about the LEC's programs. Thus, it is conceivable that applicants either already are believers or will never be believers (but find the courses intriguing).

The process by which presidents appoint judges raises questions about how easily post-appointment educational programs can change the preferences that judges bring to such programs. Presidents typically seek to appoint judges with a shared ideology. To ensure that the candidate will be faithful to a preferred ideology, the selection team will examine the candidate's pre-appointment record carefully for signs of a deep-seated commitment to the president's policy agenda. Because federal judges hold life tenure, officials who screen candidates try to identify past behavior (such as writings, judicial voting in cases on another court, or association with political campaigns) on which confident predictions about future conduct might be based. This endeavor seeks to screen out individuals who might easily be swayed by post-appointment forces, such as a shift in political fashions, peer pressure or lobbying by other judges with different tastes, or judicial education programs that expose the judge to opposing views.[11]

3.2. Non-Substantive Motives for Attending LEC Programs

Some judges may attend LEC programs for reasons that have little to do with the substance of the instructional menu. LEC courses provide a opportunity to spend two weeks in an attractive resort that features excellent accommodations and recreational activities and affords a chance to share the company of other judges in an atmosphere far-removed from the tyranny of the office routine. The instructional schedule ordinarily allows attendees numerous opportunities to avail themselves of the golf course, tennis courts, the beach, the swimming pool, hiking trials, or other recreational venues.[12] Given the number of potential recreational distrac-

10 Judges initiate the process by applying to the LEC after course offerings have been announced. Whether the judge's application is approved depends on the amount of space available at the instructional facility and the number of applicants.

11 Compare Lott and Reed (1989) (discussing approaches that voters can take to identify politicians who will steadfastly pursue a desired policy agenda, despite temptations to shirk that arise from the finite nature of a politician's life and final period problems).

12 For example, the LEC's Seventeenth Economics Institute for Federal Judges was held on March 4 through 17, 1990 at the Westward Look Resort in Tuscon, Arizona. The LEC

tions and the short length of the LEC's typical course (two weeks), one can ask how much information conveyed during the program is retained by the average attendee.

3.3. Judicial Contrarianism

Instructors who have taught LEC programs have consisted mainly of lawyers or economists who doubt the desirability of government economic regulation, including antitrust intervention. These include Armen Alchian, George Bentsen, Henry Butler, Harold Demsetz, Kenneth Elzinga, Milton Friedman, Charles Goetz, Benjamin Klein, Paul MacAvoy, Henry Manne, and Jesse Markham. A handful of LEC instructors have been academics with moderate (e.g., Philip Areeda) or liberal (e.g., Paul Samuelson) tastes for government intervention in the economy. Generally speaking, LEC instructors who teach regulation-relevant courses for judges tilt heavily toward Chicago.

On the whole, federal judges are not a credulous group. Rather, most tend to be relatively headstrong and suspicious of advocacy. The headstrong qualities are common to candidates who aspire to office and are willing to run the gauntlet that ultimately leads to a nomination. Appointments do not result from a president's dispassionate reading of attorney qualifications listed in professional directories such as *Martindale-Hubbell* or *Who's Who in American Law*. Becoming a serious candidate and ultimately gaining an appointment ordinarily require a substantial personal investment in extensive pre-appointment positioning and campaigning (albeit of a subtle nature). Those who complete the obstacle course and reach the bench usually are not wanting for a positive self-image. The timid need not apply.

Skepticism about advocacy comes naturally from the routine of deciding cases. To a large extent, the business of judging consists of watching lawyers work strenuously to solicit favorable outcomes for their clients. Few strategies and tactics of advocacy go unused. Observing relentless efforts at oral or written persuasion can imbue judges with a wariness for advocacy, whether in the form of a hard sell or subtle proselytizing.

If indoctrination is the LEC's object, its audience is a tough crowd. One way that headstrong skeptics of advocacy might react to preference-shaping efforts is to adopt a contrarian posture. Upon detecting an apparent policy bias, the attendee might proceed to hunt for logical flaws in subsequent presentations or to discount (or reject) the instructor's positive and normative representations about microeconomics and its use in evaluating and structuring legal rules. This tendency might be accentuated by the likelihood that attendees know of the controversy surround-

---

brochure that announced the program and solicited applications by potential attendees described the schedule as follows:

"Classes meet six mornings per week with some afternoon and evening sessions scheduled. Faculty/participant interchange is an important part of the learning experience. The schedule is designed to encourage this interchange, thus all meals are taken as a group. The schedule also allows ample time for recreation in a resort setting. However, participants usually spend a good deal of their time reading and studying outside of class."

ing the LEC's programs and therefore may be inclined to take all that they hear with more than a modest dose of salt. An attendee who comes to the program with expansive economic regulation preferences might finish the program with such preferences reinforced if she suspects that the instructors' presentations lack balance.

3.4. Unintended Effects of Economic Learning

Making judges more receptive to economic analysis as a tool for deciding cases does not guarantee that judges who subsequently use economic analysis more extensively will apply economic principles in ways that generate pro-business outcomes. Recent developments in industrial organization scholarship and antitrust litigation demonstrate the point. Since the late 1970s, a large number of researchers who operate within an efficiency framework have argued that proper consideration of efficiency effects justifies antitrust enforcement efforts (such as attacks upon dominant firm strategic behavior, leveraging, and vertical conduct) that extend beyond the Chicago School's antitrust agenda (Baker 1989; Shapiro 1989). The "post-Chicago" literature has exerted relatively little influence upon judicial opinion-writing to date, but past experience with the absorption of new economic literature into the judicial mainstream suggests that courts will face a greater number of cases predicated on post-Chicago arguments in the coming years.[13]

Judges who are conditioned through LEC programs to use economic analysis may decide that the post-Chicago industrial organization literature provides the best approach for accounting for economic efficiency consequences. This is particularly true for judges who come to the LEC programs with expansive antitrust preferences but are persuaded that many formative judicial decisions (such as a number of Supreme Court antitrust opinions in the 1960s) erred in their tendency to give effect to non-efficiency considerations in formulating and applying liability tests. The new literature offers a basis for expanding the zone of antitrust liability while operating within an efficiency framework.

The Supreme Court's recent decision in *Image Technical Services, Inc. v. Eastman Kodak Co.*[14] illustrates the type of results that reasoning based on post-Chicago economics can produce. In *Kodak*, the Court's analysis of tying and attempted monopolization claims spoke entirely about efficiency consequences, and the majority opinion cited several economics journals. The decision said nothing about non-economic values. However, in assessing the efficiency conse-

13 See Kovacic (1992). Some major contributors to the post-Chicago literature also are engaged in active litigation consulting practices through which they play an important role in advising attorneys in designing litigation strategies and offering economically-oriented rebuttals to Chicago School arguments before federal judges. The expanded role of the industrial organization economist as consultant-advocate provides an important mechanism for transmitting the insights of the new economic literature to federal judges. See Salop (1993).

14 112 S. Ct. 2072 (1992).

quences of the challenged conduct, the Court rejected the defendant's Chicago School arguments and embraced propositions based on information-based market power, supplier strategic behavior, and informational asymmetries to reject the defendant manufacturer's request to reinstate the trial court's grant of summary judgment against the plaintiff's claims.

Kodak shows how judges (including LEC program attendees who have been persuaded to accept the primacy of economic analysis in deciding antitrust cases) can work within an economic efficiency model and still reach interventionist outcomes that the corporate and foundation donors to the LEC presumably disfavor.[15] Even if LEC programs convince judges to use economics, they cannot ensure that judges will use Chicago School reasoning to decide cases.

3.5. Influence of Motives Other Than Efficiency-Maximization Upon Judicial Decisionmaking

In assuming that the LEC's two-week instructional programs alter judicial behavior substantially, proponents of the "justice bought and sold" hypothesis overlook the power of non-efficiency motives to determine how judges decide cases (Posner 1993). Modern research on judicial behavior indicates that judges are influenced by objectives that may have nothing to do with efficiency. One branch of commentary points out that judges may respond to the same mix of incentives (many unrelated to enhancing efficiency) that motivate elected politicians (Landes and Posner 1975; Anderson et al. 1989). Other researchers note the desire of judges to minimize reversal on appeal (Higgins and Rubin 1980); to increase the likelihood of subsequent appointment to a higher court (Cohen 1991; 1992); or to gain greater prominence within the judiciary and the legal community by issuing decisions that other courts will cite frequently (Kobayashi and Lott 1993).

Giving effect to these motivations sometimes may lead judges to endorse positions that enhance efficiency, but such an outcome is hardly preordained. Instead, pursuing these objectives can lead judges to vote for outcomes or write opinions that diminish efficiency. The preference-shaping hypothesis assumes that the LEC programs succeed in persuading judges to abandon the pursuit of these objectives when doing so would undercut efficiency. Given the potential importance that researchers have attributed to these various aims, such an assumption is questionable.

---

15 For an earlier example of an important Supreme Court decision that analyzes issues in terms of efficiency effects but reaches an interventionist outcome, see Aspen Skiing Co. v. Aspen Highlands Skiing Co., 472 U.S. 585 (1985).

4. Assessing the Impact of Preference Shaping: Some Results From Antitrust Opinions

Despite much criticism of the LEC's judicial education programs and similar ventures (Alliance for Justice 1993), few attempts have been made to test whether judges who have attended the LEC's programs have altered their behavior as a result of what they learned and have done so in ways that support the views of the LEC's business and foundation donors. This segment of the paper presents the results of an initial effort to assess whether the LEC programs have changed judicial thinking. It does so by examining reported opinions in antitrust decisions by the 58 court of appeals judges[16] who attended LEC courses dealing with antitrust economics[17] from 1974 through December of 1990.

Before discussing the antitrust opinions of judges who have attended LEC programs, an important qualification is in order. It is extremely difficult (perhaps impossible) to disentangle the effect of the LEC programs from a variety of other forces that could account for the content of judicial antitrust decisions (Kovacic 1992, 300-01). A short, incomplete list of other potentially influential factors would include shifts in Supreme Court doctrine, which lower courts must take into account in deciding new cases; differences in the abilities and preferences of law clerks, who might use their advisory role to influence the judge's analysis of antitrust issues; and changes in the sophistication and quality of advocacy of litigants appearing before the judge in antitrust cases. These and other considerations could explain the results and reasoning in antitrust decisions and would complicate efforts to assess the impact of LEC instruction.

In reading antitrust decisions involving LEC attendees, I have watched for evidence of successful pro-business preference shaping, such as a greater tendency to cite pro-business economic commentary or to write opinions that not only reach a pro-business result but also espouse analytical or doctrinal approaches that narrow the reach of the antitrust system. The identification and evaluation of such evidence

---

16 These judges are Glenn Archer, Bobby Baldock, Edward Becker, Danny Boggs, Michael Boudin, Myron Bright, John Butzner, Robert Chapman, John Coffey, W. Eugene Davis, John Duhe, Jerome Farris, Betty Fletcher, Leonard Garth, Floyd Gibson, Ruth Bader Ginsburg, Alfred Goodwin, Ralph Guy, Kenneth Hall, Cynthia Hall, Albert Henderson, William Hutchinson, E. Grady Jolly, Damon Keith, Cornelia Kennedy, Alan Lourie, Frank Magill, Boyce Martin, Monroe McKay, Gilbert Merritt, Thomas Meskill, Paul Michel, Jack Miller, Roger Miner, Pauline Newman, Helen Nies, Diarmuid O'Scannlain, James Oakes, Lawrence Pierce, George Pratt, Thomas Reavley, Max Rosenn, James Ryan, Pamela Rymer, Bruce Selya, Eugene Siler, Jerry Smith, Joseph Sneed, James Sprouse, Walter Stapleton, Richard Suhrheinrich, Thomas Tang, Gerard Tjoflat, Juan Torruella, John Walker, Harry Wellford, Harlington Wood, and Eugene Wright. This group excludes judges such as William Canby, Douglas Ginsburg, and Ralph Winter, who attended LEC programs as law professors before their appointment to the federal judiciary.

17 The LEC's antitrust-relevant courses consist of a basic economics course, which covers price theory principles, and a special course in antitrust economics.

are, of course, highly subjective processes. Even where LEC attendees write robustly pro-defendant opinions, it would be difficult to disprove the possibility that causes other than the LEC economics course (such as pre-appointment preferences or a persuasive brief) molded the judge's approach.

From my review of opinion-writing by LEC attendees, I am unable to point to opinions in which I confidently can say that the effect of LEC preference shaping is apparent. LEC attendees have written a number of strongly pro-defendant opinions, but inferring a causal link between an LEC course and such opinions is problematic. In some instances, a formative conservative opinion is authored by a judge who wrote opinions in (or simply voted in) few pre-attendance antitrust cases. Thus, it is impossible to show a shift in the way the judge frames questions, analyzes issues, and develops doctrine. For example, one cannot determine whether Judge Cynthia Hall's influential, pro-defendant opinion in *Alaska Airlines, Inc. v. United Airlines, Inc.*[18] resulted from her attending an LEC program in 1986 or from conservative preferences that she brought to the bench when she was appointed to the U.S. District Court by President Ronald Reagan in 1981 and elevated to the Ninth Circuit in 1984.

In other instances, judges who have written important pro-defendant opinions after taking an LEC course also have authored post-attendance opinions that endorse views of considerable benefit for plaintiffs. For example, Judge Edward Becker, who attended the LEC's basic economics course in 1979, authored an important pro-defendant opinion in a tying arrangement case in 1992[19] but also wrote pro-plaintiff, interventionist opinions involving vertical mergers and predatory pricing in 1988 and 1982, respectively.[20] Such a pattern suggests that the LEC program may not have effectuated a basic, consistent adjustment in the judge's preferences.

Not only is it difficult to prove much from the post-attendance, pro-defendant opinions of LEC attendees, but an examination of the post-attendance opinions of LEC attendees identifies a number of cases that tend to undercut the conservative preference-shaping hypothesis. Consider three illustrations.

Judge Harlington Wood was appointed to the federal district court in 1973 by President Richard Nixon and was appointed to the Seventh Circuit by President

---

18 948 F.2d 536 (9th Cir. 1991) (rejecting monopolization claims based upon essential facility and leveraging arguments).

19 See Town Sound and Custom Tops, Inc. v. Chrysler Motors Corp., 959 F.2d 468 (3d Cir.) (en banc) (opinion by Judge Edward Becker sustaining dismissal of tying case on antitrust injury grounds), cert. denied, 113 S. Ct. 196 (1992).

20 See Alberta Gas Chems. Ltd. v. E.I. duPont De Nemours & Co., 826 F.2d 1235, 1247 (3d Cir. 1987) (dissenting opinion by Judge Becker using economic analysis to criticize the majority's decision to affirm grant of defendant's motion for summary judgment against private plaintiff's challenge to a vertical merger), cert. denied, 486 U.S. 1059 (1988); Sunshine Books, Ltd. v. Temple University, 697 F.2d 90 (3d Cir. 1982) (opinion by Judge Becker reversing grant of summary judgment for the defendant in a predatory pricing case).

Gerald Ford in 1976. Judge Wood attended the LEC's basic economics course in 1976 and participated in 1983 on the panel that decided *MCI Communications Corp. v. AT&T Co.*[21] In *MCI* the Seventh Circuit upheld a district court's finding that AT&T had engaged in illegal monopolization by impeding MCI's efforts to obtain interconnections with the Bell System's local distribution networks. Judge Wood supported this outcome, but he dissented from the majority's rejection of MCI's predatory pricing allegations. He attacked the majority's "belief . . . that the antitrust laws should be concerned with advancing consumer welfare and should thus focus exclusively on issues of efficiency."[22] Objecting to the decision "to slight the *non-economic* dimension of the Sherman Act's concern with competition," Judge Wood said the court should not "limit [its] definition of unlawful predation to the transgression of efficiency as defined by the formulae of microeconomics."[23] If the LEC's aim is pro-business indoctrination, one presumes that LEC courses do not actively promote the perspective embraced by Judge Wood in *MCI*.

The second illustration involves the Second Circuit's ruling in *United States v. American Cyanamid Co.*,[24] which was decided in 1983 by a panel including Judge John Oakes (a Nixon appointee) and Judge Lawrence Pierce (a Reagan appointee). Judge Oakes had attended the LEC's basic economics course in 1980, and Judge Pierce had done the same in 1981. In *American Cyanamid*, the Second Circuit reviewed a district court decision to terminate a consent decree that compelled Cyanamid to buy some of its manufacturing inputs from other chemical producers. The decree originally had been entered to correct perceived foreclosure problems arising from a vertical merger. Before the district court in 1983, Cyanamid's request to vacate the decree was heard by Judge Charles Brieant, who had attended the LEC's basic economics course in 1979. Judge Brieant concluded that the anti-foreclosure safeguards no longer were necessary because "[c]ontemporary economic theory recognizes that vertical integration may foster corporate efficiency and *enhance* competition in the market place."[25]

If Judge Brieant's opinion can be said to have displayed the influence of pro-business preference shaping, it is clear that the opinion endorsed by his fellow LEC alumni on the Second Circuit did not. In an opinion by Judge Pierce, a unanimous court of appeals reversed the termination of the consent decree on the

---

21 708 F.2d 1081 (7th Cir.), cert. denied, 464 U.S. 891 (1983).

22 708 F.2d at 1175.

23 Id. at 1176, 1179 (emphasis in original). Judge Wood also quoted Professor Lawrence Sullivan approvingly for the view that "'[t]o argue, as do the Chicago economists, that antitrust ought to be used solely to inhibit expressions of market power in a technical economic sense, is not only to miss much in the history and development of the law, but to ignore much of its potential.'" Id. at 1179.

24 719 F.2d 558 (2d Cir. 1983), cert. denied, 465 U.S. 1101 (1984).

25 556 F. Supp. 361, 369 (S.D.N.Y.) (emphasis in original), aff'd in part, rev'd in part, 719 F.2d 558 (2d Cir. 1983), cert. denied, 465 U.S. 1101 (1984).

ground that Judge Brieant had failed to evaluate Cyanamid's request in light of *Brown Shoe Co. v. United States*[26] and other similarly reasoned cases dealing with vertical mergers.[27] Judge Pierce acknowledged that "*Brown Shoe* and its progeny have been the subject of considerable criticism by academicians who believe these cases apply overly harsh standards in assessing the legality of vertical mergers,"[28] but he observed that "these cases nonetheless continue to constitute the current state of the law as prescribed by the Supreme Court, which circuit and district courts are bound to follow."[29] Judge Pierce concluded that "it was error to apply 'contemporary economic theory' to the extent that it may be distinct from precedent, and fail to apply the standard framework of analysis."[30]

The third illustration deals with tying arrangements. In 1987, the Fourth Circuit and the Ninth Circuit each issued decisions involving claims by franchised dealers of Mercedes-Benz of North America that the German automaker illegally had tied its sale of new automobiles and replacement parts. In an opinion by Judge Joseph Sneed, a Nixon appointee who attended the LEC's basic economics course in 1975, the Ninth Circuit sustained the dismissal of the tying claims on the ground that legitimate business considerations justified the challenged arrangement.[31] Citing extensively from Chicago-oriented legal and economic authorities, Judge Sneed emphasized the usefulness of the tying restriction in preventing free-riding and ensuring quality control.[32]

Judge Sneed's opinion is consistent with the conservative preference-shaping hypothesis, but the opinion of his Fourth Circuit counterparts is not. The Fourth Circuit evaluated nearly identical issues, yet a unanimous panel sustained the jury's finding of liability on the tying claim.[33] The court of appeals opinion was written by Judge James Sprouse, a Carter appointee who attended the LEC basic economics course in 1985, and was joined by Judge Robert Chapman, a Reagan appointee who had attended the basic course in 1979 when he was a district judge. Judge Sprouse recognized the availability of a business justification defense to tying liability, but his opinion defined and applied the defense in a manner that defendants ordinarily will find difficult to satisfy. He emphasized that Mercedes had failed to show that tying "was necessary to police dealer misconduct" and could instead have resorted to "less-restrictive alternatives" to protect itself against warranty free-riding.[34]

26 370 U.S. 294 (1962).

27 *American Cyanamid*, 719 F.2d at 566-67.

28 Id. at 567 n.9 (citing IV P. Areeda & D. Turner, *Antitrust Law* ¶¶ 1000-19 (1980); R. Bork, *The Antitrust Paradox* 225-45 (1978); Y. Brozen, *Concentration, Mergers, and Public Policy* 402-04 (1982)).

29 Id. at 567.

30 Id.

31 Mozart Co. v. Mercedes-Benz of North America, Inc., 833 F.2d 1342 (9th Cir. 1987), cert. denied, 488 U.S. 870 (1988).

32 833 F.2d at 1348-51.

33 Metrix Warehouse, Inc. v. Daimler-Benz Aktiengesellschaft, 828 F.2d 1033 (4th Cir. 1987), cert. denied, 486 U.S. 1017 (1988).

Given the similarity of the issues and the underlying facts of the two tying decisions, the conservative preference shaping hypothesis would predict that LEC attendees would use comparable analytical approaches (emphasizing free-riding and transaction cost concerns) to exculpate the original equipment manufacturer. Instead, the LEC attendees took significantly divergent approaches in resolving the dispute and in writing opinions. The Sneed opinion is consistent with the preference-shaping hypothesis, but the Sprouse opinion (and the vote by Chapman) contradict it.

5. Conclusion and Directions for Further Research

As applied to Henry Manne's Law and Economics Center, the conservative preference-shaping hypothesis contends that the LEC provides a vehicle through which corporations and conservative foundations influence federal judges to adopt pro-business positions in deciding cases. In sponsoring economics courses for judges, the LEC's donors are said to be purchasing favorable litigation outcomes and spurring the articulation of doctrines that will minimize the business community's exposure to successful lawsuits in the future.

Antitrust law would appear to be an area in which post-appointment preference shaping of this sort might have the greatest impact. Of all federal economic regulatory schemes, the antitrust system confers unequalled discretion upon the federal judiciary. The antitrust statutes also accept (or, to state the proposition minimally, at least tolerate) the use of economics to formulate and apply standards of business conduct. Given the breadth of the judiciary's discretion in antitrust disputes, it is understandable that corporations and laissez faire foundations might decide to expend resources to educate judges to embrace analytical techniques that would narrow the antitrust system's reach.

That such a strategy would succeed in achieving its aims is hardly self-evident. The assumption that LEC programs materially alter judicial preferences overlooks a number of conceptual impediments to successful preference shaping, including important aspects of the way in which judicial LEC attendees are chosen, the range of possible motives for a judge to attend an LEC program, the process through which presidents select candidates for the federal bench, and the incentives that guide judicial decisionmaking. Moreover, the antitrust opinions reviewed for this paper dictate caution in assuming that LEC programs in fact cause attendees to adopt pro-business views. Antitrust opinions written by past LEC program attendees provide an uneasy basis for concluding that LEC courses motivate judges to favor business defendants.

If preference shaping is their objective, one could ask why corporate donors and conservative foundations would continue to fund LEC programs unless effective

---

34 828 F.2d at 1041.

preference shaping in fact was taking place. Two explanations come to mind. The first is that LEC donors do not engage in systematic monitoring activities that would be necessary to make accurate measurements of effects. A rigorous evaluation of actual impacts would involve a laborious, time-consuming review of hundreds of judicial decisions—a task that LEC donors probably are unwilling to undertake. Rather than rely on a careful empirical assessment of effects that would establish the existence (or lack) of a causal link between LEC programs and a change in judicial behavior, donors may be guided by a basic intuition that efforts to increase the economic training of federal judges will increase the likelihood that pro-business attitudes will be reflected in judicial decisions.

A second possible explanation is that donors treat the intensity of opposition by organizations such as the Alliance for Justice as a reliable proxy for effectiveness. The essential logic would be that the Alliance for Justice and other critics of LEC programs would not invest great energy in attacking economics seminars for judges unless the seminars in fact were altering judicial behavior. Given the often-expressed view of LEC critics that efficiency-oriented economic analysis is an illegitimate tool for judicial decisionmaking, LEC donors might regard vigorous opposition to LEC programs as proof that the goal of expanding the judiciary's economic learning is being achieved.

Additional data collection and evaluation would be useful to determine the soundness of the conservative preference-shaping hypothesis. A broad-based empirical assessment would have three basic elements. The first element would be a before-and-after comparison of voting results for all federal judges who have attended LEC programs. The before-and-after comparison would attempt to identify shifts in voting behavior after judges have attended an LEC program. The second element would be to compare the voting records of all LEC attendees to a control group of judges who were appointed to the bench in the same year as the LEC attendee but have never participated in an LEC program. A third element would be to conduct a similar before-and-after comparison (also with a control group of judges) of citation patterns in opinions written by LEC attendees. The review of citation patterns would be designed to detect a greater frequency of reliance on economically-oriented commentary. The use of these and other empirical tests will be necessary to assess the effect of LEC programs or other post-appointment judicial training initiatives.

References

Alliance For Justice. 1993. *Justice for Sale: Shortchanging the Public Interest for Private Gain*. Washington, D.C.: Alliance for Justice.

Anderson, Gary M., William F. Shughart II, and Robert D. Tollison. 1989. "On the Incentive of Judges to Enforce Legislative Wealth Transfers." *Journal of Law and Economics* 32: 215-28.

Baker, Jonathan B. 1989. "Recent Developments in Economics That Challenge Chicago School Views." *Antitrust Law Journal* 58: 645-55.

Cohen, Mark A. 1992. "The Motives of Judges: Empirical Evidence from Antitrust Sentencing." *International Review of Law and Economics* 12: 13-30.

Cohen, Mark A. 1991. "Explaining Judicial Behavior or What's 'Unconstitutional' About the Sentencing Commission." *Journal of Law, Economics, and Organization* 7: 183-99.

Freyer, Tony. 1989. "The Sherman Antitrust Act, Comparative Business Structure, and the Rule of Reason: America and Great Britain, 1880-1920." *Iowa Law Review* 74: 991-1017.

Higgins, Richard S., and Paul H. Rubin. 1980. "Judicial Discretion." *Journal of Legal Studies* 9: 129-38.

Kobayashi, Bruce H., and John R. Lott, Jr. 1993. "Judicial Reputation and the Efficiency of the Common Law." Mimeo.

Kovacic, William E. 1993. "Judicial Appointments and the Future of Antitrust Policy." *Antitrust* 7(2): 8-13.

Kovacic, William E. 1992. "The Influence of Economics on Antitrust Law." *Economic Inquiry* 30: 294-306.

Kovacic, William E. 1991. "Reagan's Judicial Appointees and Antitrust in the 1990s." *Fordham Law Review* 60: 49-124.

Landes, William M., and Richard A. Posner. 1975. "The Independent Judiciary in an Interest Group Perspective." *Journal of Law and Economics* 18: 875-901.

Lott, Jr., John R., and W. Robert Reed. 1989. "Shirking and Sorting in a Political Market with Finite Life Politicians." *Public Choice* 61: 75-93.

Mueller, Charles E. 1987. "Judicial Appointments and Antitrust: The '88 Presidential Campaign." *Antitrust Law and Economics Review* 19(4): 45-54.

Mueller, Charles E. 1990. "How Antitrust Fell as Economics Rose: 'Mutiny' at Justice and the FTC." *Antitrust Law and Economics Review* 22(3): 1-17.

Mueller, Charles E., et al. 1988. "Forward: The Cases, the Judges, and Economic Research in U.S. Antitrust Policy." *Antitrust Law and Economics Review* 20(1): 1-20.

Posner, Richard A. 1993. "What Do Judges Maximize? (The Same Thing Everybody Else Does)." *Supreme Court Economic Review* 3: 1-41.

Salop, Steven C. 1993. "Exclusionary Vertical Restraints Law: Has Economics Mattered?" *American Economic Review* 83: 168-72.

Shapiro, Carl. 1989. "The Theory of Business Strategy." *RAND Journal of Economics* 20: 125-37.

Sklar, Martin J. 1988. *The Corporate Reconstruction of American Capitalism, 1890-1916.* Cambridge: Cambridge Univ. Press.

7

A CONSUMERS' GROUP'S VIEW OF NEW SERVICES, QUALITY, AND REGULATION

Colin J. Mitchell

The European Mail and Express Services Users' Association, familiarly known as EMESUA, was founded five years ago with the original objective of providing a consensus consumer view to the European Commission during the drafting stages of the postal Green Paper. Users felt compelled to take this stance when they realised that the future of "postal Europe" was being influenced through the European Commission almost entirely by postal administrations and their Government owners. Even large users had experienced great difficulty in trying to negotiate on a commercial basis with the state owned bureaucracies which were responsible for providing staple services-whether universal delivery or value added. Since then, the Association, with an increasing membership across a broad spectrum of user types, has formalised the rules within its Articles of Association and has three main aims in support of its membership:

- Education and Information Exchange. Provided through: a quarterly Newsletter; conferences, seminars, and workshops; a library of books and papers relating to "Despatch"; liaison with Educational bodies and Training Councils.
- Liaison with Government and Official Bodies.
- Dialogue with suppliers of "mail" equipment and services.

EMESUA is based in the United Kingdom, and its main focus of activity is within Europe, but it nonetheless supports the interests of its members on a global basis. The Association asserts the need for a strong and active "postal" consumer association in every country. Where such an association already exists, EMESUA is glad to co-operate for the common good; where no such consumer group exists in any particular country, EMESUA would be happy to work with all interested parties to assist in the formation of such a group.

In this chapter, I address concerns from the users' point of view about new services, quality, and regulations and conclude with the users' ideal scenario for regulated postal services within Europe.

Quality of Service

It is my intention to address quality of service before considering new services, as I see no point in providing new services-whatever the levels of added value-until existing services are operated to a standard acceptable to users.

How should such acceptance be accomplished? On the basis that providers of services have undertaken sensible market research to determine user needs, or are providing a statutory universal service, they have to take a number of additional steps to achieve acceptable service to customers:

- Define and quantify the services to be provided;
- Set measurement standards which are clearly understood by providers and users alike;
- Obtain independent measurement of levels of service against the pre-set criteria;
- Publish the measured levels of service; and
- "Own" such levels of service and set targets and milestones for further improvements.

But this basic user "shopping list" in itself poses a series of practical questions:

- Who should set the targets-the supplier or the customer?
- What does "quality" mean-and to whom?
- Should quality equate to reliability?
- Are quality and fair price mutually exclusive?
- Are common standards of quality possible for trans border services in a regulated environment?

The user would argue that, the universal service notwithstanding, the supplier is offering a product which the user is prepared to purchase at the quoted market price. At this point, we should not be diverted by esoteric economic arguments concerning prices, costs, and subventions.

In any normal commercial enterprise, the customer will specify his requirements for goods or services and will negotiate with his chosen supplier on a "win-win" basis to ensure the satisfaction of both contracting parties. By the same token, users of delivery services should undertake dialogue with the suppliers of such services-whether monopoly or free market-in order to understand clearly each others requirements, strengths, and weaknesses. From such dialogue will arise a set of standards-a "Service Level Agreement."

Such agreements are commonplace between customers and free market carriers. They are becoming more common between customers and the more enlightened-or should I say commercially aware-postal administrations.

But a major problem occurs when customers hand cross border mail to a commercially aware postal administration which then passes the consignments to a less efficient administration.

The customer has undertaken his contractual obligations, using his home administration as a "one-stop shop." He does not wish, and may not be allowed by regulation, to become involved with the rest of the supply chain.

It is the responsibility of the administration of acceptance to ensure that the service level agreed with the customer is applied throughout the chain from collection to delivery. The Scandinavian experiment has proved that end-to-end quality control is possible between enlightened administrations. It is now the responsibility of these administrations to put pressure on their weaker brethren. Such organisations as PostEurop give the user hope that improvements in cross border service levels will arise in the near future.

I have argued that business relationships between customers and postal administrations should be based on service level agreements, whether express or implied. By the very nature of such agreements, one would have to agree that either party would have failed in its negotiations had it not inserted an understanding of reliability into the framework. Normal commercial remedies for compensation in the event of failure may not be available to the customer of a postal administration, but, nonetheless, the concept must be clearly understood by both parties, must be measured, and must be published.

I posed the question "are quality and fair price mutually exclusive?" There were others at the Conference far more qualified than me to review the theory of postal economics and pricing structures. In fact, some erudite papers on this subject are contained in this volume.

The user views the supplier's pricing strategy in far more simplistic terms. He requires a service which will support his business or social needs. When he understands the level, quality, and reliability of the service on offer he will determine a price which he is prepared to pay. Naturally, the more value added to the service, the more the customer will be prepared to pay for that increased value. Customers, especially those in the business sector, are sophisticated enough to realise that they cannot drive pricing down below the suppliers' bottom line without serious effect on the level of service offered. By the same token, users will not pay a premium price for a non-premium (or low quality) service, nor will they pay for value which they do not, or perceive that they do not, receive. In a free market, they will turn to other suppliers with whom they can build a business partnership based on mutual understanding, competitive prices, high levels of quality, and excellent post sales support. In a monopoly postal environment, users who do not receive satisfaction from a postal administration will turn to other forms of information transfer-for example facsimile, electronic mail, EDI, multi media services, or alternative electronic forms of advertising and order collection.

New Services

As I have already predicated, users will have no faith in new services until existing basic and value-added services operate to a high quality level of service which is measurable, measured, and published. Users wish to receive from all postal administrations minimum levels of service for jointly agreed service targets. For Universal Service deliveries users seek 95% on-time delivery levels; for special or express delivery services 99% on-time delivery levels are required. Users realise that postal administrations may have difficulty in providing early daily deliveries of universal service to rural areas: such difficulties should be overcome by negotiated later delivery service targets,**not** by degradation of standard on-time delivery targets.

So what of the future? Users now have a wide choice of methods of information movement, supported by technology which is increasing in scope at a very fast rate. At the same time, business practice is changing rapidly and operating margins are being squeezed more tightly. The result for the business user is to question every activity and cost, and to move towards outsourcing all services and non-core activities. The information movement strategy within large organisations is subject to close scrutiny and only those services will prevail which are of high quality at competitive cost in order to move more information more quickly and accurately in support of maintaining competitive business edge. To this end, the user is not concerned with *who* provides the service. His concern is for the right service to meet his needs at the right price.

Where will regulated delivery services fit into this scenario? Even before service levels have reached the 95% on-time standard which customers seek for the universal service, postal administrations *must* provide accounting and invoicing systems which reflect normal commercial practice.

Standard commercial credit terms for payment of invoices are in the region of 30 days, with possible discounts for early settlement. Pre-payment is not customary for regular, or bulk business, customers. Terms of seven days or less from date of invoice are not acceptable; no mechanised invoice clearance system can cope with such a short timeframe. As a result, payment has to be cleared manually at a cost which nullifies any competitive value of the service provided.

Postal administrations must move towards transparent pricing, especially for value added services. Users wish to know what they are paying for. Many users, in partnership with their suppliers, will wish to negotiate acquisition of goods or services on the basis of cost + N% profit margin. How many postal administrations could honestly cope with such a negotiating stance?

Postal administrations, together with the UPU, must resolve the problem of Terminal Dues. The regulated industry got itself into this mess; the private carriers exploited the system in open competition; and now the regulated industry cries "foul."

Users also seek from their suppliers technological support. This will take many forms:

EDI. The ability to pass traffic information and settle accounts electronically. But customers operating in more than one country will demand a common EDI standard, not a variety of standards or subsets of standards from differing administrations. They need Software for completion of transit documentation and waybills; for online operational information; for management and statistical data; and for costing and charging purposes. But users do not wish to be locked in by supplier hardware, or have their premises cluttered with yet another terminal and ancillary devices. They need software for installation on their own platforms.

Bar Coding Systems for Addressing and Routing. But, again, we must have standardisation. Customers currently need a minimum of three addressing formats dependent on carrier (postal administrations require full address, PO Box number where applicable, and Post Code; Express carriers require full address and telephone number, but no box number; document exchanges require exchange number and name). Several postal administrations are trialling bar codes for addressing, but there is no common system. And why, oh why, should the user be expected to pay for a technological advance which will benefit the supplier in bringing his service level up to that needed by the customer?

When service levels, accounting systems, and technology support have reached levels which customers need and trust, then they will be prepared to discuss further service offerings.

- End to end track and trace with Proof of Delivery;
- Discounted downstream injection;
- Timed deliveries (express or deferred) and deliveries to suit the domestic customer-such as evenings and week-ends;
- Third party billing;
- Discounted multi site consolidations;
- Logistics support;
- One-stop shopping;
- Mail room and despatch bay outsourcing and management; and
- Use of post office telecommunications networks to provide terminal based services at the counter, such as catalogue shopping, payment of accounts, insurance transactions, access to external databases, and much much more.

Regulation

Let me pose a series of questions which users frequently ask:

- Are existing regulators toothless?
- Who should regulate the regulators?
- Should operators become self-regulatory?
- Could codes of conduct supersede regulation?
- Should regulation be national, regional, or global?
- Should users be required to apply different techniques to the management of regulated suppliers and their services and, if so, why?

Suppliers who operate in a free market environment are not necessarily constrained by the legislation and regulation which controls, and often inhibits, monopoly services. Usually, such free market operators work within codes of conduct issued by trade associations or similar bodies. In many states, their activities will be governed by national law regarding employee protection, customer rights, advertising standards, traffic and driving legislation, etc; but their commercial practices and investment policies will not be constrained unnaturally. Apart from codes of practice, their operations, and therefore ultimately their profitability, will be governed by their ability to satisfy their customers with suitable quality products at sensible market prices.

As we know, this is not necessarily the case with regulated monopoly suppliers. Apart from the requirement to provide an universal service-a social requirement which cannot be justified purely in terms of profit-such operators are beset by statutory controls over products, pricing, business strategy, and investment policy. Many arguments have been propounded to demonstrate that postal administrations are trading unfairly and are not in open competition with non-regulated free market suppliers. Such arguments have revolved round dominant monopoly positions, VAT exemption, unfair cross subsidies and lack of transparent pricing, and unnatural government protectionism-to list but a few points. However, we have to accept that monopoly postal administrations *are* regulated and that such regulation should be carried out as fairly and freely as possible. Provision of service, or its lack, will be regulated naturally by customer demand. But the customer has no control over the regulation of the postal monopoly in individual states. In many cases, the state acts as operator *and* regulator; in others, regulation is separated, to a greater or less degree, from operation. But in the majority of cases, the regulator is a watchdog only-and usually completely toothless.

The user believes firmly that regulation and operation must be separated. A gamekeeper would surely develop a crisis of commitment were he to act as a poacher whilst on duty for his employer. Not only should the regulator be separated from the operator, but he should also be reasonably independent of the day to day controlling activities of the owner-the state. In any commercial organisation, the internal auditor is independent of the finance department, reporting directly to the Board of Directors. So should the regulator report direct to government cabinet, not to the Department of State controlling the postal administration. This regulator must be able to receive direct input from customers of the administration-across a range of products and volumes-and must have the authority to inspect the operations and books of the administration. His reports and recommendations should not be cosmetic, but should be treated with gravity and promise of action by the government to which he reports.

States with an enlightened attitude towards the standing of their postal administrations are relaxing many of the restrictive laws concerning structure, operations, and governmental financial controls. In such cases, the role of the regulator will change and will eventually diminish to responsibility for ensuring only that universal service and social obligations are carried out to the relevant agreed standards. The change in regulatory role and focus within public service industries can clearly be seen within the UK electricity industry. Here an extremely effective regulator is appointed for a five year term by the relevant Minister, and the decisions of the regulator are subject to appeal to the Monopolies and Mergers Commission—an independent Civil Service organisation which reports to the President of the Board of Trade.

Users accept that postal laws and regulations vary from state to state. Therefore, it seems logical that each state should have its own postal regulator experienced in the laws of that state.

Where rules or directives may be supra national-as may be the case with possible directives emanating from the European Commission's postal green paper-then it may be sensible for a small central regulatory unit to oversee individual state regulators and ensure that there is a common and equal application of regulatory standards throughout the group of states in question. Global regulation would not be an effective vehicle for ensuring immediate compliance with regulation. It would be too remote, too reactive, and probably too politicised to undertake the role effectively. This can be adduced through the activities of the United Nations Universal Postal Union which is an effective strategic organisation, but which could not undertake a pro-active policing role.

I stated earlier that non monopoly operators are mainly self- regulated. There is a possibility that as postal administrations become liberalised (and possibly privatised), their activities could be controlled by codes of conduct managed through some form of trade association. Postal administrations may wish to form their own association, or might even wish to join an existing association. And why not? Many administrations are now involved in joint ventures with non-monopoly carriers. But there would still need to be a regulatory watchdog to represent the rights of citizens in respect of any universal service reserved to any specific administration.

Conclusion

Postal administrations in various parts of the world are undergoing partial or complete deregulation, liberalisation, product and pricing reform, and changes in operating philosophy. Users begin to question the definition of a Post Office in these times of great change; cynical users even question whether they really benefit from some of these changes and from the improvements in productivity which certain administrations have made, or allegedly made.

But the role of this Association is not to be cynical. It is to work proactively in partnership with all suppliers to ensure that both parties profit from quality services at fair prices in support of user needs.

We are working with postal administrations and their owners to ensure:

- Existing services meet jointly agreed minimum standards of measured quality-nationally and cross border.
- Targets are set for further improvements.
- Political, legislative,and financial constraints are reduced to the minimum necessary for protection of the reserved universal service. New products are jointly developed in support of user needs.
- Regulation becomes localised, totally independent, accessible to all users and, most important, fair, fearless, and effective.

As this scenario develops, users will perceive a greater value in the range of quality products on offer from more postal administrations. They, in turn, will provide a global service organisation capable of supporting all user "despatch" needs and will profit accordingly.

8

PRICING IN POSTAL SERVICE UNDER COMPETITIVE ENTRY[1]

Michael A. Crew
Paul R. Kleindorfer

Introduction

The increased competition recently apparent in postal services takes several forms, which includes the development of new and superior services. Examples include over-night express and courier services, improved parcel and small package services, improved tracking, worksharing arrangements—primarily presorting—and downstream access to the postal network. In this paper, we confine ourselves to the discussion of the two latter forms of competition, namely, worksharing and downstream access. While our analysis is intended to be generic in application, we will draw heavily on United Kingdom and United States experience, as these are the postal authorities that we have studied most intensively.

We will examine the efficiency consequences of these competitive developments and possible implications of government and regulatory policy. As our approach is based on economic efficiency, it will recognize the benefits of competition for economic efficiency. This may mean that policies which worked well under a monopoly may lead to inefficiency once competitive entry is allowed. One example is the issue of cross-subsidies. Once competition is allowed, cross subsidies will be reduced, and failure to employ efficient prices will sooner or later result in losses.

In section 1, we develop our approach based on economic efficiency to review the impact of competition on existing pricing policies and practices. Section 2 briefly reviews the experience of changes in government policy toward entry into previously monopolized industries, with special reference to United States telecommunications. Section 3 introduces the concept of the postal value chain and the role of economic theory in developing discount structures for open access to the local delivery network. The role of efficient component pricing and discounts

1 We would like to thank Ian Reay and Paul Richards for helpful comments.

based upon long-run marginal cost are examined. Section 4 addresses the problem of downstream access[2] and how it might operate in conjunction with the two-tier pricing structure employed by Royal Mail. Section 5 provides some caveats and suggestions for future research.

1. Effects of Competition and Entry on Pricing in Theory and Practice

The underlying approach which we employ throughout is economic efficiency. This means maximizing net benefits—the excess of benefits over costs, where consumers' benefits and producers' profits count equally.[3] We employ the approach to examine the problem of setting presort discounts and the impact of competition on existing peak-load pricing policies, particularly the two-tier pricing system[4] employed in the U.K. Post Office.

The presort discount should be set so that those presorters who can perform the operations at lower cost than the postal authority do so, and those who cannot, do not. To do this, the discounts should be based on avoided cost or long-run marginal cost (LRMC) savings of the postal authority. Setting discounts in this fashion invites entry by other providers of services (e.g., presorters) precisely when they can perform the service at lower cost than the postal service. Two factors making the determination of both efficient pricing benchmarks, as well as financial viability considerations, more complex are competition and technological change. Competition in postal services is clearly evident and partly is one policy consequence of attempting to promote dynamic efficiency and technological change through new entrants and new postal technologies in various parts of the postal value chain. However, promoting efficient entry while continuing to assure the financial viability of the overall postal system is a complex matter, as we examine in detail in this paper.

Thus, while traditional postal pricing was primarily performed in the context of a secure monopoly, the trend of increasing competition makes setting discounts for various competitive services a matter not just of efficiency but also of financial viability. For example, providing too large a discount for presort or large volumes gives a cost advantage to entrants whose costs are higher than those of the postal authority (an efficiency effect) with the result that inefficient firms enter the market and simultaneously the authority makes losses (a financial effect), which in the

---

2 To our knowledge, downstream access is not generally available in any postal service. In the United Kingdom, it is only available with permission of the Post Office. In the United States, the Postal Service does allow "drop-shipment discounts" to bulk mailers.

3 In the Appendix, we develop the efficiency approach rigorously. See also Crew and Kleindorfer (1992).

4 We recognized and analyzed the contribution of the two-tier pricing system in our recent work. See Crew, Kleindorfer, and Smith (1990) and Crew and Kleindorfer (1991; 1992).

absence of direct subsidy from the government it cannot sustain.

The peak-load pricing policies of postal services, particularly the two-tier system of the U.K. Post Office, are justifiable in terms of the efficiency approach which we are employing. Indeed, in Crew, Kleindorfer, and Smith (1990) and Crew and Kleindorfer (1991; 1992), we examined, in depth, peak-load pricing in postal service, and the two-tier pricing system employed by the U.K. Post Office emerged as by far the most rigorous and widespread application of service-differentiated pricing.[5] Service-differentiated pricing provides a form of peak-load pricing when traditional peak-load pricing—i.e., time-of-day pricing—is not feasible, as in the case of postal service. Postal service faces a peak problem in that mail arrives for processing and transportation not evenly but bunched in the early evening. By being able to defer the processing of Second Class mail, the Post Office is able to utilize its facilities more evenly and thereby reduces costs. The result is the same smoothing of output that is achieved in the case of time-of-day pricing which, in contrast, operates by smoothing demand.

The two-tier system was an important pricing innovation which provided a pricing policy for a whole industry that performed the same function as the peak-load pricing theory advocated by economists for use in industries such as electricity supply and telecommunications. However, economic theory had apparently no role in the implementation of the two-tier pricing policy.[6] It was not motivated by or grounded in economic theory, as the applications in electricity and telecommunications were, but rather it was a product of practical problem solving in the U.K. Post Office introduced first on September 16, 1968.

It was not until 1990 that a rigorous basis in economic theory was provided. (See Crew, Kleindorfer, and Smith (1990).) The economic theory underlying the two-tier system was extended in Crew and Kleindorfer (1992) to take into account service quality considerations.[7] Postal authorities have to be concerned with two aspects of service quality: the time limits offered for delivery of First Class and Second Class respectively and the probability that mail will be delivered within these service guidelines. The former is obvious, as it provides the basis for differentiating First and Second Class service and the corresponding service-differentiated prices. The latter is the reliability of the service and is clearly an important aspect of service quality. It is not much benefit to mailers to be told that mail is subject to overnight delivery if it rarely makes it on time. In Crew and Kleindorfer (1992,) we examine the tradeoff between stated service standards and reliability.

5 These books and papers followed over twenty years of joint research on peak-load pricing and the preparation of testimony for the United States Postal Service before the United States Postal Rate Commission on the peak load effect. See, for example, Crew and Kleindorfer (1971; 1979; 1986) and Kleindorfer (1987).

6 The National Board for Prices and Incomes (1968) placed its imprimatur on the policy.

7 See Crew and Kleindorfer (1992) for an analysis of service quality issues in postal service and Crew and Kleindorfer (1993) for several examples of recent practice in this area.

The Post Office and the U.S. Postal Service[8] have both recently addressed the issue of service quality, especially reliability, by having independent consultants measure service quality.[9] The results of these independent surveys, as reported in the Annual Reports of the Post Office, show steadily improving service reliability. In addition, they show higher reliability in the urban areas than in remote areas. Both of these results are likely to be efficiency enhancing. The added reliability at a reasonable price is likely to be beneficial. Similarly, in the context of a uniform nationwide tariff, the lower reliability for remoter areas is a means of reducing costs for these areas, which have higher costs than the urban areas.

Overall, the postal pricing and operating policies under discussion pass the tests of efficiency rather well in the context of the measures developed in our earlier papers. With the move away from a monopoly environment, however, the question is whether some adjustments will be needed in the face of competition and technological change. We start to address this problem area in the next section.

2. Commentary on Entry Policy

Dobbs and Richards (1993) surveyed the British government's policy in promoting entry in telecommunications and gas with a view to the possible lessons for entry into postal markets. Government policy attempted to promote entry in British Telecom's and British Gas' markets by providing concessions to entrants. A similar policy was employed in the United States, which we now examine, for the insights that it provides on entry and competition policy. Prior to the Divestiture in 1984 by AT&T of its local telephone operations, other common carriers were provided access to the local network at rates considerably below those (implicitly) paid by AT&T Long Lines, the long-distance arm of the Bell System, which had over 90% of the market. Admittedly, the quality of access was somewhat lower but the rate differential more than made up for the quality differential. As a result, other common carriers were able to grow rapidly.

The system of offering lower access charges to other common carriers was changed rather radically following Divestiture. The presence of inefficient rate structures together with rather free entry resulted almost overnight in many small companies becoming providers of long-distance telephone service. These companies were in effect arbitragers taking account of the arbitrage possibilities that had artificially been created. They were able to take advantage of the price differentials by offering a discount to customers and making a sizeable profit margin. Some of the entrants were resellers who would buy in bulk and resell at a discount over

8 For additional discussion of the service standards, see Lazarowitz and Potter for testimony before the Postal Rate Commission. See also Reay (1992) for further discussion.

9 The issue has received attention in the context of international mail. Bruun (1992) examines systems of measurement and incentives for reliability for mail between the Scandinavian countries.

AT&T's retail rates to small customers not large enough to benefit from AT&T WATS rates.[10] The effect of the system was that AT&T and some of the other carriers lost traffic to resellers. The system quickly evolved with the spread of equal access to all carriers and all parts of the country, changes in access charges, and the requirement that resellers pay increased access charges. This, coupled with the increased freedom allowed to AT&T to compete, meant that WATS resellers disappeared almost as quickly as they had appeared. Once underlying cross-subsidies had been eliminated, the market was able to stabilize, with equal access becoming generally available to all carriers and with AT&T's market share falling currently to below 70% of the market.

Two other examples of entry policy in the United States are worth brief review and comment. These are AOS (alternative operator services) and the private ownership of pay phones.[11] Both of these polices had a different impact from what was expected and resulted in the exploitation of monopoly power. AOS allowed operator service to be provided by companies other that common carriers. Visitors to the United States and locals should avoid AOS because they charge in excess of the common carriers! Similarly, a privately owned payphone would charge higher rates than those of the local telephone companies and would often employ AOS. In an attempt to reduce such abuses, regulations had to be created to allow, for example, the avoidance of the AOS by the use of carrier access codes. The net effect of competitive entry in these two instances apparently did not benefit the consumer. The prime beneficiaries were the owners of the valuable sites who were able to strike better deals as a result of the competition for the right to install the payphone.

The experience in United States telecommunications provides at least a cautionary tale to policy makers considering subsidizing entry. Indeed, as far as the postal situation is concerned, we would go much further and emphasize that there is no place for subsidies to entrants and other means of encouraging entry into downstream access. Subsidies to entrants could threaten the very nature of the uniform pricing across the whole country and universal service obligations and, more importantly, would offer few significant benefits in return. Furthermore, competition in postal and delivery services, both actual and potential, is apparently vigorous, based on low entry costs and openly accessible technology for most parts of the postal value chain. This contrasts sharply with telecommunications prior to the AT&T Divestiture, where entry costs were perceived to be significant and where rapid technological progress increased the risk of investment in this sector. Thus,

10 Roughly the system involved the customer dialing the reseller's switch, for which the reseller paid a subsidized access charge. The reseller would then switch the call to AT&T's WATS service for which it received significant volume discounts. When the subsidy disappeared from access charges, a significant restructuring of the reseller market occurred. For a detailed analysis of the effects of telephone deregulation, see Vitor and Davidson (1985).

11 Previously, coin phones had been the exclusive province of the local telephone company.

there is no justification for artificially stimulating competition. As we will develop further in the next section, if competitors are allowed downstream access to the local delivery network, it should be only at economically efficient prices.

3. Postal Value Chain and Efficient Component Pricing

The postal value chain consists of all the activities that make up collection through final delivery. It is quite feasible for firms other than the postal authority to perform some or all of these activities, except perhaps local delivery because of the significant economies of scale in the local delivery function. To be the efficient producer, economic efficiency requires that the producer be able to provide that part of the value chain at the lowest price. For purposes of this analysis, we assume that the postal authority, indeed, has a natural monopoly in local delivery. But we consider all upstream activities in the postal value chain to be subject to potential entry. The question is at what level should discounts be set to achieve economic efficiency.

Let us start with an example of presorting. From an efficiency perspective, presorting should take place if presorters can perform the function at lower cost than the postal authority. As shown in Crew and Kleindorfer (1991, 51), this would imply setting the presort discount exactly equal to the marginal cost which in this case is the cost avoided by presorting. The discount should be equal to the long-run marginal cost (LRMC) which should be forward-looking in that it should reflect automation planned but not yet installed. If the presorter's costs are above the postal authority's LRMC, then they will not enter the market. If their costs are below the postal authority's LRMC, then they will appropriately claim part of the market, and this will be an efficient solution, as the sum of the costs of the entrants and incumbent of providing mail service will be lower than when monopoly alone provided mail service.

Contrast this with a situation where the regulator decides to encourage "competition" in mail service and requires the postal authority to set a discount greater than LRMC. This will result in the entry of firms into the business of providing parts of the postal value chain at higher costs than the postal authority can perform them. This would clearly be an inefficient solution, as total costs would be higher. In addition, the postal authority would lose money and have to raise rates elsewhere. Consumers would be worse off overall although some would benefit by the lower rate charged by the entrants.

The postal authority is able to reduce entry by offering discounts less than its LRMC. In addition, the postal authority has the proprietary information needed to compute LRMC whereas entrants and the government do not. This means that it is likely that a postal authority, basing discounts on LRMC, will have an incentive to understate its estimates of LRMC. However, the power of the postal authority is limited in this regard. For example, too low an estimate of LRMC for the "competitive" parts of the value chain will result in questioning through the regulatory process of the costs of the monopoly portion and the total price. There are some incentives then for postal authority to provide fairly accurate, albeit low, revelations of its LRMC.

The question is do discounts that are too high damage efficiency more that those which are too low? Absent the obligation for universal service at a uniform price, discounts above LRMC of the postal authority might still be useful, in that they might encourage competition and this itself might provide some spur to operating efficiencies of the entrants and the postal authority.[12] However, within universal service obligations at uniform prices, the effect of higher discounts could undermine efficiency and financial viability through adverse selection (cream skimming) by new entrants. The entrants would only wish to deal with high volume mail which only occurs in the low cost areas, leaving the postal authority with loss of contribution on this mail and still the obligation to serve the high cost areas.

The problem can be illustrated by means of a simple example. Assume there are two areas—low and high cost. We break the costs of the value chain into fixed-network, sorting, transportation, and local delivery for each area. Table 1 shows that the network just breaks even at a price of 20¢ at the volumes shown.

However, if discounts for drop-shipment to the local delivery network are set at

Table 1. Illustrative Example

	High Cost Market	Low Cost Market
Sorting	4¢	4¢
Transport	2¢	1¢
Delivery	12¢	10¢
Volume (pieces)	200	1,000
Fixed network costs	$54	
Price	20¢	

5.9¢, there will likely be very limited entry into the high cost market and substantial entry into the low cost area. Let us say entrants provide 10 pieces in the high cost market and 200 in the low cost market. The net result is a loss by the postal authority of $1.79. Contrast this with a situation where the discount is set at 5¢, and the entry into the low cost market drops to 30 while entry in the High cost market drops to zero. The net result is break-even, as was the case before entry. This simple example serves to illustrate that the potential damage from too high a discount may be greater than of too low a discount. Based on examples such as the above, and some specific models, Baumol and Sidak (1994) and Panzar (1992) argue that discounts should be set at LRMC. While their argument was developed in the context of a single product, it remains valid here, but some care must be exercised in its interpretation. Indeed, as the example has illustrated, where there are high

12 See, e.g., Chapter 6 of Crew and Kleindorfer (1992) for an analysis of the dynamic effects of pricing in promoting efficient entry.

and low cost areas (or services) for local delivery, the discount should be set based on the LRMC of the low cost area—not the average of the two—otherwise there may be excessive (inefficient) entry into the low cost area. If this is done, then there may actually be some benefits to the postal authority from so doing as well as providing signals for efficient entry. Only firms with lower costs would enter the market and make profits. They, in turn, would offer lower prices which would increase traffic at the local delivery network. Given the scale economies at the local delivery network, this would increase net revenues. However, given the likely magnitude of the elasticities, this effect is unlikely to be substantial. As we point out in the Technical Appendix to this paper, however, the LRMC rule itself is not generally welfare optimal if the postal authority is required to break even. In this case, application of the simple Ramsey logic would suggest markups over welfare optimal prices that would be greater for the more inelastic customers. In particular, if the more inelastic customers were the users of end-to-end postal service, we would expect a higher markup for them than for the more elastic users of downstream access. Achieving these relative markups would imply giving a discount larger than marginal cost for downstream access users. However, as the previous discussion has underlined the problems of giving excessively large discounts, the LRMC rule may represent a reasonable starting point for discounting policy even in this case.

4. Considerations for Efficient Pricing with Downstream Access

To apply this analysis to actual problems facing postal service, we have to relax some of the simplifying assumptions used above to accommodate some of the complexities. We illustrate by means of a well-known example, namely the two-tier policy of Royal Mail (RM) and its existing discount structures.

Under downstream access, the existing structure of rates would have to be modified if the benefits of the two-tier system are to be retained. (These are universal service of high quality and differentiated levels.) The basic 25p and 19p First and Second Class mail as well as Mailsort 1 and Mailsort 2 would be threatened in the event of downstream access if Mailsort 3 were to continue under downstream access. Mailsort 3 currently provides a discount in the range 25-32% off the 19p Second Class rate depending on quantity. Mailsort 1 offers the same service standards as First Class and Mailsort 2 the same standard as Second Class. Mailsort 3 offers a significantly lower service standard—delivery within 7 days. The long time allowed for delivery provides RM with considerable flexibility in terms of when it transports the mail from sorting facilities, which results in significant cost savings which RM passes on. It also embodies a quantity discount. While this may seem appealing, it may lead to arbitrage or consolidation if the discount is set too high.

Under the current situation, the discounts provided by the Mailsort tariffs have apparently not led to inefficient entry. This would likely change in the event of the adoption of downstream access to the local delivery network, if the two-tier system is to continue. Mailsort 3 would provide significant arbitrage possibilities in a situation with downstream access and the two-tier system. Consolidators could arrange for the collection of mail from small businesses as well as large businesses and offer a very low rate for local mail compared to First Class or Mailsort 1 and provide effectively the same quality of service. Consolidators would be able to take local First Class and Mailsort 1 letters to the local delivery network where it would receive the same treatment as any other mail. Mailsort 3 offers a large discount because of the flexibility it allows with originating mail and because it includes quantity discounts. Since all mail is treated identically at the local delivery stage, existing Mailsort 3 discounts would enable consolidators to undercut RM even though their costs might be higher.

What are the solutions to this problem? One possibility would be to change the local delivery networks so that they can distinguish between different classes of mail. However, this is likely to raise cost, as storing mail there would presumably require the provision of additional facilities. An alternative employed in the United States is to allow downstream access only for Third Class mail which restricts contents mainly to advertizing material and printed matter. Another possibility would be to abandon the two-tier system. Given the advantages of the two-tier system (see Crew and Kleindorfer (1992)), getting rid of it would not appear to be attractive. Let us explore some of the alternatives to this, including the LRMC proposal introduced above, all of which would involve reducing the discount on, or abolishing altogether, Mailsort 3. We analyze only one of these in detail here, but we explore other variants in the Technical Appendix. The alternative which we analyze here we refer to, following Baumol and Sidak (1994), Panzar (1993), and Dobbs and Richards (1993), as "Top-down Efficient Component Pricing" (TECP). Under TECP, the discount of each link in the postal value chain for each class of mail is set equal to the LRMC (or avoided long-run cost) of processing a unit of mail according to the service standards of the indicated class in that link of the postal value chain. We call this "Top-down" because the reference point against which discounts are set is the price of the highest cost class (First Class mail) required to make the entire price structure break even. An example will clarify our intent.

In highly simplified terms, the rates for RM under downstream access might be represented by the following structure:

First Class	P_1
Second Class	$P_2 = P_1 - d$
Mailsort 1	$P_1 - m$
Mailsort 2	$P_1 - d - m = P_2 - m$
Downstream A	$D_A = P_1 - d - m - t$
Downstream B	$D_B = P_1 - d - m - t - q = P_2 - m - t - q$

We use the following notation in the above:

d = difference between First Class and Second Class mail processing costs;

m = avoided cost of presorting;
t = avoided cost from downstream access; and
q = avoided cost arising from handling large volumes.

In the above TECP scheme, the process begins with specifying P_1; every other price is determined from this and the cost structure of the RM. Given this procedure, P_1 is set so that the postal authority breaks even. Note that this particular implementation of efficient component pricing enjoys several desirable properties. First, it is relatively transparent for regulatory purposes. Second, as noted above, it has desirable entry signalling properties, in that only entrants with lower costs than the postal authority will have an incentive to enter various activity segments. Finally, this implementation is conservative relative to the financial viability of the postal authority, in that it places the total responsibility for recovery of fixed costs on the local network where the postal authority has a monopoly.

It should be noted immediately, however, that TECP is not the only approach to break-even pricing consistent with the dictates of efficient component pricing, as laid out by Baumol and Sidak (1994). These dictates would include the following for the total pricing structure:

1. The pricing structure should lead to overall breakeven operations.
2. The revenue from any activity in the postal value chain should not exceed the stand-alone cost for an efficient producer performing that activity only.
3. The revenue from any activity in the postal value chain should be no lower than the incremental cost for the postal system to perform that activity.

It can be shown under reasonable conditions that TECP satisfies these three dictates, but there may be other price structures that also satisfy these. One possibility is a "partial" Ramsey solution, for example:

First Class	P_1
Second Class	P_2
Mailsort 1	$P_1 - m$
Mailsort 2	$P_2 - m$
Downstream A	$D_A = P_1 - d - m - t$
Downstream B	$D_B = P_1 - d - m - t - q$

This is a Partial Ramsey solution in the following sense: P_1 and P_2 are Ramsey prices and are to be determined in the usual fashion so as to maximize total welfare subject to the breakeven constraints. However, the other prices are set top down from P_1 and P_2, not with regard to inverse elasticities or some other rule. Comparing the Partial Ramsey solution and the TECP solution, we would expect that the P_1 (resp., P_2) in the Partial Ramsey solution would be greater than the corresponding P_1 (resp., less than the corresponding P_2) in the TECP solution.[13]

13 Note that, in the above Partial Ramsey solution, all downstream access prices are derived from P_1, using appropriate avoided cost discounts. An alternative Partial Ramsey solution would

As we show in the Technical Appendix, both the full Ramsey and the Partial Ramsey approaches offer greater efficiency gains than the more constrained TECP approach. However, the TECP approach is arguably more transparent. In addition, it is easier to compute and estimate than the Partial Ramsey approach. This discussion suggests several open questions concerning optimal tariff structure when competitive entry is possible. These include the following:

i. What is the structure of optimal prices subject to the above three conditions? In particular, are Ramsey prices sustainable under reasonable assumptions on the cost structure of the postal value chain?

ii. What is the welfare loss implied by using the relatively clear TECP price structure versus the (typically more complex but higher welfare) Partial or full Ramsey price structure?

iii. What are the implications of TECP and other price structures for revenue stability and short-term cost coverage in the face of entry? In particular, what is the structure of dynamic entry-efficient pricing for a multi-supplier value chain like the postal system?

While some progress has been made in addressing these questions in both a general setting as well as in the postal context (see Crew and Kleindorfer (1992)), these remain open research questions. At present, a reasonable approach would appear to be the TECP approach which motivates efficient entry,[14] yet provides a conservative approach to cost coverage for the postal system and equal access to the local delivery network.

5. Caveats and Future Research

The most important caveat relative to the above is that the state of knowledge of appropriate policy for the postal context is still not adequately developed. We have pointed above and in our several recent research publications a number of key issues which seem reasonable benchmarks for good policy at present. But the increasing pace of competition, technological change, and regulatory change certainly call for both conservative approaches, given our knowledge, but also development of our knowledge base through theoretical and practical research. The above discussion points to several topics which seem important for the research agenda.

---

derive D_A and D_B from P_2, e.g., $D_A = P_2 - m - t$; $D_B = P_2 - m - t - q$. Which of these alternative Partial Ramsey solutions would be welfare superior would depend on the usual "least distortion," principle of the Ramsey logic. We would expect that benchmarking the Partial Ramsey solution on First Class (i.e., on P_1) would yield higher downstream access prices and would be more conservative with respect to revenue stability of the postal administration.

14 Given the results of Crew and Kleindorfer (1992, Chapter 6), the level of entry implied by TECP may be lower than welfare optimal, when there is delayed reponse by potential entrants to market opportunities. In this case, larger discounts could be used to provide incentives to move more rapidly to an efficient equilibrium.

Theoretical Work: We have indicated throughout this paper some of the open issues on optimal pricing and entry, all of which seem important for future research.

Regulation: As currently organized, all postal authorities employ cross subsidies, not least the subsidies to high cost areas from the geographically uniform price. If these kind of subsidies are to continue, post offices will need to retain some monopoly power which will imply some form of regulation. In Crew and Kleindorfer (1992), we raised the idea of the possible application of the original Littlechild (1983) proposal for price-cap regulation. Under this proposal, the monopoly services, particularly First and Second Class, would be subject to the price cap and the postal authority would have more freedom on competitive services. Development of such a regulatory scheme is beyond the scope of this paper, but would be necessary in the event that competitive entry continues.

Universal Service/Uniform Pricing Obligation: These obligations are significant. If they are to remain, entry will be less than in their absence. It is beyond the scope of this paper to address these issues in detail. Absent such obligations, more entry would likely be possible and RM might wish to find that an optimal policy was one that allowed local managers to fix the fees for access to the local delivery networks under their control. A less radical alternative would be a classification system for local delivery networks into, say, low, medium, and high cost networks with cost-based prices for access to these different classes of network. Such considerations are important if government policy moves in the direction of further entry, which would need to go hand in hand with reduced universal service/uniform pricing obligations.

References

Baumol, W.J., and G.J. Sidak. 1994. "Pricing of Inputs Sold to Competitors." *Yale Journal on Regulation* (Winter): 171-202.

Bruun, C. 1993. "Nordic Measurements 1991: Service Performance and Terminal Dues Settlement." In Crew and Kleindorfer (1993).

Crew, M.A., and P.R. Kleindorfer. 1971. "Marshall and Turvey and Peak Load or Joint Product Pricing." *Journal of Political Economy* 79 (No. 6, November): 1369-77.

Crew, M.A., and P.R. Kleindorfer. 1979. *Public Utility Economics*. London: Macmillan.

Crew, M.A., and P.R. Kleindorfer. 1986. *The Economic of Public Utility Regulations*. London: Macmillan.

Crew, M.A., and P.R. Kleindorfer. 1991a. *Competition and Innovation in Postal Services*. Boston: Kluwer Academic Publishers.

Crew, M.A., and P.R. Kleindorfer. 1991b. "Peak Load Pricing and Postal Service and Competition." In Crew and Kleindorfer (1991a).

Crew, M.A., and P.R. Kleindorfer. 1992. *The Economics of Postal Service*. Boston: Kluwer Academic Publishers.

Crew, M. A., and P.R. Kleindorfer. 1993. *Regulation and the Nature of Postal and Delivery Services*. Boston: Kluwer.

Crew, M.A., P.R. Kleindorfer, and M.A. Smith. 1990. "Peak Load Pricing and Postal Service." *Economic Journal* (September): 793-807.

Dobbs, I., and P. Richards. 1993. "Policy Implications of Postal Network Access." In Crew

and Kleindorfer (1993).
Kleindorfer, P.R. 1987. *Testimony on behalf of the U.S. Postal Service.*
Lazarowitz, S. 1989. "Request of the United States Postal Service for an Advisory Opinion on a Change in First Class Delivery Standards." Docket # N89-1, U.S. Postal Rate Commission, Washington, DC.
Littlechild, S.C. 1983. *Regulation of British Telecommunications' Profitability.* U.K. Department of Trade and Industry, London.
National Board for Prices and Incomes. 1986. *Post Office Charges.* Report 58, Cmnd 3574, HMSO.
Panzar, J.C. 1993. "Competition, Efficiency, and the Vertical Structure of Postal Services." In Crew and Kleindorfer (1993).
Potter, J. 1989. "Request of the United States Postal Service for an Advisory Opinion on a Change in First Class Delivery Standards." Docket # N89-1, U.S. Postal Rate Commission, Washington, DC.
Reay, I. 1993. "Models of Reliability in Postal Services." In Crew and Kleindorfer (1993).
Rohlfs, G. 1979. "Economically Efficient Bell System Prices." *Bell Laboratories Discussion Paper* #138.
Vitor, R.H.K., and D.L. Davidson. 1985. "Economics and Politics of Deregulation: The Issue of Telephone Access Charges." *Journal of Policy Analysis and Management* 5(1): 3-22.

Technical Appendix. Modeling the Postal Value Chain and Downstream Access

In this Appendix, we consider a variation on the Ramsey problem in which the postal authority faces competition in some aspect of its service. Our aim is to provide a rigorous framework for optimal pricing for the postal context and to relate this to the discussion in the paper of "Efficient Component Pricing" and related breakeven questions for optimal drop-shipment discounts. This Appendix is intended to be self-contained and may be read independently of the preceding paper. It is based in part on Crew and Kleindorfer (1992, Chapters 2, 3, and 6).

Postal service consists of many steps (facing, presorting, barcoding, sorting, delivery to postal walks, etc.). Competition may arise from entrants who are prepared to provide substitutes for some of the mail processing steps external to the postal authority. Since this saves the postal authority resources, a prima facie case for a discount exists for companies which perform one or more of the steps required for postal service. These external suppliers compete with the postal authority and they may provide services such as presorting, consolidation, and drop-shipment to final delivery areas. Clearly, the higher the discount for each such service, the higher the incentive for firms to enter the market in providing these different services. We are interested here in describing the general approach for evaluating discounts which promote efficient entry and discourage inefficient entry. We will be also concerned with an optimal pricing/discount structure which leaves the postal authority in a breakeven position. For simplicity, we will refer to "discounts for external presorting," but the same logic would apply to "drop-shipment discounts" or any other activity in the postal value chain which could be open for competition.

We assume two classes of mail: "First-Class" mail is denoted C1 and "Second-Class" mail by C2. We assume that the level of service offered to these classes of mail is higher for C1 than for C2, and that customers are therefore willing to pay more for C1 than for C2 and that certain costs (noted below) are higher for C1 than for C2. For each class, uniform prices (P_1 and P_2) must be charged, i.e., prices not varying with time of day.

We assume a heterogeneous population of consumers denoted by $\theta \in [0,1]$, where the number of consumers of type $\leq \theta$ is given by the distribution function $F(\theta)$, which is assumed to have a continuous density $f(\theta)$. Consumers of type θ have preferences for postal services x and a Hicksian aggregate m, as represented by a separable utility function

$$U(x, m; \theta) = V(x; \theta) + m, \tag{1}$$

where m is the numeraire and $x = \{x_i \mid i = 1,2\}$; x_i represents demand for service i in period t. Consumers know that $C1$ receives better service than $C2$ and therefore the willingness-to-pay function V in (1) satisfies

$$\frac{\partial}{\partial \gamma} V(x_1 + \gamma, x_2 - \gamma; \theta) > 0, \text{ for all } \theta. \tag{2}$$

The implication of (2) is that every consumer θ prefers $C1$ service in either period to $C2$ service.

Denote $P = (P_1, P_2)$. Since the budget constraint is obviously binding given (1), demand $x(P; \theta)$ for consumer θ is determined as the solution to

$$\underset{x \geq 0}{Maximize} \left[V(x; \theta) - \sum_{i=1}^{2} P_i x_i(P; \theta)\right]. \tag{3}$$

Assuming that V is concave and monotonic increasing implies the usual characterizing conditions for demand $x(P; \theta)$. In particular, $\partial V/\partial x_i = P_i$ whenever $x_i > 0$. Since (2) implies that $\partial V/\partial x_1 > \partial V/\partial x_2$, demand for $C2$ will vanish unless $P_1 > P_2$.

A customer can either subscribe to full service, in which presorting is done by the postal authority, or the customer can contract with a presorting bureau, a competitor of the postal service, and only use the postal authority for basic mail service. Basic service is sold at a discount below full service. We assume that it costs the customer something to contract for external presorting. We model these costs as a fixed cost S per period, where one may think of S as the contracting/billing cost for a customer using an external presorting bureau. Alternatively, one may think of S as the fixed cost per period for the presorting bureau for serving a customer, a cost which is passed on to the customer. Just as in competitive bypass in telecommunications, these fixed costs imply that larger customers will find it more economical to switch to external presorting. Put differently, the key point here is that "larger" customers will be more attractive targets for competitors than smaller customers. The number of such customers who decide to switch will, of course, depend on the difference in the price between full and basic service, i.e., on the presort discount. We are interested in the determination of Ramsey-optimal prices and presort discounts which allow the postal authority to break even and encourage efficient entry into the presort market.

Let $P = (P_1, P_2)$ denote the price of full service (full service includes the cost of all operations) for $C1$ and $C2$ and let $p = (p_1, p_2)$ denote the price of basic service for $C1$ and $C2$. The price the customer actually pays if external presorting is used is then

$$p + s = (p_1 + s_1, p_2 + s_2), \tag{4}$$

where $s = (s_1, s_2)$ is the vector of unit costs of external presorting, which we assume is provided competitively. The customer also incurs a fixed cost of S, e.g., a subscription fee for the presort service, in setting up for external presorting operations.

If a customer θ uses full service, his demands are given by $x(P; \theta)$ as determined by (3). If a customer elects external presorting, then his demands are given by the solution to

$$\underset{x \geq 0}{Maximize}\ [V(x; \theta) - (p + s)x]\ , \tag{5}$$

where we have used the vector notation $(p + s)x = \Sigma(p_i + s_i)\, x_i$. Clearly, a customer will elect external presorting precisely when the benefits of so doing exceed the fixed contracting cost S, i.e., when

$$[V(x(p + s; \theta); \theta)\ -\ (p + s)\, x(p + s; \theta)\ -\ S] \geq [V(x(P; \theta); \theta)\ -\ Px(P; \theta)]\ . \tag{6}$$

To proceed further, we make the assumption that the function

$$\xi(P, p; \theta) = V(x(p + s; \theta); \theta) - V(x(P; \theta); \theta) \tag{7}$$

is increasing in θ for each fixed P, p with $(p + s) \leq P$.[15] Clearly, unless $(p + s) \leq P$, no basic service will be demanded. The import of this assumption is that the larger the customer (i.e., the larger θ), the larger the willingness to pay for presort discounts. Assuming $\partial\xi/\partial\theta > 0$, and noting from preference maximization (3) that $\partial V(x(P; \theta); \theta)/\partial x_i = P_i$, we see that

$$\frac{\partial}{\partial\theta}\ [V(x(p + s; \theta); \theta)\ -\ (p + s)\, x(p + s; \theta) - V(x(P; \theta); \theta) + P\, x(P; \theta)]$$

15 This is satisfied, e.g., when $V(x;\theta) = a(\theta)V(x)$, with $a(\theta)$ monotonic increasing in θ.

$$= \frac{\partial}{\partial\theta} [V(x(p+s;\theta);\theta) - V(x(P;\theta);\theta)] = \frac{\partial}{\partial\theta} \xi(P,p;\theta) > 0, \tag{8}$$

so that, from (6), if customer θ prefers external presorting at prices (P,p), then so does every customer $\theta' > \theta$.

Define $M(P,p)$ as the market share of the postal authority in presort service. $M \in [0,1]$ is just the largest customer type which still finds it preferable to have the postal authority presort its mail. For every $\theta > M$, (6) is satisfied. From (6) and monotonicity of indirect utility in prices, we see directly that $\partial M/\partial P_j < 0$, $\partial M/\partial p_j = \partial M/\partial s_j > 0$.

Let the total cost function $C(X, Y)$ for the postal authority depend on the demand for full service ($X = (X_1, X_2)$) and on demand for basic service ($Y = (Y_1, Y_2)$), where

$$X_i(P,p) = \int_0^M x_i(P;\theta)\, dF(\theta) \tag{9}$$

and

$$Y_i(P,p) = \int_M^1 x_i(p+s;\theta)\, dF(\theta). \tag{10}$$

We assume the following form for $C(X, Y)$:

$$C(X, Y) = G(X+Y) - H(Y), \tag{11}$$

where $G(X)$ and $H(Y)$ will be assumed to arise from appropriate cost minimization problems characterizing optimal operating policies for the postal authority (see, e.g., Crew, Kleindorfer and Smith (1990)), and where $H(Y)$ is to be interpreted as the total cost to the postal service of presorting Y, a cost which is avoided for Y by external presorting. We note that $H(Y)$ may be greater or less than the competitive market presort cost sY.

We can now state the constrained welfare maximization problem of interest. Define total welfare W as net benefits, the sum of producer and consumer surpluses, and profit Π as postal authority profits. Then W and Π may be written as follows:

$$W(P,p) = \int_0^M [V(x(P;\theta);\theta) - P\,x(P;\theta)]\, dF(\theta)$$

$$+ \int_M^1 [V(x(p+s;\theta);\theta) - (p+s)\,x(p+s;\theta) - S\,]\, dF(\theta) + \Pi(P,p)\,, \tag{12}$$

$$\Pi(P,p) = \int_0^M P\,x(P;\theta)\, dF(\theta) + \int_M^1 px(p+s;\theta)\, dF(\theta) - C(X,Y). \tag{13}$$

The first (resp., second) term in (12) is consumer surplus for those consumers who demand normal (resp., only basic) service. The third term is postal authority profits $\Pi(P, p)$, as shown in (13). We assume that external presorting is competitive, so zero profits obtain from that activity.

Taking first-order conditions for maximizing (12) subject to $\Pi(P, p) \geq 0$, and using $\partial V/\partial x_{i_t} = P_i$ as implied by (3), yields the following for Ramsey-optimal prices P and p:

$$\frac{\partial W}{\partial P_j} + \mu \frac{\partial \Pi}{\partial P_j} = - X_j(P, p) + [V(x(P;M);M) - P\,x(P;M)]\, f(M) \frac{\partial M}{\partial P_j} \tag{14}$$

$$- [V(x(p+s;M);M) - (p+s)\, x(p+s;M) - S]\, f(M) \frac{\partial M}{\partial P_j}$$

$$+ (1+\mu)\left(\sum_{i=1}^{2} \left[P_i - \frac{\partial C}{\partial X_i}\right] \frac{\partial X_i}{\partial P_j} + X_j(P, p) + \sum_{i=1}^{2} \left[p_i - \frac{\partial C}{\partial Y_i}\right] \frac{\partial Y_i}{\partial P_j} \right),$$

$$\frac{\partial W}{\partial p_j} + \mu \frac{\partial \Pi}{\partial p_j} = - Y_j(P, p) + [V(x(P;M);M) - P\,x(P;M)]\, f(M) \frac{\partial M}{\partial p_j} \tag{15}$$

$$- [V(x(p+s;M);M) - (p+s)\, x(p+s;M) - S]\, f(M) \frac{\partial M}{\partial p_j}$$

$$+ (1+\mu)\left(\sum_{i=1}^{2} \left[P_i - \frac{\partial C}{\partial X_i}\right] \frac{\partial X_i}{\partial p_j} + Y_j(P, p) + \sum_{i=1}^{2} \left[p_i - \frac{\partial C}{\partial Y_i}\right] \frac{\partial Y_i}{\partial p_j} \right).$$

Now note from the definition of the marginal consumer M that (6) holds as an equality for $\theta = M$, so that the second and third terms in both (14)-(15) cancel, leading to the following first-order conditions for optimal P_j and p_j, $j = 1,2$:

$$(1+\mu)\left(\sum_{i=1}^{2} \left[P_i - \frac{\partial C}{\partial X_i}\right] \frac{\partial X_i}{\partial P_j} + \sum_{i=1}^{2} \left[p_i - \frac{\partial C}{\partial Y_i}\right] \frac{\partial Y_i}{\partial P_j} \right) + \mu\, X_j(P, p) = 0, \tag{16}$$

$$(1+\mu)\left(\sum_{i=1}^{2} \left[P_i - \frac{\partial C}{\partial X_i}\right] \frac{\partial X_i}{\partial p_j} + \sum_{i=1}^{2} \left[p_i - \frac{\partial C}{\partial Y_i}\right] \frac{\partial Y_i}{\partial p_j} \right) + \mu\, Y_j(P, p) = 0. \tag{17}$$

While (16)-(17) are on the face of it just the conditions for the traditional Ramsey solution for the goods (X, Y), there are added complexities in the present context because of the interactions between X and Y on both the cost and the demand side. Let us analyze a few specific cases to indicate the general nature of the solution to (16)-(17).

The Welfare-Optimal Solution is Marginal-Cost Pricing

We can derive the solution for the welfare-optimal case (where $\mu = 0$) in a straightforward manner. For this case, assuming the usual non-singularity of the Jacobian matrix $\{\partial X/\partial P, \partial Y/\partial p)$, it is clear from (16)-(17) that the welfare-optimal solution is price equal to marginal cost, i.e. from (11)

$$P_i = \frac{\partial C}{\partial X_i} = \frac{\partial G}{\partial X_i}, \tag{18}$$

$$p_i = \frac{\partial C}{\partial Y_i} = \frac{\partial G}{\partial Y_i} - \frac{\partial H}{\partial Y_i}. \tag{19}$$

Since from (11) clearly $\partial G/\partial X_i = \partial G/\partial Y_i$, we see moreover that the postal authority sets the presort discount for class i at exactly its marginal cost $\partial H/\partial Y_i$ of presorting. If $\partial H/\partial Y_i < s_i$, the prevailing unit cost for presorting in the market, then the postal authority will capture the entire market. If $\partial H/\partial Y_i > s_i$, then some market share will be lost to competitors, with the magnitude of market share loss depending on $(\partial H/\partial Y_i) - s_i$ and S. We see from (18)-(19) that in this case $P_i = p_i + \partial H/\partial Y_i$.

The Ramsey-Optimal Solution and Approximations

Interestingly, even when marginal costs are constant for each class, the Ramsey solution need not satisfy $P_i = p_i + \partial H/\partial Y_i$. Thus, the presort discount under Ramsey pricing will depend on market share dynamics and on the relative unit cost advantage $(\partial H/\partial Y_i - s_i)$ enjoyed by the postal authority over the competition. The full Ramsey solution is obtainable from (16)-(17). This could be expressed as in Rohlfs (1979) in inverse-elasticity form, using "super elasticities" to reflect interactions across products. But, as is well known, this general solution is difficult to interpret.

Alternatively, following the lines of Baumol (1991) and as discussed in the paper, one could argue that there are advantages in transparency and financial stability to approximations to the full Ramsey solution. Let us consider two of these here. The first is the Top-Down Efficient Component Pricing (TECP) solution discussed in the text, and the second is the Partial Ramsey (PR) solution. In discussing these, we will use the shorthand notation:

$$G_i = \frac{\partial G}{\partial X_i} = \frac{\partial G}{\partial Y_i}; \quad H_i = \frac{\partial H}{\partial X_i}. \tag{20}$$

Top-Down Efficient Component Pricing (TECP)

In formal terms, the TECP case is modelled in the present context by appending the following constraints to the Ramsey formulation (12)-(13):

$$P_i = p_i + H_{i,} \;\; i = 1{,}2; \;\; P_1 = P_2 + d, \tag{21}$$

where d is an approximation of the difference in marginal cost between First and Second Class (full) service, i.e.,

$$d = \frac{\partial C}{\partial X_1} - \frac{\partial C}{\partial X_2}. \tag{22}$$

According to (21), the discount for presort is required to be precisely the LRMC of this operation to the postal authority and the differential between First Class and Second Class is required to be d. In the TECP approach, the postal authority is to maximize welfare (12) subject to breaking even ($\Pi(P,p) \geq 0$ in (13)) and subject further to the restrictions implied by (21). Thus, in the TECP approach, effectively only P_1 is free to vary (and is set so that, subject to other prices being determined by (21), breakeven is achieved).

In the Partial Ramsey (PR) approach, a similar approach to TECP is used except that, instead of (21), the following constraints are imposed:

$$P_i = p_i + H_{i,} \;\; i = 1{,}2. \tag{23}$$

In the PR approach, P_1 and P_2 are both free to vary (with p_1 and p_2 then determined by (23)). Note that (23) is a weaker set of constraints than (21), since fewer constraints are imposed. Thus, the welfare-maximization approach subject to $\Pi(P,p) \geq 0$ and to (23) yields a higher value of welfare than maximizing (12) subject to $\Pi(P,p) \geq 0$ and (21). Put differently, the Partial Ramsey approach which allows both P_1 and P_2 to be set according to Ramsey logic achieves higher welfare than the more constrained TECP approach in which only P_1 is allowed to vary freely. Of course, one might argue that TECP is more transparent to customers and perhaps easier to estimate than the PR approach. This sort of tradeoff between various characteristics of alternative tariff structures is common in the public enterprise pricing literature.

To compute either TECP or PR, one would append constraints (21) or (23) to the Lagrangean determining the first-order conditions and proceed as with the full Ramsey problem. For example, consider PR and assume for convenience that H_i is constant. Then, appending the constraints (23) to the maximization of (12) subject to $\Pi(P,p) \geq 0$, as in (13), and (23) (with Lagrange multipliers λ_i associated with the constraint $P_i = p_i + H_i$), we obtain the following first-order conditions mirroring (16)-(17) for $j = 1{,}2$:

$$(1+\mu)\left(\sum_{i=1}^{2}\left[P_i - \frac{\partial C}{\partial X_i}\right]\frac{\partial X_i}{\partial P_j} + \sum_{i=1}^{2}\left[p_i - \frac{\partial C}{\partial Y_i}\right]\frac{\partial Y_i}{\partial P_j}\right) + \mu\, X_j(P,p) = -\lambda_j, \tag{24}$$

$$(1+\mu)\left(\sum_{i=1}^{2}\left[P_i - \frac{\partial C}{\partial X_i}\right]\frac{\partial X_i}{\partial p_j} + \sum_{i=1}^{2}\left[p_i - \frac{\partial C}{\partial Y_i}\right]\frac{\partial Y_i}{\partial p_j}\right) + \mu\, Y_j(P, p) = \lambda_j. \quad (25)$$

Since from (23) $p_i = P_i - H_i$ and since from (11) $\partial C/\partial Y_i = \partial C/\partial X_i - H_i$, it is clear that at the optimum to the problem of maximizing (12) subject to (13) and (23), we must have:

$$P_i - \frac{\partial C}{\partial X_i} = p_i - \frac{\partial C}{\partial Y_i},\ i = 1, 2. \quad (26)$$

Thus, using (26), we can simplify (24)-(25) to obtain the following conditions characterizing the PR solution (these are conditions only on the free variables P_i, $i = 1,2$, since the variables p_i are determined from the P_i and (23)):

$$(1+\mu)\left(\sum_{i=1}^{2}\left[P_i - \frac{\partial C}{\partial X_i}\right]\left[\frac{\partial X_i}{\partial P_j} + \frac{\partial Y_i}{\partial P_j} + \frac{\partial X_i}{\partial p_j} + \frac{\partial Y_i}{\partial p_j}\right]\right) = -\mu\left(X_j + Y_j\right);$$

$$j = 1,2. \quad (27)$$

The reader may note an interesting resemblance between (27) and the general two-product Ramsey conditions. We will leave for future research the detailed analysis of (27) and the analogous conditions for TECP. We only note here the key point of this initial analysis: appending constraints to the general Ramsey formulation (e.g., of the form (21) and (23)) may help achieve clarity of the tariff structure or other qualitative benefits, but these benefits must come at the cost of some loss of welfare relative to the unconstrained approach (12)-(13). A major question for future research is to bound this welfare loss. If this loss is small under normal operating conditions for the postal authority, then the increase in clarity and revenue stability associated with the TECP or the PR solution may well be worth it.

9

AN ECONOMETRIC MODEL OF POSTAL DELIVERY[1]

Michael D. Bradley
Jeff Colvin

1. Introduction

The traditional economic justification for the state regulation of an industry is based upon its technological cost structure. To put the matter simply, if a single firm can produce the industry's output(s) more cheaply than two or more firms, then duplicating the effort must necessarily be wasteful. In such cases, therefore, the state may wish to permit or even protect the monopoly, yet regulate the price of its services to prevent abuses. It is possible in some industries, on the other hand, that the mere threat of entry will exercise sufficient gravitational pull to prevent prices from exceeding costs. In others, there may be obstructions of various kinds which prevent competitive forces from playing this socially useful role. Such obstructions include "natural" barriers to entry of sundry types, or obstructions may be deliberately erected as a matter of social policy. It may be felt that universal service carries such a positive external benefit that entry into the natural monopolist's more vulnerable products should be prohibited. Both arguments have been raised in support of restricting entry into postal services.[2]

Thus, a complete economic justification of entry restrictions would go beyond cost considerations to include an examination of demand and other issues. Be that as it may, cost subadditivity remains the fundamental necessary condition for the justification of entry restrictions.[3] In this paper, our primary purpose is to report the results of quantitative research on the cost characteristics of delivery services. We present a specific functional form for postal delivery that is strongly grounded

---

1 The views expressed in this paper are those of the authors and do not necessarily represent the opinions of the United States Postal Service.

2 See Estrin and de Meza (1991, 95). Also see Dobbs and Richards (1991, 80) for a discussion of sunk costs in postal services.

3 For a general discussion of natural monopoly in the context of the regulation of postal services, see Crew and Kleindorfer (1992, 15-20).

in statistical theory and operational reality. We then show that under positive marginal cost, this function generates subadditivity. Finally, we estimate the function and present empirical measures of economies of scope. The data strongly suggest that delivery services are subadditive; and, as discussed below, this finding has some important policy implications.

2. The Role of Delivery Costs in Postal Economics

Events of the most recent half decade have placed postal costs, and the analysis of postal costs, under a bright spotlight. Postal privatization debates have raged in major industrial countries, several countries have actually privatized all or part of their postal services, and in 1992 the EC Commission issued the *Postal Green Paper* as part of an effort to confront the many issues raised by the growth of competition in the provision of delivery services. All of this has taken place within a charged political environment, concerning utility regulation in general, in which alternatives to traditional regulation have gone beyond debate to actual implementation. These alternatives have ranged from outright privatization to price level regulation. Thus, the question of the cost justification for regulation has been placed and remains squarely on the table.

Several studies have indicated the presence of scale and scope economies in postal services. But this is not true of all studies of postal costs, and the matter is far from settled.[4] Early cost studies of overall operations did not show unambiguous scale or scope economies. Merewitz's 1971 cross sectional study of U S. Postal facilities found increasing returns in small and medium offices, but decreasing returns for large facilities.[5] Stevenson's time series study showed decreasing returns.[6] Norsworthy, Jang, and Shi (1991) found fixed costs associated with the postal network and declining marginal costs of delivery. Christensen, Christensen, Guy, and O'Hara (1993) found constant returns to proportionate changes in volume and delivery points, but a .788 elasticity of cost with respect to volume changes alone, indicating increasing returns "from delivering additional mail to a fixed set of delivery points."[7] Bradley and Baron found evidence of increasing returns to scale in their 1993 study of mail processing facilities.

Although extremely useful for a variety of purposes, it is difficult for studies of

---

4 The author of a recent principles text concludes that "careful statistical analysis of the postal service's costs has not been conclusive. Some studies support the Postal Service's claim of substantial economies of scope, while other studies find little or no evidence of economies of scope" Tresch (1994).

5 Merewitz (1979, 504-509).

6 Stevenson (1973). Gupta's 1982 update showed similar results. The data employed in these studies are quite old by now, and some postal technologies have changed. Moreover, Futz (1983) has criticized the functional forms employed in these studies (Cobb-Douglas and CES) as too restrictive to provide definitive information about the underlying cost structure.

7 Christensen (1993, 249).

overall operations to produce definitive results on subadditivity. As has been noted frequently, it is not sufficient to find scale or scope economies at current output, and it is very unlikely that time-series data on overall operations will contain observations at lower levels of output.[8] Even a cross-section of facilities, such as the one employed in Bradley and Baron (1993), is unlikely to exhibit a range of output data broad enough to test for global subadditivity.

Operation specific cross-sectional studies are more likely to have observations on a broader range of output. Such studies have pointed toward delivery as the primary source of economies. Bradley's (1987) work on purchased transportation indicated scale and/or scope economies in short-haul transportation, but Bradley found roughly constant returns in long-haul transportation. Colvin (1990) found evidence of local scale/scope economies in the delivery function.[9] From all this, it would be easy to conclude that if subadditivity is to be found in postal services, it is most likely to reside in the delivery operation.

Perhaps more importantly, the notion of economies in delivery fits nicely with common sense on the subject: just as there are scale advantages in other "networks," such as local loops in telephony and the local distribution of electric power, one would expect the average cost of delivering mail to fall as volume expands.

The somewhat paradoxical centrality of delivery costs to policy debates is highlighted in Panzar (1991). Panzar notes that competition should probably be restricted in industries characterized by subadditive costs.[10] He goes on to show that scale economies in delivery costs are of central importance because, in the absence of countervailing diseconomies in other postal operations, such delivery cost economies will "confer" large scale cost advantages on the entire set of postal operations.

Confident that economies of scale are present in delivery, Panzar concludes that postal service is a natural monopoly.[11] However, as he notes, scale returns in delivery only justify keeping the delivery operation intact; such a finding offers no obvious guidance as to whether this should be accomplished through traditional monopoly regulation, through franchise bidding, or through some other means. Panzar goes on to argue in favor of a Demsetzian scheme first suggested in Owen and Willig (1983).[12]

8 Berg and Tschirhart (1988, 43).

9 See Bradley, Colvin, and Smith (1993) for some further description of these findings and of the U.S. Postal Services' costing system. Also see Rogerson and Takis (1993) for a discussion of the USPS system in the context of natural monopoly.

10 As Panzar (1991, 221) notes, a necessary *and* sufficient economic justification for legal restrictions on entry would require an investigation into the demand side of the issue.

11 Panzar (1991, 222) is far less confident that the subadditivity of the postal cost function will ever be empirically validated. Interfirm cross-sectional data do not exist, and time-series models suffer from a degree-of-freedom problem because of the large number of parameters that require estimation. Enterprise level data may be useful, he argues, but are likely to encounter limitations because they are too aggregative and employ service categories that do not adequately reflect cost causality.

Several writers have picked up this thread of argument. Rogerson and Takis (1993) and Merewitz and Zupan (1993) compare the worksharing arrangements utilized by the U.S. Postal Service to other "contracting-out" mechanisms, including franchise bidding. Although the authors reach quite different conclusions as to the optimal form of regulation, they seem to agree that it would include some restrictions on competition in delivery. Panzar (1993) works out some of the welfare properties of access worksharing under the assumption of increasing returns in the delivery network, with constant returns elsewhere.[13] Colvin and Rogerson (1993) discuss various means of increasing competition in transportation and sorting, while maintaining the entry prohibition on the delivery network.

Other analysts, however, do not agree. Sherman (1991) argues that available data do not support an economic rationale for monopoly, and suggests experimental suspension of the private express statutes for certain types of mail, including addressed third class mail. The Postal Green Paper (1992) recommends "liberalization" of direct mail and cross-border mail, despite finding delivery to be the principal source of economies. Authors calling for the reduction or elimination of the entry restriction in the United States context include Adie (1988) and Moore (1988). In principle, such proposals consider the benefits of scope and scale economies in delivery to be outweighed by other factors.

Quantitative evidence on the subadditivity of street delivery costs can only serve to throw more light on the policy debate. Toward that end, we produce empirical evidence in this paper on the degree of scale and scope economies in delivery, among major classes of mail for the U.S. Postal Service. In addition, we establish and test conditions for natural monopoly.

3. Specifying a Model of Delivery Cost

There are both analytical and operations issues in specifying a model of postal delivery for investigating subadditivity. From the analytical perspective, the delivery model must be specified in a way which allows sufficient diversity in the definition of the "products" being delivered. Mail classes have different delivery-causing characteristics and the model must be general enough to allow for these differences.[14] Representing a broad range of mail classes will also permit the measurement of scope economies among classes. This latter characteristic is important because the decision to permit entry of some type of mail into the delivery system may turn on whether it enjoys cost complementarily with other delivered mail.

Second, the function should be as accurate as possible over large ranges in

---

12 Panzar (1991, 224 and 225).

13 Panzar (1993, 98). Also see Dobbs and Richards (1993) for an analysis of worksharing suggesting caution in pricing access to the postal network.

14 Panzar (1991, 222) discusses this problem.

volume. Subadditivity is a global concept and requires investigation of cost behavior from zero volume through the current volume. This suggests the application of a specific, rather than general functional form, if possible, to capture the cost/volume relationship as all feasible volume levels. At zero volume, for example, the model should predict zero accesses.

Finally, the model should embody certain well known analytical concepts such as measures of scale and scope, and marginal and incremental cost. Tests of subadditivity rely upon the relationship among these various cost concepts, so they should be readily computable.

From the operational perspective, the function should behave in accordance with intuitive notions concerning the incurrence of costs in street delivery. We note that we are focussing on only the "access" portion of delivery in the paper, because this accords with the traditional notion of network economies. We are thus currently ignoring the time costs of loading the mail into the mail receptacle, although we have reason to believe that there may be scale and scope economies in that delivery subfunction.[15] More importantly, the delivery cost model should capture the operational reality of how mail is delivered.

The delivery of mail can be characterized by the coverage of a network of potential deliveries or stops. All existing stops are *possible* stops, but when mail is carried to a stop, a potential stop becomes an *actual* stop or an "access." The number of actual stops or accesses that a delivery carrier has to make depends upon the amount of mail volume to be delivered on the route and the distribution of the mail volume across stops.

In specifying a model of carrier costs, several key characteristics of the nature of the delivery process should be captured in the model:

- The model should contain a direct relationship between mail volume and delivery cost. As mail volume rises, the number of accesses rises and delivery cost rises. Thus, at low levels of volume there should be low levels of total delivery cost and at high volume levels, there should be high levels of total delivery cost.
- Although total cost should rise with volume, marginal cost should decline with volume. At low levels of volume, additional mail will typically go to stops that would not have otherwise received mail and additional delivery cost will be generated. At high volume levels, most stops are receiving mail and additional volume will typically be delivered to stops that were receiving other mail anyway. In this latter case, it is obvious that no additional cost is incurred. One must conclude that in the limit, as volume increases, the marginal cost of delivery falls to zero. This limiting case should also be embodied in a model of delivery cost.
- Different types of mail have different delivery causing characteristics and the

15 For a description of how load and access cost are combined in the USPS product costing system see Bradley, Colvin, and Smith (1993, 146-150).

model should incorporate these differences. For example, a class of mail that is widely broadcast to most all households should have a higher delivery causing characteristic than a class that is intensively targeted to a smaller number of households.

- The delivery cost of a class of mail cannot be considered in isolation from other classes. The addition of new volume of Class A will cause additional delivery cost when "additional" or new accesses are generated. The existence of these additional accesses depends upon the volume of mail and delivery characteristics of *other* classes already being delivered. A delivery cost model should thus capture that the marginal cost of a particular class is a function of the volumes and delivery characteristics of the other classes.

Operational studies of mail delivery have recognized that the probability of mail arriving at any stop is governed by a generating process similar to the Poisson distribution in which the proportion of successes varies with the number of observations.[16] The distribution of mail across possible stops is then modelled as a negative exponential in which deviations from a pure Poisson are captured by estimated parameters. This previous work provides a functional form for delivery costs that embodies the desired characteristics listed above. Delivery cost rises as the number of actual stops rises. The number of actual stops rises as volume is delivered to possible stops. Reflecting this cost causing structure, we specify the delivery cost model as:

$$AS = \left(1 - e^{-\sum_{i=1}^{N} \beta_i \frac{v_i}{PS}}\right) \times PS, \tag{1}$$

where AS is the number of actual stops on a route, v_i is the volume of class i on a route, and PS is the number of possible stops on a route. Note that the volumes are normalized by the number of possible stops on the route. The β coefficients capture the deviation, by mail class, from a pure Poisson distribution. The larger the β_i, the higher the likelihood that an increase in the volume of a particular class will generate an additional actual stop.

To see that this model embodies the desirable properties discussed above let's consider the marginal cost of class k:[17]

16 For examples, see Hume(1976) and Jasinski and Streggles (1977).

17 This is not formally the marginal cost because it is only measuring the change in accesses associated with more volume, not the cost (in time) of making those accesses. If we assume the that cost of an access is constant, then marginal cost can be derived by multiplying the above expression by that constant. If the cost of an access is not constant, then marginal cost can be derived by multiplying the above expression by the derivative of time with respect to accesses.

$$MC_k = \frac{\partial AS}{\partial v_k} = \beta_k e^{-\sum_{i=1}^{N} \beta_i \frac{v_i}{PS}} . \tag{2}$$

Roughly speaking, this formulation of marginal access cost decomposes the marginal effect on actual stops into two components: one, represented by the own coefficient, the density of the *i*th mail class, and two, represented by the exponent term, the amount of mail of all classes delivered on a route. Thus, certain classes are more likely to cause a stop at any level of other classes (until coverage reaches one), but a mail type of a given density (unless it is 100% saturation mail) will have a greater (lesser) propensity to cause stops if less (more) mail of other classes is simultaneously delivered on the route. Because the exponential term is non-negative, the sign of marginal cost depends on the value of β. If all the β are positive than total cost is increasing in volume. Similarly, the change in marginal cost is given by the second derivative:

$$\frac{\partial MC_k}{\partial v_k} = \frac{\partial^2 AS}{\partial v_k^2} = -\frac{\beta_k^2}{PS} e^{-\sum_{i=1}^{N} \beta_i \frac{v_i}{PS}} \leq 0. \tag{3}$$

In addition, this model has the advantage that in the limiting case, the marginal cost will approach zero:

$$\lim_{v_k \to \infty} MC_k = \lim_{v_k \to \infty} \left(\beta_k e^{-\sum_{i=1}^{N} \beta_i \frac{v_i}{PS}} \right) = 0. \tag{4}$$

The estimated β coefficients allow different classes to have differential delivery cost-causing characteristics and equation 2 shows that the marginal cost for class k depends upon both the volume for class k and the estimated coefficient for class k, β_k. In sum, all of the desirable properties of a delivery cost function are captured in this specification.

4. Conditions Required for a Natural Monopoly in Delivery

The key question being investigated in our paper is the existence of a natural monopoly in the delivery function. To that end, we will produce empirical evidence to support or contradict the working hypothesis. The first step in producing that evidence is to establish conditions under which a natural monopoly will occur in delivery. We do this by establishing the theoretical conditions for a natural monopoly in delivery under the exponential model described above. We note that the conditions turn out to be easy to satisfy for this functional form. The evidence we present in favor of a natural monopoly in delivery is in the form of support for the exponential functional form as the correct model of delivery rather than in the form of a traditional statistical test. This is not a strong statistical test.[18] For scale and scope economies to fail for this functional form, the β's must be nonpositive. However, this would imply nonincreasing total costs in volume. Thus, while our results are supportive of scale and scope economies, we do not present a strong statistical test of either.

A multiproduct cost function exhibits the conditions required for a natural monopoly when costs are subadditive. Subadditivity is a global concept and is not ensured by either multiproduct economies of scale or economies of scope. In fact, even the simultaneous existence of the two is not enough to ensure subadditivity.

Our approach, then, in establishing subadditivity, is to follow Baumol, Panzar, and Willig (BPW) who state:[19]

> Decreasing average incremental costs of each product, up to y, and economies of scope at y imply subadditivity at y.

Incremental cost for the exponential delivery function can be derived by applying BPW's general definition for incremental costs to that function. BPW define incremental cost (IC) as the reduction in cost from the removal of one output from the vector of outputs:[20]

The incremental cost of a class $k \in N$ at volume level v is

$$IC_{k(v)} = C(v) - C(v_{N-k}). \tag{5}$$

The associated concept, average incremental cost (AIC) is just incremental cost divided by the amount of class k. Declining AIC requires that AIC falls as the volume of k rises:

$$\frac{\partial AIC}{\partial v_k} < 0, \text{ for all } v_k. \tag{6}$$

For the exponential delivery function, average incremental costs can be defined as[21]

$$AIC_k = PS\, e^{-\sum_{i \neq k} \beta_i \frac{v_i}{PS}} (1 - e^{-\beta_k \frac{v_k}{PS}})\, v_k^{-1} \tag{7}$$

and declining average incremental cost requires:

$$\frac{\partial AIC_k}{\partial v_k} = PS\, e^{-\sum_{i \neq k} \beta_i \frac{v_i}{PS}} (\beta_k \frac{v_k}{PS} e^{-\beta_k \frac{v_k}{PS}} - (1 - e^{-\beta_k \frac{v_k}{PS}}))\, v_k^{-2} < 0, \text{ for all } v_k. \tag{8}$$

Because the exponential functions, PS and vi_i^2 are all positive, it is easy to see that

---

18 We thank John Panzar for pointing this out to us.

19 Baumol, Panzar and Willig (1986, 176). We note that BPW also present an alternative set of conditions: trans-ray convexity and strictly declining ray average costs.

20 Baumol, Panzar, and Willig (1986, 67).

21 For a derivation of this and the following results, see Bradley and Colvin, "On The Existence of Subadditive Delivery Costs for the United States Postal Service." Manuscript 1994. Recall that our measure of cost is AS (Actual Stops), the number of stops receiving mail.

declining average incremental costs requires:

$$(\beta_k \frac{v_k}{PS} e^{-\beta_k \frac{v_k}{PS}} - (1 - e^{-\beta_k \frac{v_k}{PS}})) < 0, \text{ for all } v_k. \tag{9}$$

This condition will hold if β_k is greater than zero. We demonstrate this point by defining $x = \beta_k v_k / PS$. Then (9) is satisfied if $(x + 1)e^{-x} < 1$ for $x > 0$. To see that this is so, define the function $f(x) = (x + 1)e^{-x} - 1$. We wish to show $f(x) < 0$ for $x > 0$. Clearly $f(0) = 0$. Moreover, $f'(x) = - xe^{-x} < 0$ for $x > 0$. Thus, as desired, $f(x) < 0$ for all $x > 0$. This path has led us to the conclusion that the exponential delivery function will embody decreasing average incremental costs for any product that has a positive β.

The other condition that must hold for subadditivity is economies of scope. In general, economies of scope will obtain if C is differentiable function and exhibits weak cost complementarity. For the general cost function, $C(v)$, this requires:

$$C_{kj} \leq 0; \ k \neq j \text{ for all } v_k, \tag{10}$$

with a strict inequality holding for at least some v. Application of this condition to the exponential delivery function requires that for any volume $j, j \neq k$:

$$- \beta_k \beta_j e^{-\sum_{i=1}^{N} \beta_i \frac{v_i}{PS}} PS < 0. \tag{11}$$

Given that PS and the exponential function must be positive, economies of scope is ensured by positive β_j.

We come to the interesting conclusion that estimation of the exponential delivery model will yield information on the existence of economies of scope and decreasing average incremental cost base solely on the sign of the estimated coefficients. If all of the estimated β's are non-negative, and at least some of them are positive, delivery costs are subadditive and the Postal Service has a natural monopoly in the delivery of mail.

The meaning of the subadditivity of the access cost function may be expressed this way. Suppose a natural monopolist postal service delivers only two products, V_A of mail class A and V_B of mail class B. Suppose further that costs are constant not only in transportation and sorting, but in loading delivered mail as well, i.e., that the only source of economies (or diseconomies) is delivery access, or the rate at which these two mail classes cause actual stops to be made.

The finding of scope economies means that it is cheaper to deliver the two classes together (by a single firm) than by two specialized firms. However, on the basis of scope economies alone, it might still be cheaper for some entrant to deliver some fraction of class A mail and some part of class B mail, than for the monopolist to delivery the total volume of A and B together. This is what declining average incremental cost rules out: delivery of a portion of class A volume cannot be cheaper, per unit, than delivering its entire volume (at least up to the observed volume V_A). The same is true for class B.

Apart from the evidence on subadditivity, we may have interest in the degree of scope economies among individual products in delivery. Scope economies measure the additional cost incurred from the individual, rather than joint, production of an individual product. BPW provide a general definition of the degree of economies of scope:[22]

$$SC_i(y) = \frac{[C(y_i) + C(y_{N-i}) - C(y)]}{C(y)}. \tag{12}$$

This measure can be interpreted as the percentage change in cost from the individual production of product i over the cost of joint production. When SC is positive, scope economies are present and joint production is cheaper. If SC is negative, there are diseconomies of scope and total cost would be reduced by the individual production of product i.

By applying this general formula for scope economies to our delivery access cost equation, we can compute a measure of the degree of scope economies between mail class k and all other mail classes:

$$SC_k = \frac{(1 - e^{-\beta_k \frac{v_k}{PS}})\, PS - IC_k}{1 - e^{-\sum_{i=1}^{N} \beta_i \frac{v_i}{PS}}\, PS}, \tag{13}$$

where IC_k is the incremental cost of class k.

In the next section, we describe the nature of the data, and the estimation method and then, in a subsequent section, present the empirical results.

5. Data and Estimation Procedure

The data used for this study consist of mail volumes and delivery stops from a cross-section of U.S. Postal Service city carrier routes. The data were gathered as part of the U.S. Postal Service's City Carrier Cost System. This system chooses a sample of routes from the roughly 150,000 city delivery routes maintained by the Postal Service. In 1990, city carrier tests were performed on approximately 15,660 routes.[23] Mail is counted, by mail class, on ten percent of the stops on each of the selected routes, prior to street delivery. In total, over 500,000 stops were sampled.

---

22 See Baumol, Panzar, and Willig (1986, 73).

23 Appendix D of Hume (1987) contains a more detailed description of the data gathering process. Rural routes and "special purpose" routes (collection, parcel routes, relay routes) are not sampled as part of the City Carrier Cost System.

Other variables used in the analysis include the type of route from which the stop was sampled, as well as the proportion of stops of each type on each route. The eight route types reflect a categorization by the type of delivery dominating the route (business, residential, and mixed) and by the means of traversing the territory (foot routes, curbline routes, and park & loop). In addition, information was obtained on the type of stop where the mail was counted (single delivery residential, multiple delivery residential, and business and mixed stops).

This information is presented in table 1, along with the mean values of the sample volumes of mail counted. As might be expected, most stops are single delivery stops, and most routes are residential park and loop. Also note that pieces per stop are greatest for First Class Mail and commercial third class.

The exponential model is nonlinear and must be estimated with nonlinear methods. We used PROC NLIN in SAS to estimate model with nonlinear least squares. This procedure requires provision of the analytical derivatives and uses numerical methods to estimate a solution to the set of normal equations. Our application used the Gauss-Newton method of technique for finding the solutions. The nonlinear function is apparently well behaved because convergence was rapid.

Table 1. Sample Statistics for Delivery Data

MAIL CLASSES		
Class	Mean Volume Per Route	Volume Per Stop
FCM SINGLE PIECE	585.8 PIECES	1.75 PIECES
FCM PRESORTED	349.0 PIECES	1.04 PIECES
FCM CAR-RT PRESORTED	31.3 PIECES	0.09 PIECES
SECOND CLASS MAIL	141.5 PIECES	0.42 PIECES
TCM BULK REGULAR	364.0 PIECES	1.09 PIECES
TCM CAR-RT REGULAR	403.1 PIECES	1.20 PIECES
TCM BULK NONPROFIT	121.7 PIECES	0.36 PIECES
TCM CAR-RT NONPROFIT	36.7 PIECES	0.11 PIECES
FOURTH	8.2 PIECES	0.02 PIECES
OTHER	122.8 PIECES	0.37 PIECES
ROUTE & STOP CHARACTERISTICS		
% BUSINESS FOOT		2%
% BUSINESS MOTORIZED		3%
% RESIDENTIAL FOOT		12%
% RESIDENTIAL PARK & LOOP		59%
% RESIDENTIAL CURBLINE		18%
% MIXED FOOT		1%
% MIXED PARK & LOOP		4%
% SDR STOPS		75.3%
% MDR STOPS		11.2%
% BAM STOPS		13.5%
POTENTIAL STOPS	33.53 POTENTIAL STOPS	

6. Results

Estimation of the exponential delivery model requires a slight modification of equation (1). Two types of control variables are included in the equation to account for possible heterogeneity across carrier routes. First, a dummy variables for the route types are included in the equation. These dummies account for the fact that the distribution of mail across stops could be different for, say, business routes as opposed to residential routes. The variable *RCAT* is included in the estimated exponential delivery equation to account for this possibility.

It is also well known that the distribution of mail to stops depends upon the stop type. In particular, a given volume of mail may have a different cost-causing effect if it is distributed across different types of stops. In particular, three classes of stops have been identified: single delivery residential stops (SDR stops), multiple delivery residential stops, like apartment buildings (MDR stops), and business and "mixed" stops (BAM stops) where a mixed stop includes both business and residential addresses. To determine the degree which stop composition affects access cost the proportions of stops of each type on a route are also included in the exponential delivery regression equation. The equation to be estimated is

$$AS_j = \left(1 - e^{-\sum_{i=1}^{N} \beta_i \frac{v_{ij}}{PS_j} + \sum_{k=1}^{K} \gamma_k RCAT_k + \delta_1 S + \delta_2 M + \delta_3 B}\right) \times PS_j + \varepsilon_j, \tag{14}$$

where S is the proportion of SDR stops, M is the proportion of MDR stops, B is the proportion of BAM stops, ε is the stochastic term, and j indexes the route (e.g., AS_j is the number of actual stops on the jth route).

The estimated parameters are given in table 2. Inspection reveals that all of the estimated β coefficients are nonnegative and most appear to be positive. Although inference in nonlinear least squares regressions is only asymptotic, the size of the asymptotic t-statistics and the fact the estimation is based on over 15,000 observations increases our confidence that the estimated β_i are positive. In addition, the results accord with our expectations about different classes. Classes that have relative large volumes, like First Class or third class, have relative large estimated coefficient indicating a relative large responsibility for causing accesses. In addition, the presorted rate categories have the highest coefficients, reflecting the characteristics of these rate categories to be broadly broadcast over possible stops.

The effect of the route category variables is relatively unimportant being small in both absolute magnitude and of uncertain statistical significance. The stop type proportions appear to be significant and appear to help explain the generation of accesses on any given route. These coefficients measure the response in accesses to a change in the mix of stops for a given level of volume and potential stops.

Our primary result is empirical evidence indicating the presence of subadditive delivery costs for the U.S. Postal Service. We find evidence for declining average incremental costs and economies of scope in delivery. Of some interest may be the degree of scope economies for each of the mail classes or rate categories. Those

Table 2. Estimated Delivery Cost Model

Variable	Estimated Coefficients	Asymptotic t-statistics
MAIL CLASSES		
FIRST CLASS SINGLE PIECE	0.4472	37.79
FIRST CLASS PRESORTED	0.6818	45.21
FIRST CLASS CAR-RT PRE-SORTED	1.2193	19.37
SECOND CLASS	0.5986	18.09
THIRD CLASS BULK REGULAR	0.5294	35.77
THIRD CLASS CAR-RT REGULAR	0.9871	62.73
THIRD CLASS BULK NONPROFIT	0.5967	15.22
THIRD CLASS CAR-RT NON-PROFIT	0.9446	13.68
FOURTH CLASS	0.3271	1.71
OTHER MAIL	0.7269	22.97
ROUTE & STOP CHARACTERISTICS		
% BUSINESS FOOT	0.5393	4.26
% BUSINES MOTORIZED	0.0474	0.43
% RESIDENTIAL FOOT	-0.3475	-4.28
% RESIDENTIAL PARK & LOOP	-0.2825	-3.49
% RESIDENTIAL CURB	-0.2588	-3.17
% MIXED FOOT	-0.3219	-3.6
% MIXED PARK & LOOP	-0.2618	-3.07
% SDR STOPS	0.5242	6.41
% MDR STOPS	0.3533	3.54
% BAM STOPS	-0.9192	-9.96
# OF OBSERVTIONS	15660	

Table 3. Measures of Scope Economies

Mail Class	Measure of Scope Economies
FIRST CLASS SINGLE PIECE	54%
FIRST CLASS PRESORTED	51%
FIRST CLASS CAR-RT PRESORTED	11%
SECOND CLASS	22%
THIRD CLASS BULK REGULAR	44%
THIRD CLASS CAR-RT REGULAR	67%
THIRD CLASS BULK NONPROFIT	19%
THIRD CLASS CAR-RT NONPROFIT	10%
FOURTH CLASS	1%
OTHER MAIL	24%

measurements are given in table 3.

7. Policy Implications

This section highlights the policy implications of the analysis and makes suggestions for further research. The empirical work presented above validates the claim that delivery costs are subadditive. Hence, unless the cost subadditivity in delivery is overwhelmed by diseconomies somewhere else in the system, postal services are a natural monopoly. Of equal importance, the work supports those who have argued for restricting entry into delivery services.

With regard to the overweening question regarding the economic justification for regulation, this analysis addresses an important part, but only a part, of the picture. The other part has to do with the question: does a set of prices exist which will allow a postal natural monopoly to break even, yet prohibit wasteful entry? If not, if every set of break even prices offers the potential entrant the opportunity to make a profit, then the incumbent regulated firm will be unable to sustain its monopoly without legal restrictions on entry.[24] Of course, under such conditions, entry would reduce welfare, because the incumbent is able to produce the entire set of products at the lowest cost. Hence, regulation is justified on economic grounds.

How can such a thing happen? Under the assumption that the demands for all postal products are independent, a price vector will be nonsustainable only if some price exceeds the stand-alone cost of production. In the case of the U.S. Postal Service, it is unlikely that any of its existing products are cross subsidized. On the other hand, cross subsidies within mail classes are possible and would offer the most likely opportunity for wasteful entry.[25] Delivery on some routes, such as routes with high coverage or routes in densely populated areas, is probably cheaper than on others. Nevertheless, the price is uniform across these varying cost circumstances. Under such conditions, entrants would be able to skim the cream of low cost deliveries, leaving the natural monopolist, operating under an obligation to serve, with the high cost remainder. A similar case, perhaps an even stronger one, can be made concerning intra-class cross-subsidy in the collection function.

This familiar argument is difficult to evaluate with existing data, which are organized by the classes and subclasses that are actually priced.[26] Measured costs of production represent averages across a variety of cost conditions. Even if data

---

24 We ignore here questions concerning the reaction of the natural monopolist to attempts by potential entrants to take a portion of the market by undercutting the monopolist's price. That is, we assume that potential entrants have Bertrand-Nash expectations. See Estrin and de Meza (1991) for a discussion of the welfare impacts of different assumptions about the incumbent's reaction.

25 Postal Green Paper (1992), Estrin and de Meza (1991), Dobbs and Richards (1991), and others have made similar arguments.

26 For a discussion of the extent of cross-subsidy within the delivery function, see Cohen (1993); also see Colvin and Rogerson (1993) for a discussion of cross-subsidy in the collection activity.

were available by cost groupings other than the actual product line, estimates of incremental access costs would have to be added to similar cost estimates for other operations, since no price exists for "delivery access" alone.

Moreover, it is unlikely that demands are independent.[27] In this more general case, as Panzar and Willig (1977) show, subsidy-free prices do not guarantee sustainability. All of this said, those seeking quantitative answers to questions concerning sustainability may nevertheless find something of interest in the way we have investigated subadditivity. Recall that we have established our main result by showing the access cost function to possess two key properties: declining average incremental costs and economies of scope. It turns out that much can be learned about the sustainability of a natural monopoly by examining the relative strengths of these two sources of natural monopoly, and comparing them to the appropriate cross price elasticities of demand.[28] In particular, domination by declining average incremental costs tends to lead to entry vulnerability for the natural monopolist. To put the matter as simply as possible, if a product has a very strong substitute in demand, then a natural monopolist may not be able to offer the product at a sustainable price without losing the advantages of declining incremental costs in the production of the substitute. Such a phenomenon would be swamped, on the other hand, by powerful scope economies.

References

Adie, Douglas K. 1988. "Privatization of the United States Postal Service." *Testimony before the President's Commission on Privatization.*

Berg, Sanford V., and John Tschirhart. 1988. *Natural Monopoly Regulation: Principles and Practice.* Cambridge University Press.

Baumol, William J., John C. Panzar, and Robert D. Willig. 1988. *Contestable Markets and the Theory of Industry Structure*, Revised Edition. San Diego: Harcourt Brace Jovanovich.

Bradley, Michael D. 1987. *Testimony before the Postal Rate Commission.* Docket No. R87-1.

Bradley, Michael, and Jeffrey Colvin. 1994. "On the Existence of Subadditive Delivery Costs for the United States Postal Service." Manuscript.

Bradley, Michael, Jeffrey Colvin, and Marc Smith. 1993. "Measuring Product Costs for Ratemaking: The United States Postal Service." In *Regulation and the Nature of Postal and Delivery Services*, edited by M.A. Crew and P. R. Kleindorfer. Boston: Kluwer Academic Publishers.

Bradley, Michael D., and Alan R. Robinson. 1988. "Determining the Marginal Cost of Purchased Transportation." *Journal of the Transportation Research Forum* 30 (1).

Bradley, Michael D., and Donald M. Baron. 1993. "Measuring Performance in Multi-Product Firms: An Application to the U.S. Postal Service." *Operations Research* 41 (3).

Christensen, Dianne, Laurits Christensen, Charles Guy, and Donald O'Hara. 1993. "U.S.

27 See Tolley (1994).

28 Panzar and Willig (1977).

Postal Service Productivity: Measurement and Performance." In *Regulation and the Nature of Postal and Delivery Services*, edited by M.A. Crew and P. R. Kleindorfer. Boston: Kluwer Academic Publishers.

Cohen, Robert, William Ferguson, and Spyros Xenakis. 1993. "Rural Delivery and the Universal Service Obligation: A Quantitative Investigation." In *Regulation and the Nature of Postal and Delivery Services*, edited by M.A. Crew and P. R. Kleindorfer. Boston: Kluwer Academic Publishers.

Colvin, Jeffrey L. 1990. *Testimony before the Postal Rate Commission.* Docket No. R90-1.

Colvin, Jeffrey L., and Cathy M. Rogerson. 1993. "An Operation-Based Approach to the Regulation of Postal Services." Presented at the Workshop on Postal and Delivery Economics, Daun, Germany, June 1993.

Commission of the Economic Community. 1992. *Postal Green Paper* (English Version).

Crew, Michael A., and Paul R. Kliendorfer. 1992. *The Economics of Postal Service.* Boston: Kluwer Academic Publishers.

Dobbs, Ian, and Paul Richards. 1993. "Policy Implications of Postal Network Access." In *Regulation and the Nature of Postal and Delivery Services*, edited by M.A. Crew and P. R. Kleindorfer. Boston: Kluwer Academic Publishers.

Dobbs, Ian, and Paul Richards. 1991. "Assessing the Welfare Effects of Entry into Letter Delivery." In *Competition and Innovation in Postal Services*, edited by M.A. Crew and P.R. Kleindorfer. Boston: Kluwer Academic Publishers.

Estrin, Saul, and David de Meza. 1991. "Delivering Letters: Should it be Decriminalized?" In *Competition and Innovation in Postal Services*, edited by M.A. Crew and P.R. Kleindorfer. Boston: Kluwer Academic Publishers.

Futz, Melvyn A. 1983 "Cost Allocation: How can the Costs of Postal Services be Determined." In *The Future of the Postal Service*, edited by Joel Fleishmann. Aspen: Aspen Institute.

Gupta, S. N. 1982. *Production and Cost Functions of the Unites States Postal Service*. Ph.D. dissertation, George Washington University.

Hume, Peter. 1987. *Testimony before the Postal Rate Commission.* Docket No. R87-1.

Hume, Peter. 1976. *Testimony before the Postal Rate Commission.* Docket No. R76-1.

Jasinski, K.M., and T.J. Steggles. 1977. "Modelling Letter Delivery in Town Areas." *Computer & Operations Reseearch* 4: 287-294.

Merewitz, Leonard and Marc Zupan. 1993. "Franchise Bidding, Contracting Out, and Worksharing in the Production of Postal Services: Can They Collect, Sort, and Deliver?" In *Regulation and the Nature of Postal and Delivery Services*, edited by M.A. Crew and P. R. Kleindorfer. Boston: Kluwer Academic Publishers.

Merewitz, L. A. 1971. "Costs and Returns to Scale in U.S. Post Offices." *Journal of the American Statistical Association* 66 (335): 504-509.

Moore, Thomas, G. 1988. "Testimony on Privatization of the U.S. Postal Service." *Testimony before the President's Commission on Privatization.*

Norsworthy, J.R., Jang Show-Ling, and Wei-Ming Shi. 1991. "Productivity and Cost Measurement for the United States Postal Service." In *Competition and Innovation in Postal Services*, edited by M.A. Crew and P.R. Kleindorfer. Boston: Kluwer Academic Publishers.

Owen, B. M., and R. D. Willig. 1983. "Economics and Postal Pricing." In *The Future of the Postal Service*, edited by Joel Fleishmann. Aspen: Aspen Institute.

Panzar, John. 1993. "Competition, Efficiency, and the Vertical Structure of Postal Services." In *Regulation and the Nature of Postal and Delivery Services*, edited by M.A. Crew and P. R. Kleindorfer. Boston: Kluwer Academic Publishers.

Panzar, John, and Robert Willig. 1977. "Free Entry and the Sustainability of Natural Monopoly." *Bell Journal* 8: 1-22.

Rogerson, Cathy, and William Takis. 1993. "Economies of Scale and Scope and Competition in Postal Services." In *Regulation and the Nature of Postal and Delivery Services*, edited by M.A. Crew and P. R. Kleindorfer. Boston: Kluwer Academic Publishers.

Sherman, Roger. 1991. "Competition in Postal Service." In *Competition and Innovation in Postal Services*, edited by M.A. Crew and P.R. Kleindorfer. Boston: Kluwer Academic Publishers.

Stevenson, R. E. 1973. *Postal Pricing Problems and Production Functions*. Ph.D. dissertation, Michigan State University.

Tresch, Richard W. 1994. *Principles of Economics*. Minneapolis: West Publishing Company.

10

THE SCOPE OF THE RESERVED AREA

Ian Reay

Introduction

The justification for the letter monopoly is now generally based on a combination of social and economic arguments. The letter service may be an "unsustainable natural monopoly," particularly if the socially desirable requirement of the provision of universal service within a uniform and affordable structure of tariffs is imposed.[1]

Recently the attitudes of governments and industry regulators in all economic sectors have tended towards a greater emphasis on the efficiency benefits of increased competition. This change has evolved together with a growing willingness to remove public service industries from direct public ownership and control and to "privatize;" encouraging techniques of financial control developed within the commercially-oriented private sector.

The Green Paper[2] reflects this changing emphasis towards liberalization. It seeks to provide a framework for postal services within the European Union (EU) which will enable a balance to be set between an agreed obligation to provide a universal service and the extent of the letter monopoly (the reserved area) required to support it. The Green Paper recognizes the current evolving views of regulators towards increasing competition by providing within the framework a process for periodic review of the reserved area. The clearly acknowledged agenda is that, over time, the level of monopoly protection will gradually reduce and competition will play an increasing role.

The Universal Service Obligation and the Reserved Area

The Green Paper proposes the development of a common definition of a universal postal service requirement (or obligation); to take into account social and economic

---

1 See Crew and Kleindorfer (1992).

2 Green Paper on the Development of the Single Market for Postal Services, European Commission, COM (91) 476

needs and commitments to the Universal Postal Union. It also proposes the development of a set of reserved services, which should also be established at "Community" (now Union) level. By the principle of proportionality, the size of this reserved area should be "no larger than is needed to secure the universal service objective"[3]—this objective presumably includes the *affordability* of the price.

The Green Paper envisages that the conditions in some Member States may be such that they only require a set of reserved services which is less than the set defined at Union level whilst still ensuring the common universal service. The common list of reserved services is to be regarded as a maximum—that is to say, no Member State should have a larger reserved area than it needs for this purpose. However, the Green Paper suggests that if a Member State finds that the community defined reserved area is insufficient to guarantee "the universal service" that Member State could apply to the Commission for an extension of its reserved area.[4]

However, the Green Paper is silent on the issue of whether or not a Member State which wishes to ensure a more extensive universal service obligation than the community-agreed definition, thereby is entitled to increase the size of its reserved area. For example, in the United Kingdom, the postal service currently delivers mail not only to every address but twice a day to addresses covering approximately 85% of the country. The United Kingdom's government may, for domestic political reasons, require that this provision remain and form part of the universal service obligation. It is unlikely that this provision would form an element of the community-wide definition of a universal service obligation. Will the United Kingdom's government, or its appointed postal regulator, have the discretion to provide for a reserved area which is more extensive than the community defined one, in order to fund this second delivery? In general, although it is to be expected that there will be an agreed universal service, this will be a minimum requirement. Many states may already provide for, or will wish to provide for, a more extensive obligation. In general, such a provision will be a matter of public policy very much concerned with domestic political perceptions and expectations and will be very largely determined by the current level of provision. The same considerations apply to the *affordability* of the price of the universal services.

As measured by Purchasing Power Parity, the letter tariffs of Member States of the European Union vary by a factor of more than two. Affordability of the public tariff, like the form of universal service obligation, will be a concern of public policy of the Member State.

There are close links between the extent and nature of the universal service obligation, the extent of the reserved area, and the perceived affordability of the tariff. Given the particular national considerations of Member States in determining these, it is argued that the reserved area should only be defined at European Union level in very general terms and that a large degree of discretion should be

3 Op. Cit.
4 Green Paper, page 233.

permitted by Member States or their appointed regulators.

The Scope of the Reserved Area in European Union States

The scope of the reserved area is expressed, at least throughout the EU, in terms of a combination of weight, price, and contents. Proposals to reduce the scope have included eliminating direct mail (linked to "printed papers" in some countries) and lowering the weight/price threshold, as well as network bypass proposals such as downstream access. Most European countries (but not the United Kingdom) include a weight-based element in their reserved area definition, but, for comparison purposes, the price of the threshold weight step can be used.

The range is very substantial. In 1990, the monopoly threshold in the United Kingdom was 5 times the price of the first class basic weight step (currently—1994—it is 4 times). In Italy, the ratio is 27 (this threshold is in fact a weight limit converted into the price for that weight). In some countries, printed papers, public fax, express mail, and parcels are also in the reserved area.

Clearly, any move to harmonize on the monopoly threshold—even in terms of using the same multiple of the basic weight step tariff—would impact very differently on the Member States. For example, to a threshold set at 10 times the basic tariff might increase the competitive opportunities in eight countries (in some substantially) while leaving four untouched.

But how would reducing the monopoly price threshold in this manner allow competition to develop, what are the potential risks to the incumbent, obligated universal service provider, and how should this threshold be set?

The Pace of Change

We should, perhaps, not be asking the "absolute" question—what should the reservation threshold be?—but the "incremental" question—to what extent should the threshold be reduced now (i.e., in the present political, economic, technological, and regulatory situation)? Both questions may depend on considerations which vary from country to country. Recently, Sweden has abolished its letter monopoly totally—few other countries have yet been prepared to take such a radical incremental step.

A highly significant factor bearing on the need for change in postal delivery services is the rapid rate of change in technology. The growing diversity of telecommunications based means of exchanging data and their rapidly reducing costs is creating a range of alternatives to the letter post. This is affecting especially the business-to-business element of the mail which, in the United Kingdom, has reduced from 35% to 28% of all letter mail in the last 5 years.

In the United Kingdom, the rapid rate of decrease in telecommunications prices relative to postal prices is expected to continue, indeed to accelerate, because of the very severe price cap (RPI-7.5%) which has been imposed on the dominant telecommunications supplier (BT) by the regulator Oftel and the number of alternative high capacity networks which are being established. Between 1987 and 1997, unit telecommunications prices will fall by 40% from their initial value in real terms, whereas postal prices are only forecast to reduce over the same time period by 5%-10% in real terms.

Despite this technological impact on communications in general and despite substantial plans by postal operators to introduce automation in sorting (mail processing), the cost reductions that can be achieved by this means are comparatively limited. This is partly because the largest single cost area—the delivery operation itself (the postman's walk)—is not amenable to significant, incremental, technological enhancement without affecting the service to the recipient of the mail.

This cost area is, on the other hand, amenable to gradual unit cost reduction through volume growth (economies of scale). In the United Kingdom, the marginality of the cost of the delivery operation itself (excluding the indoor, preparatory tasks) has been estimated at less than 50% (even over the long run). Real wages tend to grow (in the United Kingdom at about 2% per annum) and a small annual volume growth is a means of holding real unit prices constant and even maintaining a gradual medium term reduction in real prices while preserving competitive wage levels and satisfactory levels of recruitment.

We have a potentially destabilizing situation as far as postal prices and services are concerned (at least in the United Kingdom). Competition is growing rapidly from telecommunications and there is evidence that this is affecting letter volume growth. The effective mechanism of maintaining a high quality postal service at constant or gradually reducing prices in the medium to long-term—volume growth—is also being threatened by moves from regulators (in the United Kingdom and EC) to reduce the reserved area protection in the interests of promoting direct competition. The result could be higher postal prices and a long-term spiral of decline in the provision of postal services.

Reducing the Reservation Threshold

A discussion on the extent to which the Reservation Threshold should be reduced would have to consider.:

- the nature of, and costs of providing, the universal service;
- the indirect competition which is emerging through technological change regardless of any changes to the extent of the reserved area;
- the attractiveness of these activities to potential operators (new firms starting from little or nothing or large organization—possibly of international scale—who might expand their operations on the margin);
- the speed with which such operations could grow, attract substantial diversions from the incumbent, become profitable and able to maintain viability;
- the impact on the volume, costs, and revenues of the incumbent—short term as well as long term.

The remainder of this paper discusses potential direct competition which may evolve to exploit a reduction in the Reservation Threshold. A wide range of new forms of competition may emerge, but only two examples will be considered:

a) The emergence of one or more competitors specializing in distribution, who will offer a high reliability (next-day) service at a price close to the Reservation Threshold.
b) The development of "facilities management" companies which specialize in such functions as accommodation maintenance, computing services, security, and mailroom services.

Competitors Offering a Reliable Next-Day Service

With the Reservation Threshold in the range 2 to 4 times the basic letter tariff (x2 to x4), the market that becomes available to competitors is that of a product in between the next-day service at the reliability of the incumbent universal service provider and a guaranteed next-day courier service. Another element of this potential market is (higher weight) packet items priced within the range that becomes exposed to competition. The risk to both these elements (the attractiveness of a competitor) depends on the comparable service qualities of the incumbent and competitor (not only the reliability but also customer care in general), brand strengths, access, and marketing effort.

The vulnerability of a universal service provider to competitive entry must depend importantly on its present service performance and customers' willingness to pay for an improvement. Market Research can be used to estimate this, but the results of such research will depend on the current performance of the incumbent universal service provider and (perhaps more importantly) on the perception of that performance by customers. The size of this market is therefore variable and cannot be known with confidence, but a range of between 0.5% to 5% of first class mail volumes has been estimated in the United Kingdom if the Reservation Threshold is lowered to x2.

The question arises of the financial viability of a competitor able to price in the range x2 to x4 of the basic letter tariff and to provide a (relatively) high, but not guaranteed reliability while handling between 0.5% to 5% of the incumbent's (first-class) mail volume. The cost function of a delivery service is well known to demonstrate substantial scale economies, so this question is critical. The competitor's costs will, of course, also vary according to whether it is obliged to provide a universal service or can limit its operations to major cities.

Figures 1a and 1b show estimates of competitor unit costs based on a model of a hypothetical competitor to Royal Mail providing a highly reliable (but not guaranteed) next-day service. The costs are expressed as a multiple of the basic (first-class) letter tariff. These costs include collection, trunking, and delivery (using motor cycles), an administrative overhead, and profit contribution. The "delivery" component of this model explicitly reflects the scale economies in delivery to be found in representative environments in the United Kingdom. A description of the basic features of this model can be found in Jasinski and Steggles (1977).

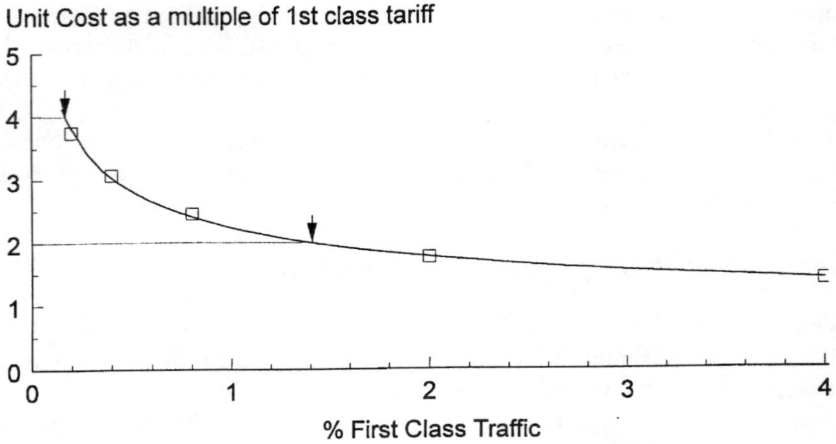

Figure 1a. Competitor Unit Costs as a Multiple of Basic Tariff for a National Operation

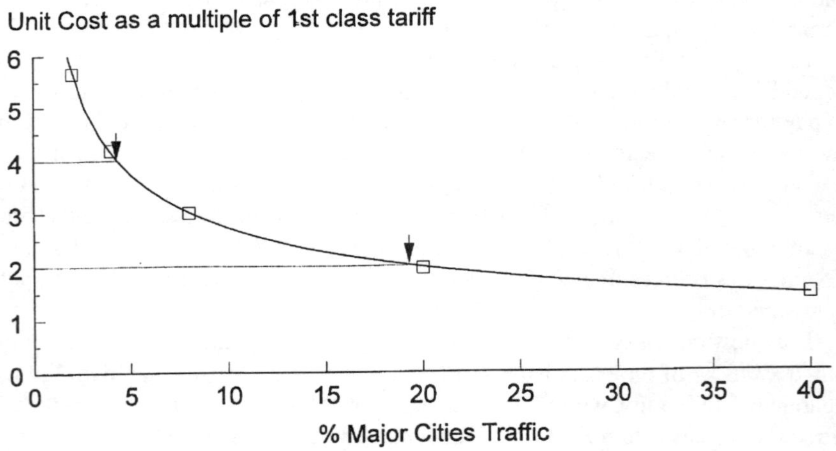

Figure 1b. Competitor Unit Costs as a Multiple of Basic Tariff for a Major Cities Operation

It can be seen that this model predicts that a stand alone competitor (i.e., not exploiting economics of scope with other operations such as express parcels or couriers) will be financially viable at a Reservation Threshold of x4 when handling 0.5% of first-class mail (nationwide) or 2% of first-class mail within and between major cities. With the Reservation Threshold lowered to x2, a competitor will be financially viable handling 2% of first-class mail (nationwide) or 14% of major cities first-class mail if it is permitted to limit its operations to this element. Converting this to annual turnover, assuming the competitor charges exactly the Reservation Threshold price (figure 2), shows that a minimum viable competitor

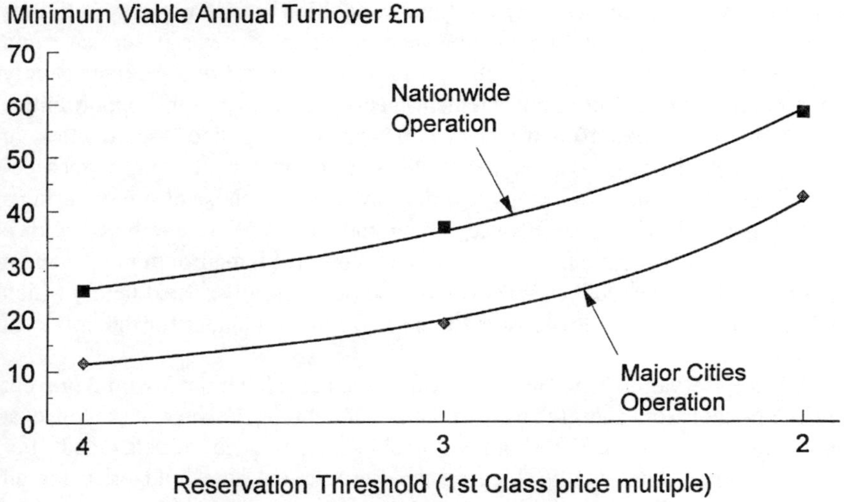

Figure 2. Minimum Viable Competitor Size

would have a turnover of £40m at a Reservation Threshold of x4 rising to £70m at x2. By restricting operations to major cities, a smaller operation is feasible—£13m turnover at x4 rising to £50m at x2.

Since these estimates assume no economies of scope with other operations, they are almost certainly over estimates of the minimum viable size of a competitor's operation. By simply lowering the Reservation Threshold, it will not be possible to oblige competitors to offer a universal service, and it is to be expected that they would limit their operations to major cities. Lower cost operations would also be possible if competitors restricted their collections to major volume posters and similarly restricted their deliveries to business addresses.

The conclusion from this analysis would seem to be that lowering the Reservation Threshold down to the region of x4 to x2 of the basic letter tariff exposes the incumbent to small volume losses—but the items at risk will be highly profitable. In other words, opportunities for cream skimming will occur, and the financial viability of the incumbent will be at risk to a greater extent than indicated by the raw figures of traffic at risk. Nevertheless, with the Reservation Threshold in this range, the incumbent may be able to defend its position against this form of competition provided it could maintain very high levels of service quality—particularly for mail within and between major cities.

Facilities Management

As companies restructure their operations and organization and move to concentrate on their core business, a trend is developing for companies to contract out subsidiary activities. The total potential market for these activities in the United

Kingdom has been estimated at £25 billion. In addition to such non core activities as catering, cleaning, building maintenance, security, secretarial services, and computer support services; mailroom and messenger operations are increasingly being undertaken by facilities management specialists. This presents opportunities for such an organization to control entry into the postal "pipeline"—particularly in the situation of a low Reservation Threshold. For example, mailroom and messenger services are frequently concerned with more than one physical site requiring a transport network to operate between them and may also be combined with a logistics transport operation. An operator may combine a mailroom management operation with its own delivery network (for some externally posted items) which will enable it to skim off low cost mail and leave the remainder for the universal service provider.

While a Reservation Threshold higher than the basic letter tariff would prevent such an operator from charging a cost-related price for the delivery of the low cost items, a low Reservation Threshold will enable such a barrier to be evaded. For example, although nominally charging the Reservation Threshold price for all external (to the client) items that the mailroom operator delivers itself, these additional revenues could be used to support its, other facilities management operation (for the same client)—nominally cross-subsidizing from its external postage revenues to its other operations. Reasonable guesses as to the proportions of mail handled in this way, with a Reservation Threshold of x4 to x2, indicate that it is likely that an internal cross-subsidy of 2% to 5% of the facilities management operation for a client might be required (Appendix 1). A lower Reservation Threshold reduces the level of this.

The attitude of a regulator to such an internal cross-subsidy by a competitor to a universal service provider will be important. On the face of it, such pricing arrangements are artificial but may not be anti-competitive if the organization concerned does not hold a dominant position in the postal or associated markets. The freedom to price in this way would enable a facilities management company with an associated delivery or logistics operation to cream skim the incumbent, the provider of a universal postal service within a uniform tariff structure.

Conclusions

The postal service is under threat from developing competition arising from a number of independent developments:

- Rapidly changing technology in the telecommunications sector and lower costs leading to a wider range of means of transferring information electronically and to growth in the availability and use of electronic alternatives to the postal service;
- Throughout the world economy public utility regulators are placing increasing emphasis on competition as a means of encouraging efficiency gains. These benefits need to be weighed against the potential losses of "cream skimming" activity.

- Changing approaches to the organization of large business operations leading to the contracting out of "non-core" activities to specialist facilities management companies. This enables mailroom service providers to control entry into the postal pipeline.

Lowering the Reservation Threshold into the range of between 2 and 4 times the price of the basic letter tariff will enable alternative forms of competition to develop and grow and may create incentives for the incumbent universal service provider to deliver a high service reliability and customer responsiveness. It will not, however, meet the objective of preventing cream skimming activities which will increasingly become possible as the Reservation Threshold is lowered through this range.

For both of these reasons, the result may be a real price increase in the basic letter tariff which would increase the vulnerability of postal services to telecommunications.

Appendix. Calculation of Internal Cross Subsidy for Facilities Management Operation

Suppose that a facilities management company (FMC) provides a packaged service to a client company (which would include mailroom services and mailing operations as well as, for example, a security service). Suppose the total price of the package is £M of which £P represents the revenue that would normally be spent on external mailings of the client company. Suppose also that the FMC can deliver 100x% of the external mail for 100s % of the cost of the public tariff (e.g., local and city center mailings). Finally, let the Reservation Threshold be T times the basic tariff.

In this example, the FMC culls out from the client's external mail the mail it can deliver itself. The remainder is mailed with the universal service provider.

The cost of external mailings to the FMC (including both those it delivers itself and those passed to the postal operator)	$= £P(1-x) + £Pxs$
The nominal cost of the external mailings to the client company (where the FMC delivered mail is nominally charged at the Reservation Threshold, T)	$= £P(1-x) + £PxT$
The nominal cross subsidy from the external mailing operation to rest of FMC's services to client company (difference between nominal charge and actual mailing costs)	$= £Px(T-s)$
This can be expressed as a percentage of the total FMC charge to the client	$= \frac{P}{M} x(T-s) \times 100\%$

Table 1 shows a feasible range of values for these variables and Figure A.1 the corresponding internal cross subsidies.

Table 1

	Estimate		
	High	Mid-Range	Low
Percentage of clients' mail FMC can deliver more cheaply	25%	10%	5%
Proportion of public tariff at which FMC can deliver selected items (incremental cost to FMC)	70%	80%	90%
Proportion of total price FMC charges to client represented by external mail costs (at basic public tariff)	20%	12%	5%

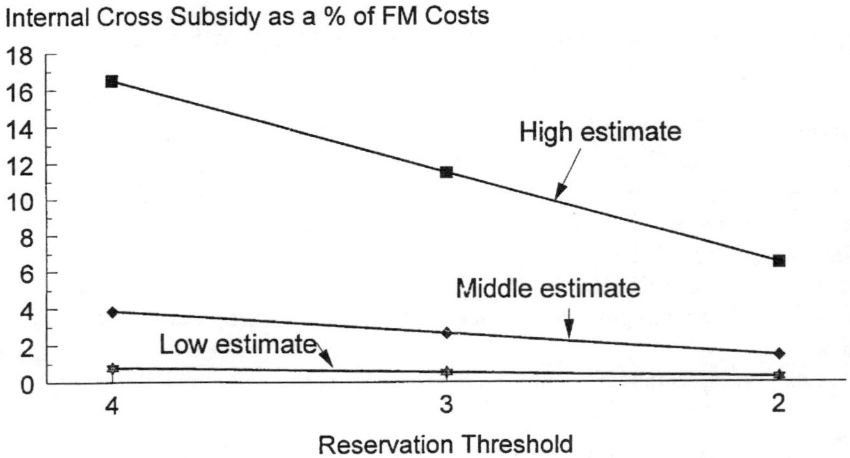

Figure A1. Facilities Management Operation Internal Cross Subsidy

References

Crew, Michael A., and Paul R. Kleindorfer. 1992. *The Economics of Postal Service*. Boston: Kluwer.

Jasinski, K.M., and T.J. Steggles. 1977. "Modelling Letter Delivery in Town Areas." *Computing and Operations Research* 4:287-294.

11

PRICE CAPS FOR POSTAL SERVICE

Walpurga A.K. Speckbacher

1. Introduction[1]

In contrast to the structure appertaining to most other countries, Deutsche Bundespost itself was simultaneously a ministry and a self-governing enterprise providing postal and telecommunications services. This changed on January 1, 1990, and since then Germany has had a Federal Ministry of Posts and Telecommunications responsible for public services in the areas of postal services, telecommunications, and postal banking. So that this responsibility could be properly executed, the public services were split into three different independent enterprises, one of which is Deutsche Bundespost POSTDIENST (DBP P).

At present, DBP P is a public enterprise. If the drafted law for Postreform II as currently discussed in parliament becomes effective on January 1, 1995, the three enterprises of Deutsche Bundespost will be transformed into joint stock companies: Deutsche Post AG, Deutsche Telekom AG, and Deutsche Postbank AG, whose major shareholder (over 50 percent) will be the government. In the case of Deutsche Post AG, the government will be the only shareholder for a period of five years.[2]

A large part of DBP P's services–two-thirds of total turnover[3]—is provided on a reserved basis, roughly identical with the letter service. Regulation is essential to prevent the possible abuse of monopoly power. However, regulation should allow the postal service the highest possible degree of flexibility in business decisions and offer incentives to provide high quality, as well as innovative, services. The forthcoming corporatization and privatization of DBP P makes the search for an appropriate regulatory regime even more important.

---

1 Part of this paper is based on Neu, Speckbacher, and Stumpf (1992). John Dolling, Stephen Gibson, Ian Reay, Jeanne Golay, and Gottfried Tappeiner provided helpful comments on an earlier draft, as did a number of colleagues from other postal services. Nonetheless, the views expressed herein represent those of the author and not those of Deutsche Bundespost POSTDIENST or its owner. The usual disclaimer applies.

2 For a detailed discussion, see Pieper and Stumpf (1994).

3 According to the business plan for 1993.

This paper is organized as follows. First, it briefly discusses changing market conditions for postal services and the possible implications for price caps of substitution and competition. The price-cap model is introduced, and services which should be included in price caps are discussed. Consequences of restrictions partially imposed on regulated tariffs and possible ways of introducing separate baskets for regulated services to avoid undue cross-subsidization are outlined. The paper discusses different indices which could be used as a reference index and also addresses considerations to determine the X factor in the price-cap formula. The paper concludes by illustrating some of the practical problems DBP P will face once price caps are introduced.

2. Changing Market Conditions

As a framework for analyzing postal markets, the traditional structure-conduct-performance paradigm can be used; however, to do this would extend the scope of this paper. Therefore, the analysis is strictly limited to those factors that most influence regulation.

The public enterprise DBP P is a hybrid.[4] As an enterprise, its behavior is influenced by the markets as shown in this section. However, as a public organization, its behavior is subject to pressure from politicians, regulators, and the postal unions. In the case of the public enterprise, the evaluation of performance will always lead to political decisions which influence the regulatory framework. One of the most prominent conditions for market entry–the prices of the public enterprise–is subject to regulation. One of the important objectives for DBP P with regard to profitability is stated in the Postverfassungsgesetz.[5] The Deutsche Bundespost enterprises[6] are required to cover their full costs with their revenues. This is a rather vague goal without any explicit definition whatsoever. As Vogelsang (1990) has shown, the objectives of a public enterprise vary with the goals pursued by the various actors in the enterprise's hierarchy.[7] This paper addresses mainly the pricing issues. Institutional factors are regarded as given facts and only some of DBP P's constraints are discussed in section 8.

In the seventies, postal markets were relatively static and dominated by administrations or public enterprises. Since the early eighties, postal markets have changed rapidly; postal services are subject to structural change, i.e., they are being transformed into public enterprises or joint stock corporations and the scope of their reserved area is shrinking. Private competitors have entered the postal markets, at

---

4 See Vogelsang (1990, 6).

5 Law concerning the Constitution of the Deutsche Bundespost, Bonn 1989.

6 They are DBP Telekom, DBP Postdienst, and DBP Postbank.

7 These may be within DBP P (the Management Board and its Chief Executive Officer, labor representatives, the workforce) or outside it (civil servants in various ministries, politicians, the regulator, the owner).

first only offering high-branded courier services, but then penetrating the international letter segment on a growing scale and recently even operating domestically. The product cycle for the classical postal monopoly services is characterized by stagnation. Therefore, product differentiation is likely to grow.

There is a growing tendency to replace the traditional letter service by new telematic services, like EDI and e-mail. Fax is used intensively between some customer groups. Market research studies indicate that the use of telematics will increase, especially in the business-to-business segment. DBP P caters to this growing demand by offering a hybrid service called ePost. This service is likely to replace part of the traditional direct mail business and letter mail. Public utilities may send invoices via this new hybrid distribution system.

Because of the changing market conditions DBP P's monopoly is under pressure. Increasing competition is affecting most postal markets. Whether it is in the form of direct competition or substitution effects, increasing competition will affect price-cap regulation. There is considerable theoretical ground to believe that price-cap regulation allows the regulated enterprise to develop an optimal price structure for the services offered. In the case of direct competition and substitution, the tendency to adopt optimal price structures does not hold strongly (Neu, Speckbacher, and Stumpf 1992). The critical point is that regulation should ensure the efficient provision of services by the enterprise without neglecting innovation.

In the context of regulation, efficiency is as important as the rate of technical innovation. It can be assumed that there is inefficiency in postal services because of the constraints of market entry in the past. Price caps are likely to encourage the regulated enterprise to operate efficiently within a clear framework.

3. The Price-Cap Formula

Objectives of economic regulation for the postal service are:

- to prevent possible abuse of monopoly power;
- to allow the management of postal services the highest possible degree of flexibility in business decisions;
- to attempt to offer incentives to the regulated enterprise to provide high quality, as well as innovative services;
- to limit the costs of regulation; and
- to attempt to mimic the likely operation of a competitive market.

Having studied two alternative approaches to regulation (Braeutigam and Panzar 1989), one arrives at the conclusion that price-cap regulation enables a postal business to achieve the afore-mentioned goals, avoids the negative effects inherent in cost-of-service regulation, and ensures that the average level of tariffs will decline in real terms, provided that X is negative. Compared to cost regulation, it is easy for the regulator to administer once it is implemented.[8]

The main elements of price-cap regulation can be described as follows:

- Price limits are linked to a general index of inflation, reflecting input price changes of the regulated enterprise.

- The price cap, or ceiling is applied to the average tariffs concerned. Consequently the weights are given by the percentage of revenue contributed by each tariff item in the previous year. The price increase proposed for each item is multiplied by that particular weight.
- The X factor reflects productivity gains and should be deducted from the price-cap index.

A simplified version of the price-cap formula for the postal service is

$$\sum_{i}^{n} w_{i,t}\left[\frac{p_{i,t}-p_{i,t-1}}{p_{i,t-1}}\right]\leq I_t - X, \tag{1}$$

where $n =$ number of regulated services;
$p_{i,t} =$ price of service i in year t;
$w_{i,t} =$ share of revenue from service i of total revenue in the previous year t–1;
$I_t =$ value of inflation in the relevant year t, measured in rates of change of the price index; and
$X =$ productivity factor.

Price-cap regulation allows a continuous adjustment of tariffs by changing the cap concerned. However, characteristics of some postal services, in particular the letter mail service, complicate this possibility, since some tariffs are only adaptable in relatively large price steps. In Germany and some other European countries, it would be very difficult in practice to raise tariffs by, e.g., 2 Pfennigs, which would imply a stamp of the very impractical amount of 82 Pfennigs. In the past, tariff increases consisted of at least 10 Pfennigs, which is, in relation to the price level, a considerable increase.[9]

A solution to this problem may be found in imposing restricted conditions for changing regulated tariffs. A restriction could be imposed partially on regulated tariffs; e.g., the price for the basic letter with a stamp. Such services, with imposed restrictions, should be in a separate basket. This basket would only embrace such restricted services[10] that need more flexibility for tariff adjustments. Restricted means that changes in tariffs are subject to certain conditions like round figures.

The price-cap formula for a basket of restricted services is as follows:

$$\sum w_{i,t}^{R}\left[\frac{p_{i,t}^{R}-p_{i,t-1}^{R}}{p_{i,t-1}^{R}}\right]\leq I_t - X + I_t^{ng}, \tag{2}$$

8 For a summary of the discussion, see Braeutigam and Panzar (1993, 194).

9 In the Netherlands, for example, there are no coins smaller than the value of five cents. Therefore, prices for stamps can only be raised in five-cent steps.

10 The term "restricted services" should not be confused with the term "reserved services" from the Green Paper.

where R indicates restricted services. The difference between formula (2) and (1) is the term I^{ng}, which takes into account the permissible–but in practice not exploited–tariff increases of the previous years. It is possible to carry out tariff adjustments on the basis of accumulated price margins. Changes in tariffs can only be made once the technical restrictions are met.

4. DBP P's Regulatory Framework and Price Caps for the Letter Mail Service

At present, there are the following kind of postal services with regard to the regulatory setting:

(a) Monopoly services;
(b) Mandatory services;
(c) Competitive services.

According to the Postverfassungsgesetz[11] the resolutions of the Supervisory Board concerning the tariffs for the letter mail service shall require the approval of the Federal Minister of Posts and Telecommunications. At present, political and regulatory aspects are somewhat in suspense, since the letter mail service as it is offered today is not completely identical with the monopoly area. According to the Postgesetz,[12] any item including a written message or any other message directed to a specific person is subject to the Beförderungsvorbehalt, a restriction specifying that it may only be forwarded by DBP P. Unaddressed advertising mail, books, or small packets containing samples without a letter do not fall within the monopoly area but are still part of DBP P's Briefdienst.[13] Therefore, by law, both monopoly and competitive services are subject to price regulation. There is also a price limit for letters transported by private firms. It is ten times the postage payable for a standard letter, that is to say 10 Deutschmarks at present. The Federal Ministry of Posts and Telecommunications has been looking into the question of lowering the price limit for items delivered by bicycle courier.

There is an increasing tendency towards competition in the market for letter mail services. For some months, the Federal Ministry of Posts and Telecommunications has been examining the possibility of opening the market for the segment of addressed advertising mail. This is made possible by the granting of licenses. Already forty firms have applied for a license to distribute addressed advertising mail and catalogues. If the price limit is lowered and one segment is liberalized, the problem of by-passing may arise. If segments of a monopoly sector are opened to competition, the core business will also be affected. I should like to illustrate this by an example. Let us assume that the Ministry would grant licenses on the

---

11 Law concerning the Constitution of the Deutsche Bundespost.
12 The Postal Law.
13 The whole of the letter mail service.

condition that the distribution of addressed advertising mail is offered on a nationwide scale. Then, the possibility of bills or bank statements also being delivered in the process could not be precluded. Controls are often proposed as a solution. But are such controls compatible with the idea of free competition? Such a restriction would only entail further encroachments. Thus, a partial opening of the market is not an optimal solution.

Services offered in free competition can be declared Pflichtdienste (mandatory services). The regulator can impose obligations with regard to coverage and quality. The Mandatory Services Order came into effect on February 1, 1994. The transportation and delivery of parcels up to 20 kg–the so called over-the-counter-parcel–is defined as mandatory service. International parcels, parcels containing dangerous goods, and parcels where a commercial customer has done specified preparatory work are exempted. The tariffs for mandatory services shall be subject to the right of the Federal Minister of Posts and Telecommunications to object.

The competitive services constitute the third category. DBP P is obliged to inform the Advisory Board and the regulator only when tariffs are changed. Free services may possibly be subject to an examination by the Federal Cartel Office (e.g., undue cross-subsidization, misuse of market power).

Only monopoly services should be subject to price-cap regulation. Tariffs provided in competitive areas should not be regulated. To regulate postal prices in Germany, the regulator could distinguish between monopoly and competitive services as follows:

- The Federal Minister of Posts and Telecommunications approves tariff changes for monopoly services, if they stay below the approved price cap; and
- Tariff changes for competitive services are set, without being controlled further.

Thus, the regulator should only set a ceiling in noncompetitive markets and allow DBP P to enter into competitive markets and produce whatever output levels it desires in competitive markets. This is consistent with the most recent publication of the Postdienstverordnung[14] which requires the services offered by DBP P to be split up into monopoly services and competitive services. Tariff setting for monopoly and competitive services has to be done separately for each respective service group.

5. Definition of Service Baskets

Since the possibilities for substituting vary differently for different user groups, it can be concluded that postal services used by business organizations are subject to heavier competitive pressure than services used by private and small business users.

14 The Postal Service Ordinance.

Generally speaking, there is still a need for more information about the composition of user groups, possibly also about the different weight steps of the products and how their demand differs according to different customer groups. In April 1993, DBP P introduced a new concept for prices and products in the letter mail service, thus abandoning the numerous weight steps and variety of products. There are now four products, determined by size (volume) and weight, resulting in four price categories. The brand names are Standard-, Kompakt-, Groß-, and Maxibrief. They apply to Briefpost and Infopost. The difference between the latter two product categories are their contents. Briefpost is individual communication and Infopost contains mainly addressed advertising mail. However, Postwurfsendungen, which is unaddressed advertising mail,[15] is the third product category within the letter mail service. Therefore DBP P's letter mail service mixes monopoly and competitive services.

From the perspective of competition theory and welfare theory, it could be advisable to limit DBP P's degree of freedom in lowering tariffs for a specific group of services and raising tariffs for another. Changes in the price structure can be crucial if they occur in those groups of services subject to substitution. If an overall cap is applied, it introduces the risk that tariffs in certain service areas are deliberately kept high to compensate for low prices in the competitive areas. As a consequence, changes in prices for the less competitive services would be higher than the cap on average. Therefore, certain groups of services should be put into a separate basket. In certain areas, the possibilities to substitute are better for business users than for private households. As was shown in section 2, fax, EDI, and e-mail represent possible alternative means of communication for most large business users.

Therefore three baskets could be applied:

Basket A: letter mail services, which are primarily used by households and small businesses; including inland services and international services;

Basket B: letter mail services, which are used by business organizations; inland letters only;

Basket C: letter mail services, which are used by business organizations; international letters only.

The services in all three baskets should be subjected to price-cap formulae on the basis of identical specifications. If the proposals to liberalize some areas of postal services according to the EC Green Paper come to fruition, this would have an effect on price caps. Services which are now in the monopoly area could be in the competitive one and could be freed from regulation. Basket C could vanish. However, even if outgoing cross-border mail in Germany were still within the exclusive privilege, there would be competition in actual fact. In practice, DBP P's

15 Unaddressed advertising mail is not within the scope of DBP P's monopoly.

monopoly for cross-border mail is put at risk in the customer segment of large business users since they give their mail to private operators or to competing foreign postal services. Therefore, it is questionable if basket C should be implemented at all. Rebalancing is limited principally by the need to avoid undue discrimination between customers.

However, if DBP P has to step further on the path towards liberalization, the scope of the service baskets has to be adapted accordingly. It is feasible that only tariffs of the basic letter (the scope has to be defined by the regulator) are subject to a price-cap regime. Another possibility is the separation of baskets between the two major user groups. Price caps could only be applied to letter mail services for private households. If Posts and Telecommunications Reform II comes to fruition, more concrete work can be done in defining the scope of the service baskets.

6. Selection of the Price-Cap Index

The changes in the price-cap index (PCI)[16] should represent external impacts on the input prices of the regulated enterprise. It should be ensured that the PCI cannot be influenced or manipulated by DBP P. The PCI should be relatively easy to administer, and the system of gathering the relevant data should not be overcomplicated. The PCI should be plausible and easy to understand in the public perception, because postal tariffs are still political prices. The PCI is represented in our model as index of reference (REFI).

The following published price indices are considered:

- The Einzelhandelspreisindex (EHPI), which is the retail price index for Germany.
- The Erzeugerpreisindex der gewerblichen Wirtschaft (EPI), which is the producer price index for Germany.
- The Index der Tarifgehaelter der Angestellten bei Gebietskörperschaften (GEHI), which is the average earnings index for salaried employees in the public sector.

The study analyses which index best reflects the development of DBP P's costs. A cost index for DBP P's letter service has been constructed on the basis of an analysis of costs and output in real terms. The rates of change of the cost index show the development of costs incurred in producing a unit as expressed in table 1. For some peculiar reason the category of cost of materials[17] shows considerable variations over time.[18] To smooth away some of those variations, moving averages over a three-year period have been applied to the cost data.

16 Term I_t in equation (1).

17 Until the year 1989, in DBP P's cost accounting there were only three cost categories: labor costs, capital costs, and Sachkosten, which are all other costs, mainly for the purchase of goods and materials.

18 The variations are due to the purchasing behavior of DBP P, the payment procedure for

Table 1. Rates of Change of Cost Index for the Letter Mail Service, 1974 - 1989

Year	Rates of Change Cost Index	Cost Index Smoothed
1974	——	——
1975	7.35	5.87
1976	2.90	3.97
1977	1.65	2.91
1978	4.17	4.52
1979	7.73	5.56
1980	4.78	6.91
1981	8.21	5.95
1982	4.85	6.29
1983	5.81	3.32
1984	-0.72	2.20
1985	1.49	-0.02
1986	-0.85	0.55
1987	1.01	-0.92
1988	-2.91	1.14
1989	5.31	2.57
Mean value	3.39	3.39

Note: Moving averages over a three-year period have been applied to the cost data in column 3.

Table 2. Rates of Change of Smoothed Cost Index (KIG), Retail Price Index (EHPI), Producer Price Index (EPI), Average Earnings Index (GEHI), and Price-Cap Index (REFI)

	Rates of Change				
	KIG	EHPI	EPI	GEHI	REFI
1975	5.9	5.4	4.6	5.8	5.6
1976	4.0	3.2	3.7	3.5	3.5
1977	2.9	3.9	3.0	5.0	4.6
1978	4.5	2.4	9.7	4.4	3.6
1979	5.6	3.5	4.8	4.0	4.1
1980	6.9	5.4	7.6	5.6	6.0
1981	5.9	5.3	7.8	3.6	4.4
1982	6.3	4.7	5.6	3.8	4.2
1983	3.3	2.6	1.5	3.6	3.2
1984	2.2	2.1	2.8	1.0	1.4
1985	0.0	1.6	2.5	3.2	3.1
1986	0.6	-0.2	-2.5	3.4	2.2
1987	-0.9	0.4	-2.5	3.4	2.2
1988	1.1	0.6	1.3	1.8	1.7
1989	2.6	2.2	3.1	1.9	2.2
Mean value	3.4	2.9	2.9	3.6	3.5
Correlation with KIG		0.90	0.83	0.56	0.79

Comparison of the Kostenindex geglaettet (KIG), the smoothed cost index, with the three different indices mentioned above show, in table 2, that the development of all rates of change are roughly in line with the development of KIG.

The mean value of the rates of change differ for the respective indices. In comparison, the mean values of GEHI and REFI seem to converge better with KIG than EHPI or EPI. For data in time series, where rates of change are employed, the mean value is a better indicator for fitness than the correlation coefficient. Since the EHPI reflects price changes mainly in consumer goods and DBP P's costs are dominated by wages and salaries, no further consideration is given to this index. Since 20 percent of the costs are non-labor related, the GEHI in itself cannot be regarded as sufficient. A purely wage-based index may also be difficult to communicate to the general public. Therefore, no single index is suitable for use as an index of reference. The highest cost input for the DBP P is labor; it represents about 80 percent of total costs. Capital costs represent 5 percent and all the other costs 15 percent. A composite index of reference should reflect this cost structure of DBP P's letter service.

In our model, the price-cap index (REFI) is a synthetic index composed of indices mirroring DBP P's input price changes:

$$REFI = 0.8 \times GEHI + 0.2 \times EPI.$$

The average earnings index (GEHI) is used to reflect labor costs and the producer price index (EPI) indicates capital costs and other costs.[19] Figure 1 shows the development over time of the rates of change for the price-cap index (REFI) and the smoothed cost index (KIG). Figure 2 demonstrates the development over time in a different way. The gap between the cost index (KIG) and the retail price index (GEHI) diverges over time, whereas the average earnings index (GEHI) or the price-cap index (REFI) follow the development of the cost index (KIG) much more closely.

7. Determination of the X Factor

The size of the X factor is inevitably subject to negotiations between the regulator and the regulated enterprise, based on a plausible scenario for demand and cost conditions in the future (Crew and Kleindorfer 1992). Some argue (Bös 1990) that X should not be determined economically. Cabral and Riordan (1991) show the risks involved if the regulator sets X too high, thus reducing efficiency-seeking efforts of the regulated enterprise. Some other literature discusses the determination of the X factor in depth, suggesting that X should be composed of a fixed and a

terminal dues, and specific cost accounting techniques in the past.

19 The management of DBP P cannot influence the wage setting process (see section 8).

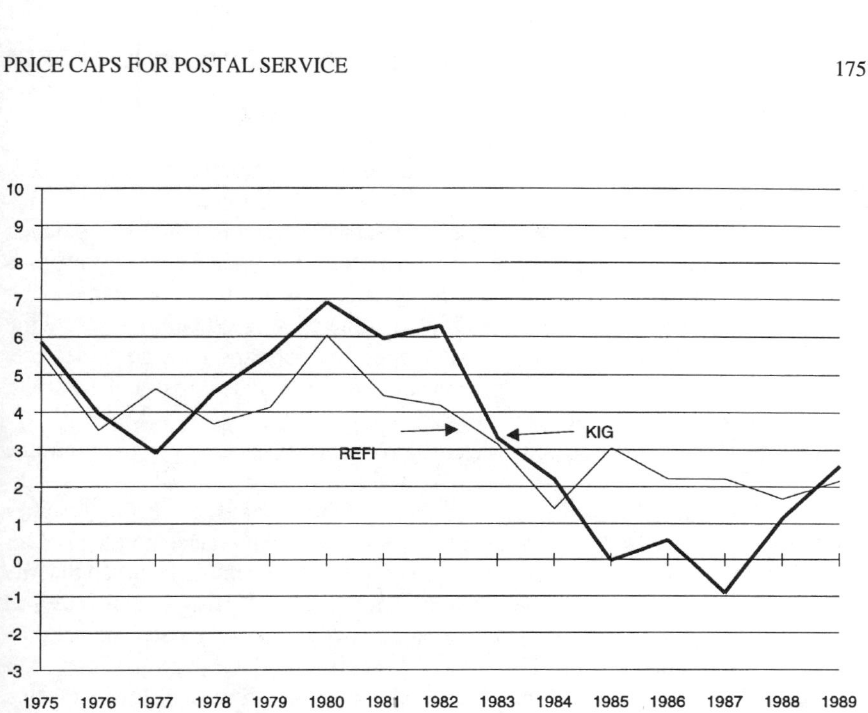

Figure 1. Developments of Rates of Change of Price-Cap Index (REFI) and Smoothed Cost Index (KIG)

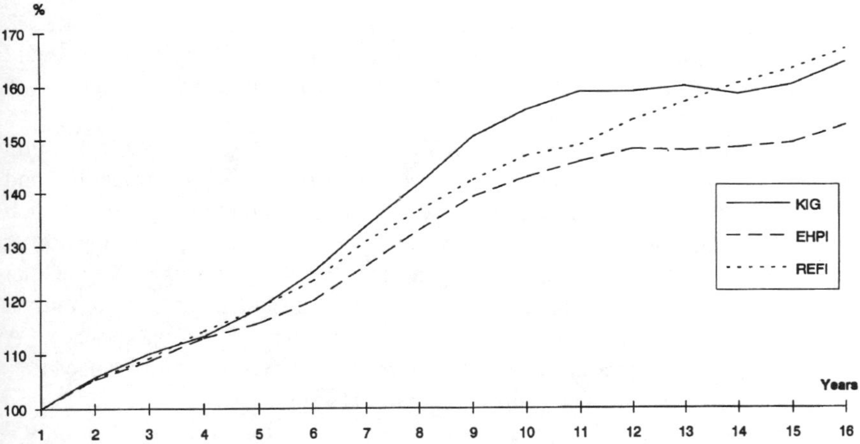

Figure 2. Comparison of Indices

variable part. The latter being a function of observable indicators, reflecting the development of the costs of the enterprise.

Kiss (1991) discusses the changes in volume of service due to developments in the business cycle, whereas Noam (1990; 1991) considers the quality of services to be incorporated in price-cap regulation. From a theoretical point of view, these different approaches seem to be interesting. However price-cap regulation then becomes very complex and loses one of its major advantages, which is its simplicity.

The X factor determines the extent to which tariff increases should be reduced as a result of gains in productivity. With an increase in volume, X would grow, thus allowing a smaller tariff increase since the average costs decrease simultaneously. If the quality of services is lowered, a higher value of X could be imposed by the regulator. The value of X is critical for the success of price caps in the postal service. When the size of X is determined, the imbalance of the level in tariffs at the starting point should be taken into account.

The data used in our study point towards an X factor of 0. However, to encourage efficiency and based on experience in Australia and New Zealand, Neu, Speckbacher, and Stumpf (1992) suggest an X factor with the value of 2%. On the other hand, the experience in the Netherlands shows that a postal service with a productivity factor of 0 value seems to operate quite efficiently. It should be noted that the value of X is also related to the index of reference used. If a general index of inflation, e.g., RPI is used, then a deduction of X would have a greater impact than if a wage-based index is used. The latter also implies productivity variations.

Quality of service must be monitored, and sanctions imposed, to assure that service quality does not decrease under price caps.

8. Markets, Ministers, and Price Caps

The regulator should commit himself to implement price caps for periods of at least five years. Imposing very short periods between formal price-cap reviews should be prevented, since neither DBP P nor the consumers will benefit from such an approach.

The critical point is that almost any analysis of DBP P requires explicit attention be given to both sets of influences: markets and ministers.[20] The workability and success of price caps in the postal service in Germany depend to a large extent upon the ability of the ministers to refrain from any pressure, even if price caps are set and provoke political debate. Braeutigam and Panzar (1993, 197) argue that price-cap regulation "is an effective means of controlling the prices of dominant firms when the control of their profits is left to the competitive marketplace." A critical point is the necessity that DBP P be free to make entrepreneurial decisions and to achieve the results determined by price-cap regulation.

The following example serves to illustrate this. Although wages of postal employees are negotiated between the three enterprises of Deutsche Bundespost on the one hand and the labor unions of postal workers on the other, the resulting Tarifabschluesse (collectively bargained settlements) are in fact in line with those for the employees in the public sector. The latter are negotiated between the

20 According to Vogelsang (1990, 7), bureaucrats, politicians, and special interest groups are embraced by the term ministers.

respective labor unions and the Federal Minister of the Interior. In the past, results of the collectively bargained settlements for the employees in the public sector have been assigned more or less to the civil servants as well. 53 percent of the total workforce in DBP P are civil servants. Therefore, DBP P's autonomy in the wage-setting process exists only in theory. As a consequence, this institutional constraint limits DBP P's possibilities to control and influence directly one important parameter of the development of labor costs. This might change when Postreform II,[21] Posts and Telecommunications Reform II comes into effect. However, the draft law suggests assigning wage-setting autonomy to the newly created holding company in the form of an institution under public law–the so called Bundesanstalt fr Post und Telekommunication.

Most of DBP P's cost savings can only be realized by laying off labor. As explained earlier, more than half of the total work-force in DBP P are civil servants. Their status is quite unique as they have a lifetime guarantee of employment. DBP P is also subject to special regulations concerning redundancy policy. The so called Rationalisierungsschutzabkommen[22] makes it very difficult to lay off surplus staff. If, as a consequence of rationalization within the organization, certain posts become superfluous, DBP P is not allowed to make people redundant without negotiating with the labor representatives to obtain their agreement. At present, the management can only achieve labor-saving effects by not replacing people who retire or hand in their notice. The natural retirement and quit rate in DBP P is about 5 percent annually.

However, the retirement and quit rate differs among various Laufbahnen, the four different service grades within any administration in Germany. Civil servants of the upper grade, the second highest grade, mainly perform administrative duties in regional headquarters or large post offices. In this area, rationalization is a main target for DBP P's management to achieve higher efficiency. But it is impossible to make those people redundant, and it is virtually impossible to transfer them to other jobs in other locations, if they are not willing to do them. On the other hand, the people working in operations, the sorting centers, are blue-collar workers. The retirement and quit rate there is already high. In the field of operations, efficiency gains will be achieved by increasing fully automated processing (including machine legibility) of all letters to 80 percent.

Consequently, in the short term, it may prove very hard to realize efficiency gains with a X factor of 2% in the current political situation. The institutional

21 Postrefom II will turn the three Deutsche Bundespost enterprises into joint stock companies. Constitutional amendments to enable privatizations have been introduced into the German Parliament, with an initial stake in the company DBP Telekom set for floatation in 1996 and DBP Postdienst in 1998. Germany's privatization will be unusually complex, partly because of the exigencies of a cross-party agreement with the opposition Social Democrats necessary to get the required parliamentary majority for the privatization legislation. It is likely that the German Posts and Telecommunications Reform II will be completed by the end of June 1994.

22 An agreement affording protection against the effects of rationalization measures.

constraints will be crucial for the success of price caps for DBP P's monopoly services, since institutions determine the residual rights of control.

The discussion of whether public or private ownership is more likely to promote social welfare is an ancient and central question in economics. According to Laffont and Tirole (1993, 638), private ownership implies a more diffuse allocation of residual rights of control and generates externalities among the parties exerting these rights. At present, DBP P is a public enterprise whose assets are owned by the government, who therefore performs both internal and external control. Public ownership gives the Federal Ministry of Posts and Telecommunications the means to achieve social goals that include, but are not confined to, profit maximization. As explained in section 2, DBP P is only required to cover its full costs with its revenues. There is no explicit profit maximizing goal. In this context, the absence of residual claimants attenuates the incentives of price caps for efficiency.

The draft law for Postreform II is currently discussed in parliament. It will transform the enterprises into joint stock companies from January 1, 1995 on. For a five-year period, the government will be the only shareholder of Deutsche Post AG which runs the postal service. This forthcoming corporatization and privatization imply further distinctions, as the ownership structure matters according to Laffont and Tirole (1993, 642) in two basic respects. "First, (even partial) public ownership reduces the acquisition of (noncontractible) information about the firm's managers' activity by outsiders, namely stock market participants. Second, public and private ownership imply owners with different objectives and therefore different behaviors in case of contract incompleteness."

There is a distinction to be made between the question of the relative cost efficiency of the public and private sector and the case when contingencies occur. In respect to relative cost efficiency, currently neither the theory nor the empirical literature are conclusive.[23] Ownership makes a difference when contingencies occur that are not covered by the contract between the government and the firm. This might be the case if price caps are to be introduced in the current ownership structure of DBP P. The residual claimant determines who can dispose of the assets in such contingencies. In this case, one cannot expect the same response under public and private ownership (Laffont and Tirole 1993, 644). Under the ownership structure as put forward by Posts and Telecommunications Reform II, the problem of capture may still occur. The shares of the joint stock company Deutsche Post AG will be hold by the Bundesanstalt fuer Post und Telekommunikation, which will be controlled by and will act on behalf of the Federal Ministry of Posts and Telecommunications. The Bundesanstalt will act as an agent for the State and perform its rights as an owner, and it will negotiate the general structure of wage agreements with the Postal Workers Unions. The Federal Ministry will act as a regulator. However, the relationship between the two bodies may provoke certain

23 For a more extensive discussion of the arguments, see Laffont and Tirole (1993, 654).

problems. Regulators can be captured by interest groups. It is very likely that the government will be constrained in the use of its instruments. For instance, the negotiation of the general structure of wage agreements for the forthcoming Deutsche Post AG will be carried out by the Bundesanstalt fuer Post und Telekommunikation and not by the management of the firm. How the earlier mentioned cost savings are to be achieved with price caps within this future structure remains an open question. However, price caps seem to give DBP P more entrepreneurial and commercial freedom during the transition to competition.

So far, consideration of the impact of the price-cap formula has been simplified by analyzing the situation when there is no change in volumes. In fact volume changes will prove to be important, as the costs are largely fixed for a given time period in the postal service, so that changes in volumes have a sharp impact on profits (Spring 1992). When X is relatively high, the price-cap index low, and volume changes minimal or negative, the cost requirement becomes much tougher each year than in the opposite case.

9. Conclusion

This paper proposes a price-cap formula applicable to postal services and identifies some of the technical features of tariff adjustment under a price-cap regime, related to the characteristics of the letter mail service. It proposes different baskets for different kind of services and user groups respectively. It discusses various types of general indices to be used as a price-cap index. In particular, it identifies an index of reference applicable for price-cap regulation of DBP P's letter mail services. The suggestion is made that setting the X factor too high could cause political and financial stress for DBP P. A solution for the institutional constraints is yet to be found. Nevertheless, it seems that price-cap regulation for the postal service is most effective as transition step on the road towards deregulation and competition and would give DBP P more entrepreneurial and commercial freedom. In order to promote further practical work in this area, the paper suggests some issues that ought to be resolved before price caps can be implemented.

References

Altmannsperger, H.J. 1989. Gesetz über das Postwesen, Kommentar, Stand Dezember 1989, Heidelberg.

Bauer, B. 1992. "Ansaetze zur Erfassung und Regulierung der Qualitaet im Monopolbereich der DBP POSTDIENST." WIK-Diskussionsbeitrag Nr. 85.

Bös, D. 1990. "Notes on Price Caps Regulation." Discussion Paper A-278, Sonderforschungsbereich 303, Universitaet Bonn. Bonn.

Braeutigam, R.R., and J.C. Panzar. 1989. "Diversification Incentives Under 'Price-Based' und 'Cost-Based' Regulation." *Rand Journal of Economics* 20: 373-391.

Braeutigam, R.R., and J.C. Panzar. 1993. "Effects of the Change from Rate-of-Return to Price-Cap Regulation." *American Economic Review* 82:191-198.

Brennan, T. 1990. "Regulation by Capping Prices." *Journal of Regulatory Economics* 1:133-147.

Cabral, L.M.B., and M.H. Riordan. 1991. "Incentives for Cost Reduction under Price Cap Regulation." In *Price Caps and Incentive Regulation in Telecommunications*, edted by M.A. Einhorn, pages 159-165. Boston: Kluwer.

Crew, M.A., and P.R. Kleindorfer. 1992. *The Ecomonics of Postal Service*. Boston: Kluwer.

Der Bundesminister für Post und Telekommunikation (Hrsg.). 1988. *Gesetz zur Neustrukturierung des Post- und Fernmeldewesens und der Deutschen Bundespost. Text und Einführung*. Heidelberg: Springer.

Glynn, D.R. 1992. "The Mechanism of Price Control." *Utilities Policy*: 90-99.

Hillmann, J.J., and R. Braeutigam. 1989. *Price Level Regulation for Diversified Public Utilities*. Boston: Kluwer.

Kiss, F. 1991. "Constant and Variable Productivity Adjustments for Price-Cap Regulation" In *Price Caps and Incentive Regulation in Telecommunication*, edited by M.A. Einhorn, pages 159-165. Boston: Kluwer.

Laffont, J.J., and J. Tirole. 1993. *Incentives in Procurement and Regulation*. Cambridge, MA: MIT Press.

Littlechild, S.C. 1983. *Regulation of British Telecommunications Profitability*. Report to the Secretary of State. London: Department of Industry.

Neu, W. 1988. "A Theoretical Look at Price Capping Mechanisms: Some Clarifications and One Recommendation." WIK-Diskussionsbeitrag Nr. 47.

Neu, W., W. Speckbacher, and U. Stumpf. 1992. "Preisregulierung im Monopolbereich des Postdienstes." WIK-Diskussionsbeitrag Nr. 92.

Noam, E. 1991. "The Quality of Regulation in Regulating Quality: A Proposal for Integrated Incentive Approach to Telephone Service Performance." In *Price Caps and Incentive Regulation in Telecommunications*, edited by M.A. Einhorn, pages 167-189. Boston: Kluwer.

Noam, E. 1990. Rate-Case 89-C-022. "Proceeding on Motion of the Commission at to the Rates, Charges, Rules and Regulations of Rochester Telephone Corporation." In State of New York Public Service Commission. Opinion No. 90-8, issued and effective: February 14.

Richards, P. 1989. "Pricing Regulation of Letter Services: The Impact on Prices, Profits and Efficiency." Presentation at WIK.

Spring, P. 1992. "The RPI-X system of Price Capping Regulation Re-examined." *Utilities Policy*: 186-203.

Vogelsang, I. 1988. "Price Cap Regulation of Telecommunications Services: A Long-Run Approach." A Rand Note N-2704-MF. Santa Monica.

Vogelsang, I. 1990. "Public Enterprise in Monopolistic and Oligopolistic Industries. *Fundamentals of Pure and Applied Economics"* 36, Chur.

12

USE OF TECHNOLOGY ARISING FROM CUSTOMERS' NEEDS

Hannu Tuominen

Just in the last decade, the development of new technology-based postal services has started expanding. In recent years, this trend seems to have become more systematic and based on surveys on business and public sectors customers' true needs. A special contribution to this development has been given by structural changes which have been and still are under the way, especially in Finland and in other industrialized countries. The significance of new advanced-technology-based services to the major customers has clearly been indicated, frequently in customers' retention and satisfaction surveys on total quality of postal services in Finland.

1. Introduction

Structural changes are currently taking place in business and social sectors in Finland, as well as in other advanced industrialized countries. The changes strive to respond to demands for increased efficiency and rationalization in both the private and public sector. These trends are also creating pressures for changes in companies' communications and transportation processes, i.e., their information and materials management systems. In addition, they put extraordinary pressure for cutting tariffs for traditional basic services and for ensuring that the quality of these services remains reliable. Clearly, decreasing tariffs call for reductions in costs.

These requirements for change are more urgent in Finland than in other respective countries for three main reasons: the prevailing recession, poor demand in the domestic market, and the high rate of mainly structural, but to some extent also seasonal, unemployment.

Postal services in Finland have traditionally been organized under the same organization umbrella as telecommunications services owned by the State. Digitalization of telecommunication networks during the 1980s in this country of 5 million people living in an area of 337,000 km has guaranteed the availability of high-quality telecom services. They have promoted the adoption of telecom-based communications and transportation services by companies and private consumers.

Until July 1, 1991, Finland Post had a statutory monopoly in letter services. Post has never, however, enforced this right, e.g., by complaining about its competitors. In fact, actual competition in letters has existed in the form of national and local courier companies since the beginning of the 1970s. In spite of the free competition prevailing in its main range of services, i.e., letter services, the Post has been able to make a profit during the last ten years.

Finland Post and Telecommunications was designated a status of a State enterprise at the beginning of 1990, which meant releasing it from strict governmental budgetary management and control. The new form of management and control included requirements regarding the setting of quality standards for basic services (1st class letters and distribution of newspapers and magazines). The logical next step was to grant corporate company status for the Post and Telecommunications at the beginning of 1994. It is still 100% owned by the State. This means that the government exercises management and control in the normal manner for a shareholder. They are carried out by the executive board of the P&T corporation, Post's executive board, and by the annual meetings of shareholders.

At the same time, a special Act on Postal Services was enacted in order to ensure that domestic and international postal services would be available at affordable prices in high quality to companies and private consumers. The Act made the provision of any extensive basic postal services subject to a special concession to be issued by the Ministry of Transport and Communications, in order to guarantee reliability and high quality. Basic postal services are defined as applying to items of up to 2 kg in weight which can be delivered to a standard-sized letter box. The concession has so far only been granted to Finland Post Ltd.

The incorporation of the Finnish postal and telecommunications services has increased the opportunities for the Post to optimize the range of services which it offers. The additional regulations issued by the Ministry of Transport and Communications under the Act above imposed more stringent requirements on companies providing basic postal services under a concession agreement.

The communications market as a whole has expanded significantly during recent decades. Despite predictions to the contrary, volume of domestic letter services has increased at the same pace with Finland's gross national product. The most recent predictions indicate, however, that the traditional basic letter services has reached the apex in its life-cycle. It seems that the volumes are about to enter a decline, the steepness of the trend being dependent on the GNP.

Letter volumes began to decline during the recession, in 1991-93. This can also be regarded as a sign of a permanent structural change, which is related to the increased payment of bills by direct debit systems and the use of receipt-free bookkeeping and accounting systems. One third of all traditional letters have been replaced by data transfers, telefax, and electronic mail services. The trend is likely to continue at an accelerating pace.

The declining volumes of traditional services have compelled Finland Post Ltd. to strive to restructure its services and operations in order to guarantee affordable pricing of the respective basic services and to ensure that the quality of these services remains high as required by the Act. This can also be regarded as a means of ensuring profitability and a sufficiently high annual dividend to the company's shareholder, the State.

For this reason, Finland Post Ltd. has consequently set out to create value-added services, especially in its current freight and direct mail business areas. Today, the Post is offering and creating new, tailored comprehensive communications, transportation and delivery services, at least for key customers, i.e., services closely associated with modern information and materials management systems. The development of new service concepts in the communications sector was initiated in the form of ePost (i.e., PEM) and customer address information services in the mid-1980s. Innovative services associated with freight, i.e., materials management, were started at the beginning of the 1990s.

2. Impact of the New Services on the Total Quality Experienced by Business Customers

Competition requires focusing on the quality and reliability of services. For this reason, Finland Post Ltd. has for the last three years been devoting considerable resources to the development of total quality in accordance with the ISO 9004-2 standard and the Malcolm Baldrige Quality award criteria. Two essential measures of quality and company performance seem to be customer satisfaction and customer retention.

Post Ltd. has commissioned frequent customer satisfaction surveys at given intervals during the last two years in order to analyze the total quality of its operations and services. Figure 1 illustrates some of the findings. The weights on the factors in figure 1 tend to vary according to differences in customers' service

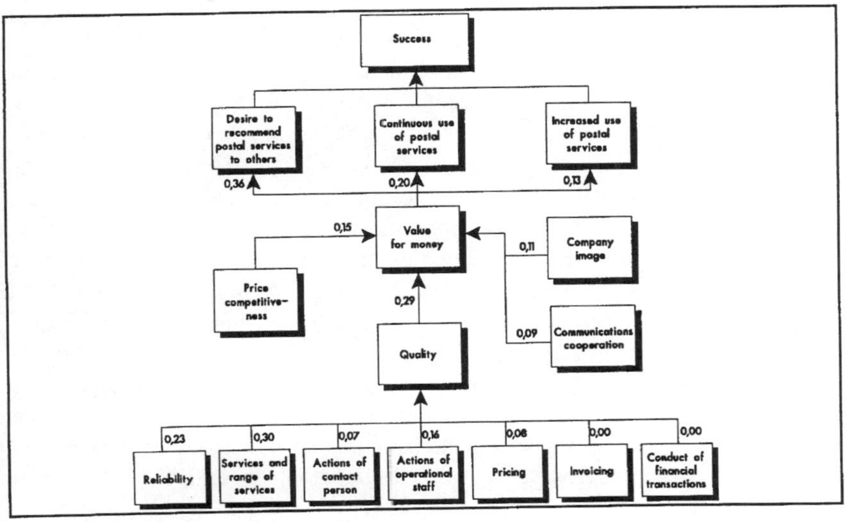

Figure 1. Weights of Individual Factors of the Postal Services

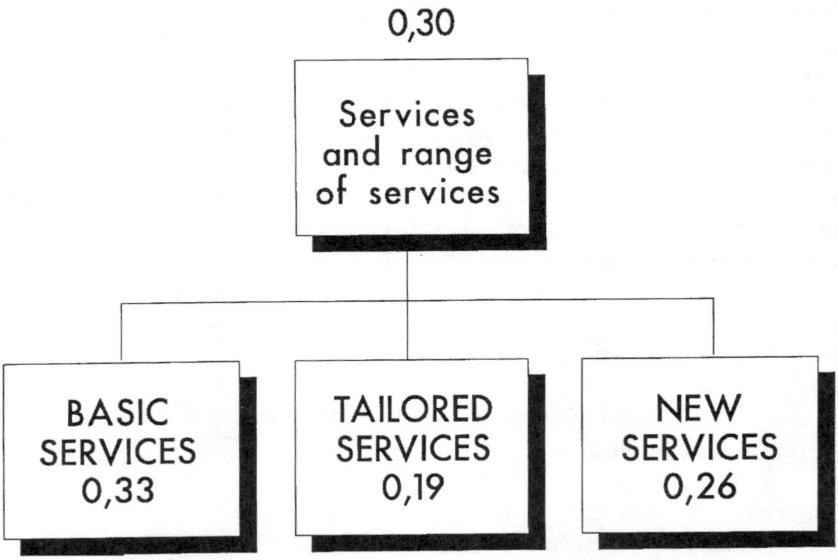

Figure 2. Weights of Services and Range of Services in Total Quality.

requirements. So continuous quality monitoring and management is an essential part of the operation and management system. The surveys indicate the weight which is attached to each of these factors influencing customer satisfaction and customer retention, and on the extent to which customers feel they receive value for money. According to the most recent survey, the latter seems to be mainly dependent on the quality of services, which in turn is determined by their range and reliability. Another aspect evaluated is the role of traditional, tailored, and new services within the total range.

As shown in figure 2, business customers' evaluations of the quality of postal services and their range are mainly determined by the traditional services. The most essential factors are their feasibility and risk-freeness to the customers.

The second most essential factor is the quality of new services, the evaluation of which is dependent on three main features according to the survey findings. The most important factor is how well customers are kept informed. The second factor is the feasibility and reliability of the services, which requires major input in testing their feasibility and the ease with which they can be adopted. The third factor is an active attitude towards development of services, which requires developing new service concepts and services, e.g., employing advanced technology, and acting in cooperation with major customers.

Customers indicated that they were most satisfied with development and use of advanced technological solutions applied in the new domestic communications and goods transport services. In accordance with the survey outcome, customers seem to expect more resources to be assigned to the development of direct marketing and international services.

3. Existing New Services Based on Customers' Needs

Home Shopping Services

The new Home Shopping concept is a complex of services, which was started with a major customer, featuring an entirely new concept of direct sales and consisting of alternative letter mail, telematic, freight, logistic, and financial transaction services. It involves traditional services which are combined in an entirely new way and exploit the full potential of electronic management and control systems. Alternative service solutions can be used to ensure that all companies can benefit from this new concept irrespective of level of technology available to them. At the same time, the concept will offer them access to integrated communications services utilizing a wide range of advanced technology.

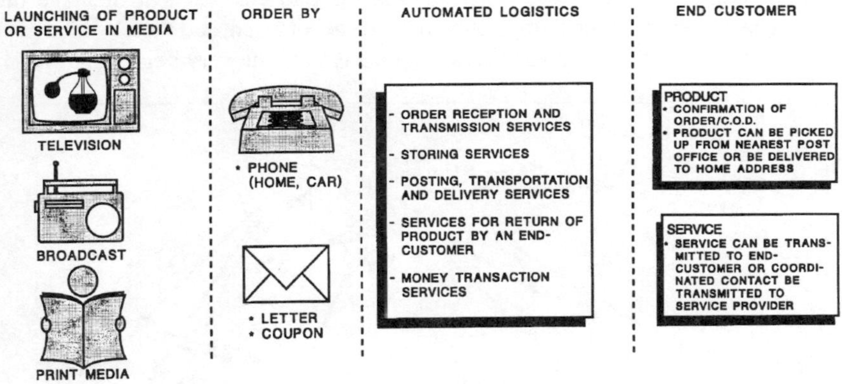

Figure 3. The Home Shopping Concept–Fulfillment Service Concept.

The Home Shopping concept is based on the use of a centralized logistic system to manage supply chains. The Home Shopping concept offers complete services to companies irrespective of the media employed, ranging from reception of orders to delivery of the goods and invoices to an end customer. Use of the concept minimizes the fixed costs to a business customer. It lowers the threshold for using direct marketing and sales. Further more, it accelerates warehouse turnover and cash flow. In addition, it has been verified that it reduces substantially credit risks and the number of returned items. The services concept makes possible rapid ordering and delivering goods to an end customer. These services in the concept are regarded as safe from the point of view of the end customer, as the consumer protection legislation on mail order services is also applied to them. Meanwhile, returns and refunds can be dealt with easily and reliably.

Outcome of the most recent surveys has indicated that more than 85% of the end customers, i.e., the customers of the companies making use of the Home Shopping concept, have been satisfied with the service provided. They seem to assign the greatest value to the ease of ordering, reliability of delivery, and suitability of the available means of payment.

Logistic Services: From Transport to Value-added Services

Post Ltd. participated in the multiclient Enator/T&LS (Transportation & Logistics Services) Survey in 1991 to figure out the use of information technology in logistics. At the time of the survey, a major chaining company of retailers dealing in books and computer and office equipment was seeking new means of improving and facilitating its purchasing functions. This company joined forces with the Post to devise a pattern of operation which enables the end customer to effectively promote cost efficiency and improve quality of the purchasing process. The service concept is intended for retail chaining companies dealing in special articles, as these can profit most from a situation in which the number of customers and suppliers is large.

The model makes a clear distinction between purchase decisions on goods and decisions on logistics services. This enables the end customers to manage the service chain right from the point at which goods are ordered, and thereby take over their own information and materials management from the very beginning.

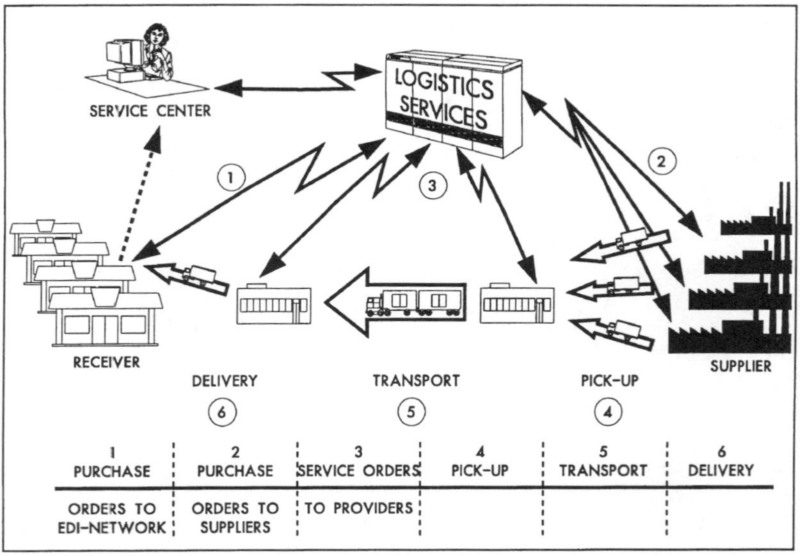

Figure 4. Process Description of the Logistics Services.

The purchasing process in an ordinary supply cycle proceeds in the following manner. Retailers/shopkeepers order articles through EDIFACT, by phone or by some alternative communication means. Then the orders are transferred to the required supplier by the logistic data system. An order may cover various entries and types of goods and be intended for communication to a number of suppliers, to whom the entries will be distributed by the information system. After that, the service orders are simultaneously transmitted to the transportation network of the Post, on the basis of which the items are picked up from the suppliers. In the end, the consignments from the various suppliers are combined for a single delivery to the end customers.

This new type of service concept enables companies to save approximately 30% of their freight and staff costs and up to 50% of their warehousing costs, as it speeds up warehouse turnover and reduces the capital bound up in warehoused goods. In addition, simpler purchase routines can be employed. Less time is required for making orders. The coordination of deliveries to a single consignment also ensures that staff resources do not have to be assigned to reception of goods. Business customers have recognized improvements in their operations and services. Deliveries are now faster and more punctual.

4. New Services Being Developed

Total Communications Sorting System

Post is currently engaged in a project to develop a total communications system which combines electronic and physical facilities for conventional and electronic messages and which will be based on customers' changing needs. The system is mainly intended for the transmission of messages and data from organizations to individuals. Its pattern of operations is built up in a bottom-up manner, setting out from actual needs. The aim is to achieve soon concrete results.

The information to be communicated may consists of a continuous flow of individual messages or of occasional bulk communications. The system enables the sender to communicate his message to the center in the form that is most convenient for him. From the center it will be passed on in the form most convenient for the recipient. A private person as a sender does not need any special communications equipment, as the Post will transfer it in the form determined by the sender but in the manner desired by the recipient.

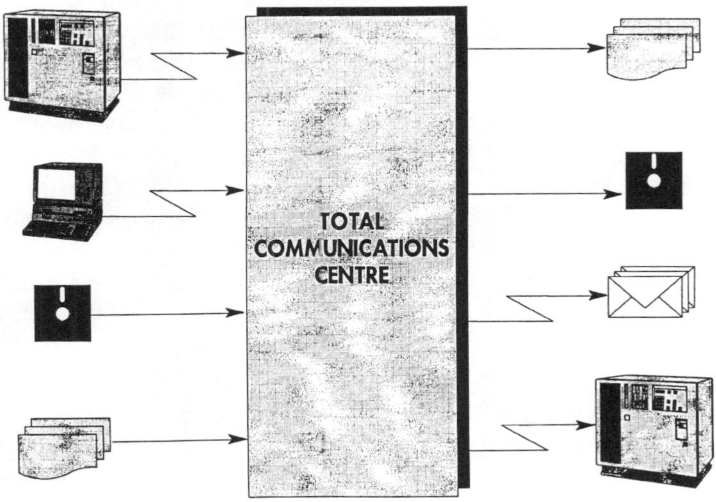

Figure 5. Operation of a Total Communications Center

The project aims at offering new alternative services which will enable business customers to concentrate on their core business, to accelerate their operations, and to intensify their use of resources and of advanced technology. In addition to companies, banks, and research institutes, the potential user groups include the government, local councils and their social welfare and health sectors, and various authorities responsible for issuing licenses and permits.

The total communications center can be used also to ensure that communication between companies and other instances takes place at the right time and in the correct form and that messages are delivered reliably to the desired address. This also improves data protection. In addition, use of the center will guarantee that companies receive high quality printouts. Companies can also make most profit from the system in financial terms, most notably as a result of reduced need for investments in data preprocessing equipment or maintenance of computer software and hardware for external communications.

End-to-End Services

The basic aim of the European End-to-End (ETE) services and the concepts which lie behind them, is to support the strengthening of the postal organizations in the various countries as providers of communications services in the face of the inevitable decline in the volumes of traditional services based on increased use of electronic alternatives. The aim is to introduce special value-added services in electronic information and messaging communications.

The End-to-End (ETE) project mainly focuses on communication between companies. It is intended to make increasing use of individual systems communicating directly with one other. In the system the messages will always exist in an electronic form. The service entities will consist basically of two primary sets of products, the more important one being business applications, a combination of communication services. The combination can be integrated into customers' computerized applications. The other set comprises basic communication services. Both sets contain alternative combinations of letter, telematic, freight, logistic, and financial transaction services. It combines the services and service concepts of the total communications centers with traditional transport and distribution services.

The applications can be divided into three categories:

- First, postal-based applications which add to traditional services can utilize the significant, distinct synergic advantages offered by the joint operations management of all postal services, in which electronic communications play an important role.
- Second, non-postal applications will be based on business processes, in which the electronic communications support initiation and maintenance of these process and which are dependent on the ones from one organization to an other.
- Third, business applications can be accessed by means of electronic databases, which are used to support new types of business activities and concepts

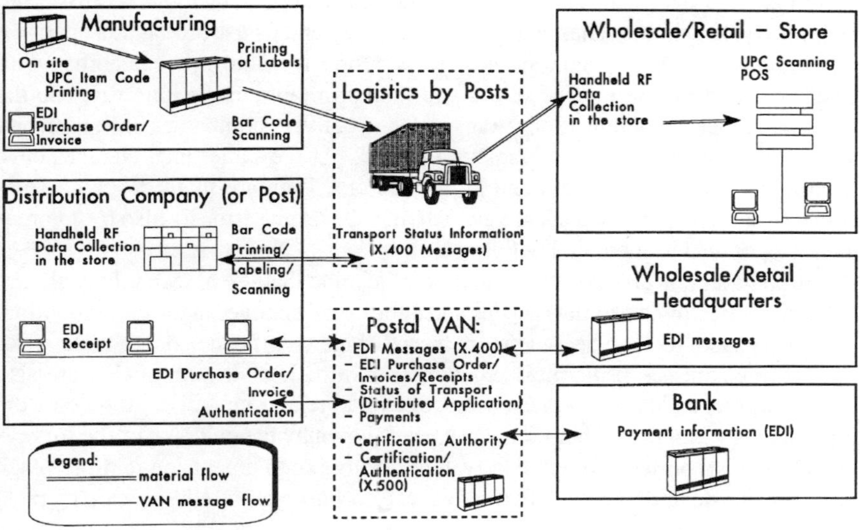

Figure 6. General Operations Model for ETE Applications.

and can be implemented only by means of electronic communications.

The services require good basic means of data transfer and communications in general which are comprehensive in both national and international terms, e.g., electronic mail, EDI, etc. A further aim is to concentrate efforts on application-level solutions which support the business activities concerned. The primary EDI users in Finland are retail and wholesale traders and the transport sectors. Banks and many companies make major use of electronic financial transactions, which allows them more time to concentrate on their core business.

Many branches of the industrial and service sectors, e.g., retail and wholesale trading, mechanical engineering, electronic engineering and computers, clothing, forestry and paper industries, shipbuilding, insurance, and the public sector, are currently re-evaluating and streamlining their functions and means of operations. At the same time, a change in trading practices and systems is under the way. With great probability, they will be increasingly based on telecom-services in the future, as these improve in speed and reliability.

The short-term requirements in the case of technically advanced systems are that their users must be committed to them for longer period.

5. Conclusions

In previous decades, introduction of new services in traditional communications and transportation were relatively inexpensive and labor-intensive. In the past, these new services were based on the providers' assumptions on customers' needs of the day and in the near future without any adequate data on them. Now that customers' service requirements have indicated the need for more sophisticated technology, the situation has changed. Technology and its use are capital-intensive and require extensive planning and true adaption to achieve acceptability with customers and to become successful and thus profitable in the long run. So the Posts and other communications, transport, and delivery companies have been and are currently going through a transition period. At the same time, changes have been taking place in business and public sectors. They are likely to give rise to major structural changes in society, which must be taken seriously also by communications, transportation, and delivery sectors.

Throughout this process, it should be kept in mind that use of technology always starts from existing customers' needs and anticipated changes in these. In addition, customers seem to have become more aware of the significance of technology for their core business. Furthermore, customers' evaluations of total quality are also essentially dependent or the new services available and on active attitude of the providers in introducing them. This has been shown by the outcome of the surveys from Finland reported above. Clearly, these factors supplement and reinforce each other in the development of new advanced-technology-based services to meet customer needs.

13

ON THE STRUCTURE OF INTER-FIRM POSTAL DEMAND

Toru Azumi

Introduction

This paper aims at analyzing inter-firm postal demand within a traditional micro-economics framework. The first section of the paper sets forth the concept of three networks: transportation, settlement, and communication. The second section gives an analysis of the process of determining the total volume of communications accompanying transportation (logistics communication), settlement (transactional communication), and dialog-type communication, employing the concepts of economies of scale and scope. The third section describes the generation of inter-firm postal demand mainly from the perspective of the nature of inter-firm communication for logistics, settlement, and other communication. The major drivers of this communication in the inter-firm context are then summarized and discussed in an international comparative context.

The micro-based, structural analysis presented here, being complementary to macro long-run analysis, will hopefully offer answers to such questions as: What is postal service? Why has demand for postal service continued its growth rate in line with the economic growth rate during the course of the 1980s despite extensive and growing competition? and What kind of elements will affect future demand trend?

1. Methodology and Basic Concepts

It is commonly believed that executives in the firm do not control communication costs. Although postal and telecommunication costs may be considerable for the individual firm, the executives of the firm typically have little opportunity to regard these costs in a strategic manner. The same can be said of transportation costs, which until recently were also relegated to relatively low tactical executives and therefore received little strategic attention. Similarly, settlement costs have been largely neglected. These costs differ from financial costs such as interest expense which executives have been quite keen to save. Settlement costs relate to the structure and timing of receivables and are associated with such operational functions as invoicing and other order fulfillment functions.

If these facts are assumed, then how it is possible to analyze the demand for services supporting inter-firm communications, with postal demand being an integral part of them? The approach taken here is to consider the demand for these services through the associated networks of transportation, settlement, and communication which mediate and support such inter-firm communciations.

A network is a mechanism for intermediating the exchange of something. More rigorously, a network can be defined as: "Any mechanism which intermediates the exchange of goods, money or information between different points without transferring ownership to its operator."

If "different points" are taken to mean different geographical locations, then three types of networks result: transportation networks, settlement networks, and communication networks, with providers of these networks called transportation carriers, banks, and communication carriers respectively.[1]

Our main interest here is in the inter-firm communication network, and in particular in that part of it which uses postal service as its medium of communication. It should be noted, however, that the communication network is intimately connected to both transportation and settlements networks. For example, goods transportation is accompanied by such information as the invoice. Moreover, although settlement used to mean actual exchange of bank notes, it is often replaced today by special forms of communication. Accordingly, it is convenient for purposes of analysis to distinguish inter-firm information exchange into the following types: "communication accompanying transportation;" "communication accompanying settlement;" and finally ordinary "dialog-type communication."

While executives of a firm may not directly control the costs of using any of the three networks of interest here, the demand for these networks is clearly influenced by other managerial decisions made by the executives. Thus, executives of the firm control the transportation volume and its cost by determining the size of the establishment, while controlling the settlement and communication volume and their costs by deciding the size of the firm itself. The next section will focus on these points in more detail.

2. Determination of Total Communication Demand

The concept of the network is not dealt with in ordinary economics, where transportation cost, settlement cost, and communication cost are usually neglected. It further supposes that any goods produced are to be immediately transferred to the next production stage or to be consumed at once. Nevertheless, should economics be used to successfully analyze the real economy, it must implicitly provide

1 If we expand the concept of "different points" to the time dimension, networks also include warehouses, money deposits, life insurance, and mailboxes. We restrict the concept of network here to the geographical dimension.

tools for analyzing the network. In this section, we analyze the determining element of demand for the network with the help of the two concepts of "economies of scale" and "economies of scope." An attempt is made here to expand on and generalize these concepts, which provide new insights into the source of these economies.

2.1. The Volume of Communications Accompanying Transportation

Forms of communications accompanying transportation include delivery notices, shipment instructions, goods orders, and goods receipts, which are characterized as not including price information at all or only nominally. The demand for these types of communication is generated inevitably by transportation, and it is fulfilled exactly as necessary. The totality of transportation in one whole economy is determined as the executives of the firm decide the size and geographical distribution of the "establishment"—a term used to denote physical economic units such as factories, warehouses, logistics centers, stores, sales offices, and branch offices—by taking into account the transportation costs, i.e., transportation costs of materials, products and staff, and, in the case of stores, the access cost of consumers.

Assume that two establishments, which produce the same kind of goods g at the volume level of g^1 and g^2 respectively, merge into one, realizing economies of scale (see figure 1). Letting C be the cost function of an establishment and V that of transportation, then the following relationship stands if scale economies are present:

$$C(g^1) + V(g^1) + C(g^2) + V(g^2) > C(g^1 + g^2) + V(g^1 + g^2). \tag{1}$$

If we assume further that constant returns to scale prevail within the establishment, then equation (1) can be rewritten as

$$\begin{aligned} C(g^1) + C(g^2) &= C(g^1 + g^2) \\ V(g^1) + V(g^2) &> V(g^1 + g^2). \end{aligned} \tag{2}$$

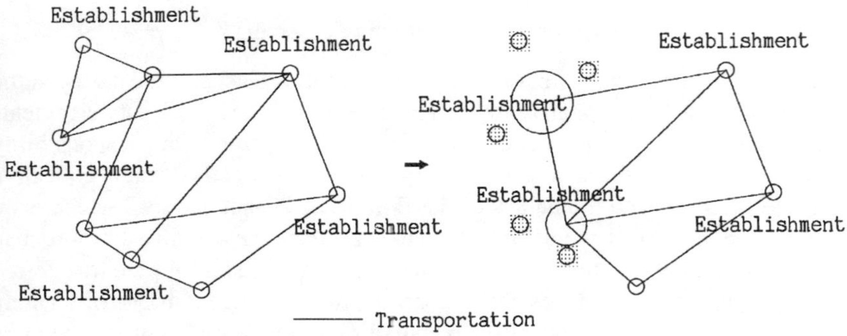

Figure 1. Formation of Establishment by Economy of Scale

The reasons for the gradual decrease in transportation costs include improvement in transportation efficiency and construction of additional infrastructure. However, as one establishment merges with other establishments located in other areas, transportation costs tend to increase, since transport distance becomes longer. Since the profits of each establishment are maximized at the equilibrium point under the given transportation rates (r^t), the following relationship holds:

Marginal Economies of Scale = Marginal Diseconomies of Scale.

At this point, the economy determines the output level (*GNP*) and the totality of transportation (*TT*) simultaneously, which is expressed as:

$$TT = TT(GNP, r^t). \tag{3}$$

Now with the total transportation determined, the volume of communications accompanying transportation (denoted *T*) is also determined so as to minimize the cost, given unit communication price (r^c):

$$T = T(TT, r^c). \tag{4}$$

The following equation then results from the above equations:

$$T = T(GNP, r^t, r^c). \tag{5}$$

2.2. The Volume of Communications Accompanying Settlement

Types of communications accompanying settlement include contract instruments, invoices, promissory notes, checks, and dividend notices, the main content of which is price information. As stated above, settlement is originally a process of actual exchange of bank notes, but there are only a very few examples of cash settlement in the firm's transactions. These are usually replaced by communications of special form. Kinds of communications accompanying inter-firm settlement are generated from two types of external contracts the firm makes: a commercial contract and a financial contract. Letting *S*, *F* be the corresponding settlement communications respectively, then

Communications Accompanying Settlement = $S + F$

Settlements generated from a commercial contract are usually transacted at the firm's headquarters. Although settlement is sometimes done at such establishments as a branch office, a sales office, or even a factory within the responsibility transferred to it, invoices are, in principle, bundled together for a collective settlement according to the names of the firm at the "headquarters," which is an establishment providing special functions to coordinate the activities of more than two establishments (see figure 2). If all settlement responsibilities are transferred from the headquarters to the establishments, there would be no merits of forming a single accounting unit, i.e., the firm, by bundling several establishments together.

Accordingly, the totality of settlements determines when the firm, with an

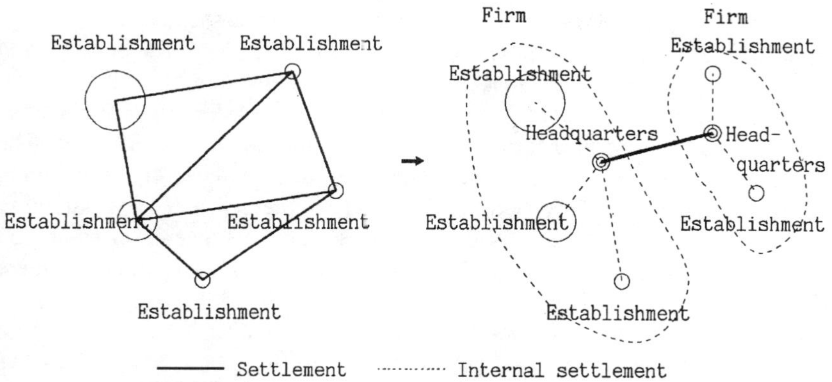

Figure 2. Formation of Firm by Economy of Scope

independent headquarters function carrying out collective settlements, chooses its own size while pursuing greater settlement efficiency. In other words, should the size of the establishments be given by the principle reviewed in the previous subsection together with the GNP, the totality of settlements still decreases as the firm becomes larger. This is applicable in the case of the horizontal merger, such as a supermarket expanding its chain stores, but is more apparent in the case of a vertical merger such as a manufacturer merging with its suppliers.

If we assume that the respective establishments produce only one kind of product which differs from that of another, then it is equivalent to the realization of the "economies of scope" for the several establishments to form one company. For example, let two establishments produce goods g_1 and g_2 respectively. They are assumed to have no independent headquarters, which means the unit of the establishment exactly corresponds to the unit of the firm. Suppose these establishments merge into one firm by creating a new independent headquarters in order to economize on settlement cost between their common business partners. Letting C be a cost function of establishment, H that of headquarters, $C(g \mid H)$ that of the establishment after having created an independent headquarters (to economize on settlement cost of a commercial contract), then the following relationship stands:

$$C(g_1) + C(g_2) > H(g_1, g_2) + C(g_1 \mid H) + C(g_2 \mid H). \tag{6}$$

This then is a special form of the following definitional equation for economies of scope:

$$C(g_1) + C(g_2) > C(g_1, g_2). \tag{7}$$

However, if we expand the concept of establishment to one floor of a building or even to one corner of a floor, and modify the concept of headquarters to simply a coordination function, (6) can also be regarded as a general form of economies of scope. This equation clearly indicates that the rationalization of settlement and the headquarter's communication function are among the largest elements essential to realizing communications economies of scope. In general, the source of economies of scope is considered to be the existence of common facilities, but it should be understood, more precisely, that it lies in the rationalization of settlement cost by organizing one firm and not renting common facilities. For example, a telephone company provides telephone service and data transmission service together. The source of the economies of scope does not lie in the existence of the common facilities in itself but in the economization of the settlement which is otherwise necessary whenever two services having different sources of revenue use common facilities. Thus, the degree of the economies of scope is a function of a settlement technology, i.e., the settlement cost.

The firm can reduce the number of settlements generated from a commercial contract by merging its counterpart establishments in so far as the firm has transactions with them or has common business counterparts with them. However, as the firm merges establishments one after one, the number of transactions or common counterparts with an additional establishment will gradually be reduced, causing a greater "diseconomies of scope." This is because of an increase in other costs due to unnecessary communications with its additional staff, who are no longer engaged in a common business, in order to maintain the corporate organization.

If we call the cost for settlement generated from a commercial contract the "transaction cost," and the cost for various kinds of communications between the firm and its staff to maintain its corporate organization the "organizing cost," the equilibrium point, yielding a minimum of the total of these costs, is given by the following equation:

Marginal Transaction Cost = Marginal Organizing Cost.

This equation can also be expressed in the terminology employed here:

Marginal Economies of Scope = Marginal Diseconomies of Scope.

We return to this equation after dialog-type communication is discussed.

The question of concern here is how communications accompanying settlement are generated from a financial contract such as payment of interest or dividends. Some cases arise in which financial reasons play a significant role in causing the firm to merge. However, these circumstances differ significantly from company to company. Moreover, the numbers of financial settlements are not always reduced as a result of merger since several contracts are sometimes concluded in parallel between the same firm and the same financial organization. The numbers of financial settlements depend eventually on financial market conditions. Thus, they are simply expressed as a function of the profit of financial institutions PFT^F as

$$F = F(PFT^F, r^C). \tag{8}$$

2.3. The Volume of Dialog-Type Communications

Dialog-type communication is a general term used to cover business communications other than those accompanying transportation and settlement. Dialog-type communication can be divided into two categories: Marketing-type communication (I) between establishments which produce different products or services from each other; and intra-organization communications (B) taking place within the space of the firm to which respective establishments belong. Thus,

$$\text{Dialog-Type Communications} = I + B.$$

There is an obvious cost-benefit relationship in marketing-type communication compared to other forms of communications. Accordingly, executives of the firm control this kind of communication in a strategic manner. However, since its optimal volume is related to human ability to comprehend the information, it is considered to depend on the number of employees and is relatively independent from the formation of the establishment or the firm which is essentially an institution. If we assume that the economic value of decision making is parallel to the information acknowledged, then the volume (I) of marketing-type communication is a function of the number of employees (N) and, representing the economic value of decision making by GNP, we can write:

$$I = I(N, GNP, r^C). \tag{9}$$

Intra-organization communication (B) is typically represented by the "business document." The business document includes paper materials prepared by the headquarters for its branch offices such as management policies, sales targets, personnel information, detailed product information, technical information, as well as similar such reports from branch offices to the headquarters.

2.4. The Volume of Communications Accompanying Settlement and the Volume of Dialog-Type Communications (Revisited)

Communications accompanying a commercial settlement S and intra-organization communications B were left undetermined during the course of presenting the above argument. The purpose of this subsection is to determine these using the following micro equilibrium condition, previously noted:

$$\text{Marginal Economies of Scope} = \text{Marginal Diseconomies of Scope.} \tag{*}$$

Economies of scope are related solely to the communications of one firm to another firm, i.e., communications accompanying commercial settlement S under the assumptions of this paper. On the other hand, the source of diseconomies of scope is the increase in unnecessary communications in order to maintain the firm's organization, which may have little relationship to business activity itself.

Consider a marginal (i.e., a small) establishment of size n which is a candidate for merger with a headquarters and other establishments. For any firm at the equilibrium condition, realizing the profit maximization, the benefit of saving a commercial settlement by merging with this marginal establishment is arguably equal to the increase in the intra-organization communication cost. Denoting the cost of settlement communications by C^S and the cost of intra-organization communications by C^B, the equilibrium condition (*) may be expressed using a micro-framework as

$$\frac{\partial C^S(s, n)}{\partial n} = -\frac{\partial C^B(b, n)}{\partial n}, \tag{10}$$

where lower case letters refer to firm-level decisions and upper-case letters refer to generic or economy-wide aggregates.

2.5. Summary

Denote by V the Total Communications Volume. Then, we can summarize the above analysis by the following equations.

$$\begin{aligned} V &= T + (S + F) + (I + B) \\ &= T(GNP, r^t, r^c) + S + F(PFT^F, r^c) + I(N, GNP, r^c) + B, \end{aligned} \tag{11}$$

where, for given N (or n), B (or b) and S (or s) satisfy (10) as well.

3. Media Structure of Inter-Firm Communications

The firm fulfills its communication demand by choosing suitable media, taking into account the prominent media characteristics and relevant costs. Communications media can be divided according to their characteristics into "telecommunications (including facsimile)," and "documentation." We assume that the mix between these two media choices for a particular firm is set to minimize total communications cost. Let us discuss transportation and settlement communications in more detail.

3.1. Media Choice for Communications Accompanying Transportation

Among the communications accompanying transportation, as to those such as shipment instructions and goods orders, telecommunication is generally preferred, while documentation is usually chosen for delivery notices and goods receipts. The communication mode is basically the same regardless of whether or not it occurs inside firm (e.g., from factory to warehouse) or between the firms (e.g., warehouse to store).

The telephone has played an undeniably central role among the various telecommunications media, but nowadays demand is shifting to facsimile and data communication. The same type of substitution is also observed in the office, supporting testimony that major substitution is from one form of telecommunication, i.e., telephone, to another form of telecommunication, i.e., facsimile or data communication.[2]

The nature of communication accompanying transportation is to convey and confirm the facts related to transportation. Thus, goods receipt is usually documented, and the reason for this is that the document gives the minimum solution cost whenever a dispute arises concerning facts about the receipt. Increasingly, Electronic Data Interchange and other interfirm computer-based communications media are being used to increase the efficiency of transportation-related documentation. Nonetheless, some shipment instructions or goods orders are still documented and sent by mail. But we assume that they will sooner or later be replaced by telecommunications in so far as they do not have a contract element (or a price decision element). In Japan, the ratio of inter-firm mail to total volume has decreased from 35.6% in 1988 to 28.7% in 1991. As for communications accompanying transportation as a whole, including delivery notices, a major tendency is being observed toward shifting to more advanced telecommunications, and it is assumed that such a trend continued to produce a major substitution from mail to telecommunications.

3.2. Media Choice of Communication Accompanying Settlement

Laws and customs require that communications accompanying settlement should always be, in principle, documented between the parties concerned. However, the degree of documentation throughout the whole process varies depending on the method used. This implies that part of the process can be handled by telecommunications inside or between financial institutions.

Nevertheless, three types of communications, "contract," "charging," and "receipt," are, in most cases, documented in some way regardless of the settlement method utilized. Specifically, an invoice is generated from every commercial transaction, and, as far as Japanese business customs are concerned, is always documented whatever the settlement method employed after its receipt. According to the result of our interviews with major Japanese companies, there were only a few examples in which a core part of the invoice is sent by telecommunications—that between a parent company and its full subsidiary or on an experimental basis. The preparation intervals of the invoice, namely, the settlement intervals, however, depend on the kind of the business concerned. The literature indicates that this custom differs from country to country and from business to business even within a country.

If we define a security as a document stipulating the right-obligation relationship, various other documents such as entrance tickets, discount vouchers, meal tickets, complimentary tickets, hotel coupons, and exchange slips are all included here. They all require documentation and can be exchanged either by means of face-to-face delivery or mail.

Among communications accompanying settlement, the invoice and the check show the highest mailing-ratio in general. In this field, it can be said that postal service is competing with various non-cash settlement methods offered by the bank.

2 This substitution is part of our reason for dividing media into telecommunications as a whole and documentation.

On the other hand, intra-organization communication is usually documented. For this type of communication, being a kind of official communication in the sense that it is a communication intended for the institutional firm space, documentation is, in general, the least expensive way to share such official information among many people. In other words, it is even possible to define the firm in a more substantial manner as the space in which costly documented information is freely exchanged. Nevertheless, it has recently become possible to realize this kind of information sharing through the intra-firm networks, and this system serves as a substitute for documentation.

As to business documents, mail is competing with a large market called "internal mail." According to our interviews with major Japanese companies, they use internal mail for offices generating a large communication volume such as a regional head office, while they use ordinary mail for offices producing a smaller volume.

3.3. Construction of a Macro Model

The individual firm decides on its management size which then leads it to determine the communications accompanying its commercial settlements and intra-organization communications. Building on the previously constructed micro model (see 2.5), we begin with the equilibrium condition that marginal economies of scale should equal marginal diseconomies of scale, i.e.,

$$\frac{\partial C^S(s,n)}{\partial n} = -\frac{\partial C^B(b,n)}{\partial n} \tag{12}$$

Letting y be the sales of the firm and assuming the total cost function leading to (12) is of the form $C = C(s(y(n)), b(n))$, we get

$$\frac{\partial C}{\partial s}\cdot\frac{\partial s}{\partial y}\cdot\frac{\partial y}{\partial n} = -\frac{\partial C}{\partial b}\cdot\frac{\partial b}{\partial n}\,. \tag{13}$$

Thus, using subscripts to denote partial derivatives, we obtain from (13)

$$C_s\cdot\frac{s}{y}\cdot\eta_{sy}\cdot y_n = -\text{`}C_b\cdot b_n\,, \tag{14}$$

where η_{sy} is the elasticity of s with respect to y. Therefore, we obtain the following equation to give the number of invoices for the firm:

$$s = -\frac{1}{\eta_{sy}}\cdot\frac{C_b}{C_s}\cdot\frac{b_n}{y_n}\cdot y\,, \tag{15}$$

where

s = communications accompanying settlement;
y = sales;
C_b = marginal cost to produce one unit of internal communications (one sheet of a business document);

C_s = marginal cost to conduct one settlement;
b_n = number of units of internal communications (number of sheets of business documents) per marginal staff; and
y_n = sales per marginal staff.

From (15), we can deduce that:

1. The number of settlements is parallel to sales.
2. The number of settlements decreases when the marginal cost to produce one sheet of a business document drops.
3. The number of settlements increases when the marginal cost to conduct one settlement drops.
4. The number of settlements increases when the number of sheets of a business document per marginal staff rises.
5. The number of settlements decreases when the sales per marginal staff rises.

If we assume that $\eta_{sy} = 1$, then there exists a constant k such that

$$-\frac{C_b}{C_s} \cdot \frac{b_n}{y_n} = k, \tag{16}$$

and settlement expenses are proportional to the firm's sales y, i.e., for a given firm i,

$$s_i = ky_i\,, \tag{17}$$

and for the economy as a whole

$$S = \sum_i S_i = k \sum_i Y_i = kY, \tag{18}$$

assuming that linear aggregation across firms is reasonable. Using (10) to determine b as a function of s and n, we obtain for firm i

$$b_i = B_i(s_i, n_i, r^{c)} = B_i(y_i, k, n_i, r^{c)}. \tag{19}$$

Thus, (18) implies at the macro level the following relationship:

$$B = B(S, N, r^c) = B(Y, k, N, r^c). \tag{20}$$

With B and S determined at the macro level by (18) and (20) and with the other communications volumes determined by aggregating the corresponding terms (for T, F, and I) in 2.5, we have thus specified the total communications volume in the economy. Assuming that media selection is cost-minimizing, we can then split this total volume into the volume served by mail and that served by other forms of communication. The result is a model of total mail volume for the economy, which could be further split into volumes of various classes of mail. Building on the above discussion, we an represent the process of aggregating across firms to obtain total communications volume in the economy and then disaggregating total communications volume into document communications and then mail volumes as follows:

V = **Total Communication Volume**

$$V = T + (S + F) + (I + B)\}$$

$$= T(GNP, r^t, r^c) + kY + F(PFT^F, r^{c)}\} + I(N, GNP, r^c) + B(Y, k, N, r^c) \quad (21)$$

D = Total Document Communication Volume

$$D = \alpha_1 T(GNP, r^t, r^c) + \alpha_2\, k\, Y$$

$$+ \alpha_3 F(PFT^F, r^c) + \alpha_4 I(N, GNP, r^c) + \alpha_5 B(Y, k, N, r^c), \quad (22)$$

where α_i ($i = 1,5$) is the documentation-to-communication ratio for each indicated type of communication.

M = **Total Mail Volume**

$$M = \beta_1 \alpha_1 T(GNP, r^t, r^c) + \beta_2 \alpha_2\, k\, Y$$

$$+ \beta_3 \alpha_3 F(PFT^F, r^c) + \beta_4 \alpha_4 I(N, GNP, r^c) + \beta_5 \alpha_5 B(Y, k, N, r^c), \quad (23)$$

where β_j ($j = 1,5$) is the mailing-to-documentation ratio for each indicated type of communication.

From the foregoing analysis, this can be rewritten as

$$M = \gamma_1 kY + \gamma_2 F(PFT^F, r^c) + \gamma_3 I(N, GNP, r^c) + \gamma_4 B(Y, k, N, r^c) + Z, \quad (24)$$

where Z is a residual. Note that we have neglected the term in (23) representing communications accompanying transportation, recognizing that such communications are not important as a determinant of mail demand. Equation (24) indicates that the mail volume consists of settlement communications and dialog-type communications. The final point to be analyzed is which element will play a more crucial role in the future trend of postal demand.

3.4. International Comparison of Postal Demand

The postal market is characteristically different from country to country. For example, the numbers of postal items posted per capita per year are: Japan 190.4, Sweden 200.4, Germany 263.4 (countries with relatively small volumes of mail.), the United Kingdom 284.0 (modest volume), Canada 312.3, France 379.5, and the United States 648.5 (countries with larger volumes of mail).

People generally ascribe this disparity to the cultural differences of the country, saying that some peoples write a great many letters while other peoples do not. However, peoples all over the world have the same tendency with regard to personal letters—a tendency not to write so frequently. From where then does this stark difference arise? It is commonly observed in all industrialized countries that the economic activities are run mainly by the firm. Since the firm is engaged in business

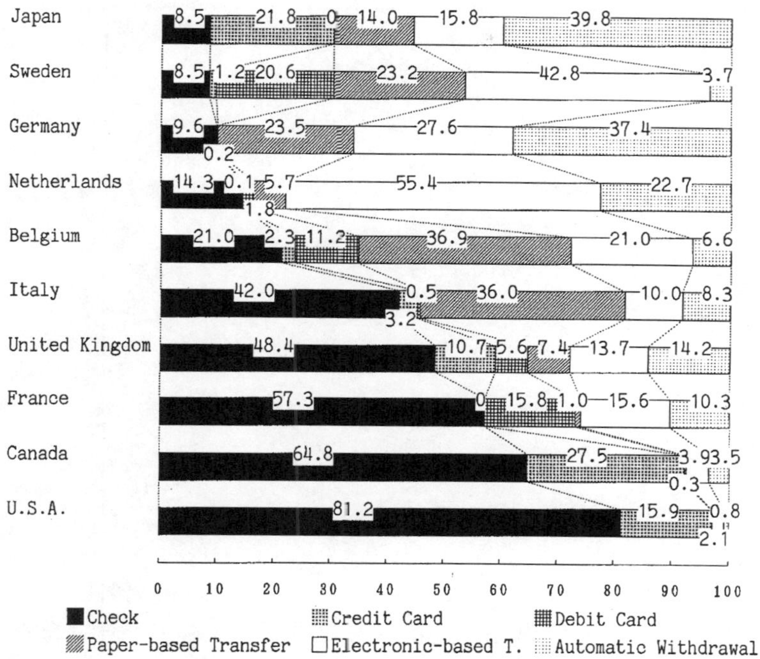

Figure 3. Constituent Percentage of Non-Cash Settlement (1991)

Source: Battel

for the same purpose everywhere, specifically, to make as much profit as possible, its organization and behavior principles are basically the same. Similarly, banks are committed to non-cash inter-firm settlement. Thus, there appears to be no differences in the nature of settlement costs, nor the motivation to minimize them, across countries. Despite all of these circumstances, the actual settlement institutions vary remarkably from country to country.

Figure 3 indicates the constituent percentage in the number of non-cash settlements by country. Here, non-cash settlements are classified into six categories: check, credit card, debit card, paper-based money transfer, electronic-based money transfer, and automatic withdrawal. In the case of credit card settlement, after the credit transaction takes place between the consumer and the store, the store makes another settlement with the credit card company, and this is repeated between the credit company and the consumer. Those settlements may be by check, money transfer, or automatic withdrawal. Postal demand may be generated from paper-based money transfer but it is much smaller in volume since several settlement documents are bundled together. It is even smaller with regard to electronic-based money transfers, and, in the case of automatic withdrawals, the successive processes are handled by the computer. Accordingly, the check is the most important

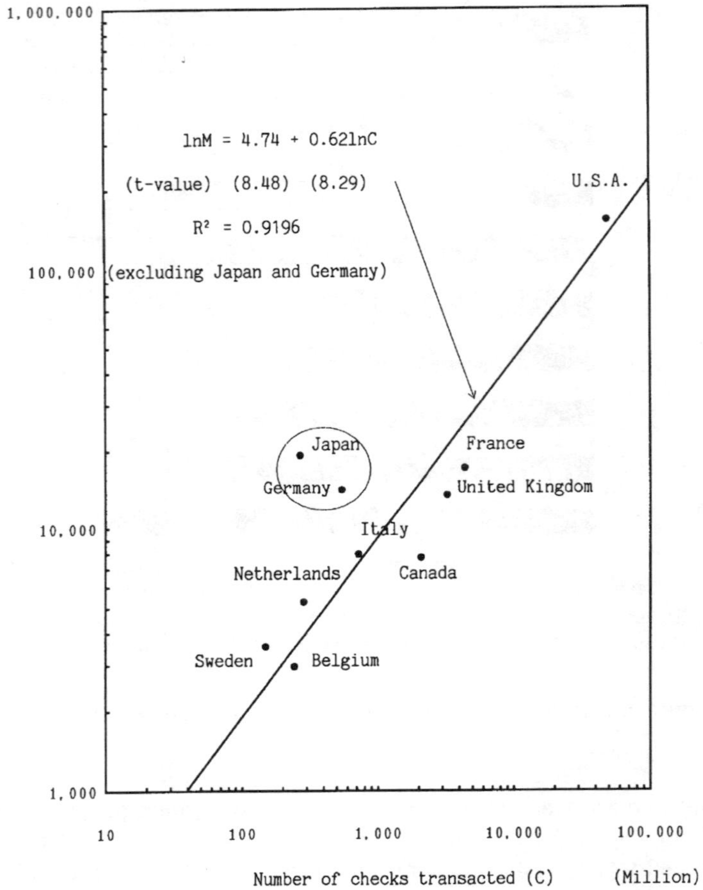

Figure 4. Correlation between Numbers of Checks and Postal Items (1987)

Source: Battel

driver of mail volume among these methods, followed by the credit card in "check" countries. The check thus seems to generate the largest postal demand.

Although the constituent percentage of check settlements seen here seems in itself to be closely related to the number of postal items posted per capita, this is even clearer in figure 4, which demonstrates the correlation between the number of checks transacted and that of total postal items processed. This figure also indicates the remarkably large number of settlements made in the United States. This is probably due to the lower cost of check settlement, assuming settlement efficiency in the United States economy. It appears that the "universal service" offered by the post office is, in fact, that of settlement.

4. Conclusions

People naturally feel a sense of nostalgia when the word "mail" comes up. However, even when the modern post was established, people who used the postal service most must have been merchants. Documents such as contract instruments, order forms, goods receipts, and promissory notes have been actively exchanged.

On the other hand, American Express, which used to be engaged in the transportation of gold, transformed itself into a financial institution by replacing gold transportation with communications. The nature of any financial institution is to intermediate transactions by means of replacing an expensive gold settlement with communications. The postal service has been deeply committed to this settlement process from its inception.

"The postal service is a financial service" is then the conclusion of this paper. This point is applicable not only to inter-firm post but also to the postal items we receive during our daily life. The postal items posted from a public enterprise or a credit card company are all related to settlements. Recently, direct mail has tended to include entrance tickets to a special bargain sale, discount vouchers and other such items. These are all settlement documents in the sense referred to in this paper. This trend is more and more apparent along with the development of telecommunications which is playing a central role in streeamlining logistics. Thus, it would be no exaggeration to say that the future of the postal service lies in its function to contribute extensively to improving financial efficiency through the post-mediated settlement processes described in this paper.

14

ANALYSIS OF ECONOMIES OF SCALE IN SMALL PACKAGE CARRIER SERVICE IN JAPAN[1]

Toru Azumi
Ken Umemura

Introduction

At present, Japan's small package carrier service is divided into two categories: parcel post as conducted by the Ministry of Posts and Telecommunications, called "Yupack," and parcel delivery service rendered by private long-distance trucking firms. In 1992, the Ministry handled 426 million postal packages, while Yamato Transport Company, Ltd., which ranks first in scale within the nation's commercial parcel delivery industry, handled 515 million. Nippon Express Company, Ltd., placing second in the industry, carried 324 million parcels. Thus, public and private sector services are intermingled and in competition with each other. In this paper, we deal with the parcel delivery service market.

The first section of this paper shows that the oligopoly of the individual parcel delivery services market is more conspicuous than its corporate counterpart and that this is because economies of scale peculiar to the individual market are operating. The second section demonstrates that the individual and corporate markets differ with respect to the method of order acceptance and explains that economies of scale, as peculiar to the individual market, work at the stage of consignment acceptance. And it is theorized that, specifically, the factors seen in the economy of scale are those lying in consumer demand, such as the costs they incur to find out about the quality and contents of services offered and to reach the nearest transport firm outlet, or agency. The third section presents the results of examining the economy of scale as taking place in the individual market by constructing a model of service production in the parcel delivery industry and measuring agency elasticity of demand as well as that of service awareness among

1 The authors thank Professor Kenichi Fukumiya of Meiji University for his invaluable advice. Without his help, this paper could not have been completed.

potential customers by use of statistical data. The fourth section contains conclusions germane to the analysis.

1. The Current State of the Small Package Carriers' Market

Private-sector small package carrier service began in 1976. Prior to that time, services had been provided by the Ministry of Posts and Telecommunications and the Japanese National Railways (JNR), both of which were governmental. With private firms joining the market, however, the volume of parcel consignments to JNR decreased, and its services in this regard eventually faded to oblivion. The amount of parcel post shipments also dropped sharply for a while, but the Ministry regained competitiveness by renewing its nationwide shipping system, the relaxation of restrictions on weight and developing new products (figure 1).

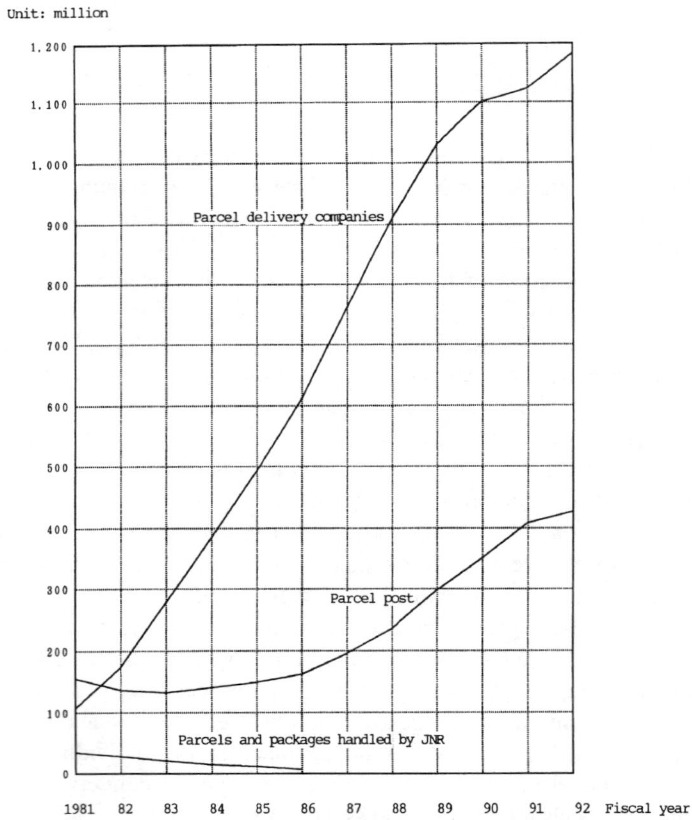

Figure 1. Transition in the Number of Parcels Handled by Japan's Small Package Carrier Services

Source: Ministry of Posts and Telecommunications, Ministry of Transport
Note: Parcels and packages handled by JNR were abolished by the end of FY 1986.

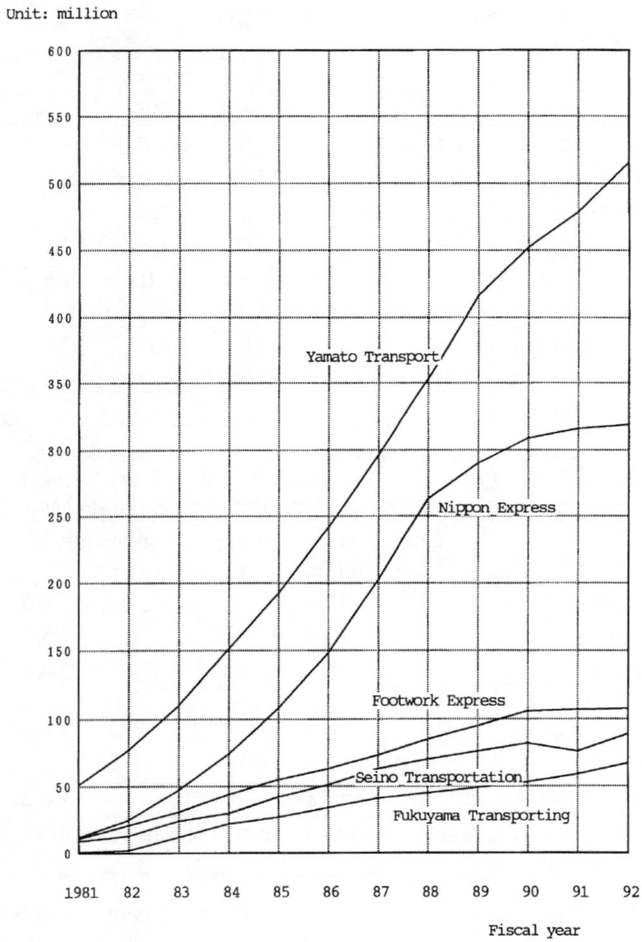

Figure 2. Transition of the Top Five Companies in the Parcel Delivery Business

Source: Ministry of Transport

Yamato Transport was the first to launch parcel delivery service as a business, and its sucess catering especially to individual consumers inspired many other trucking firms to joint the market. Business swiftly expanded when this service was extended to carrying small packages consigned by corporations (figure 2). Throughout the 1980s, parcel carrying accounted for one of the fastest growing industries in Japan. And, in fact, the aggregate number of parcels handled had recorded a constant two-digit annual increase until 1990.

A close look at the market structure of Japan's current parcel carrying industry, though, will reveal that it has a marked tendency toward oligopoly. In 1992, with respect to the total number of parcels handled, 87 percent of the market was

Table 1. Transition of Market Shares Held by Parcel Delivery Service Companies

	Fiscal Year					
Companies	1982	1984	1986	1988	1990	1992
Yamato Transport	44.1	41.9	39.3	38.7	41.1	43.5
Nippon Express	14.4	19.1	23.2	28.9	28.1	26.9
Footwork Express	11.9	11.6	10.3	9.3	9.6	9.1
Senio Transportation	7.5	7.9	8.4	7.7	7.5	7.5
Fukuyama Transporting	1.1	5.7	5.6	5.0	4.8	5.7
Others	21.1	13.8	13.3	10.5	9.0	7.2
Two Top-ranking firms	58.5	61.0	62.5	67.6	69.2	70.4
Four Top-ranking firms	77.9	80.5	81.2	84.6	86.3	87.0

Source: Ministry of Transport

Table 2. Comparsions of Shares of the Entire Parcel Delivery Service Market (Individual , and of the Individual Market and Corporate Markets)

Companies	Entire Parcel Delivery Service Market (%)	Individual Market (%)
Yamato Transport	43.5	64.6
Nippon Express	26.9	25.3
Seino Transportation	9.1	4.2
Footwork Express	7.5	1.8
Fukuyama Transporting	5.7	1.4
Others	7.2	2.7
Two top-ranking firms	70.4	89.9

*Individual market shares were established based on data obtained from the 1994 IPTP report (Reference 10).

commanded by four top-ranking companies, with 70 percent controlled by only two (table 1). In terms of parcels consigned by individual customers (the individual market), the oligopolistic feature became even more pronounced.

IPTP estimates that in the individual market of parcel delivery service, first-ranking Yamato Transport ruled a 65 percent share, while Nippon Express, as second-best, held 25 percent, with the two combined dominating all of 90 percent of the entire market (table 2). This being the case, we can safely say that other than Yamato Transport and Nippon Express virtually all other firms engaged in the trade have dropped out of the individual market.

Why do the individual market and the corporate market (transport of consignments from companies) of parcel delivery differ in degree of oligopoly? In economics, market oligopoly within a specific industry is ascribed to concepts of economy of scale. For this reason it is presupposed that, in view of the individual market's oligopoly being more conspicuous than that of the corporate market, economy of scale is more prominent in the former variety.

In the next section, the characteristics of the individual market are clarified by examining where and for what reasons economy of scale works in this market.

2. Economies of Scale in the Individual Market

Characteristically, in a service type industry like parcel delivery, service is rendered only upon request, and unlike with commodities service cannot be stocked for later use. Strictly speaking, service varies in content depending on where and how demand occurs. Thus when analyzing the production costs of this form of endeavor, it is not enough to assess only supply side factors; rather, cost analysis must also include peculiarities of the demand side (expenses incurred by consumers when they use the service).

2.1. Supply-Side Factors—Accepting Orders

As stated in the preceding section, the oligopolistic situation of the individual market is far more apparent than in its corporate counterpart. In this section, by first examining supply-side factors, an analysis will be made to determine which phase of parcel delivery operation has generated an economy of scale pronounced enough to draw the market toward a natural monopoy.

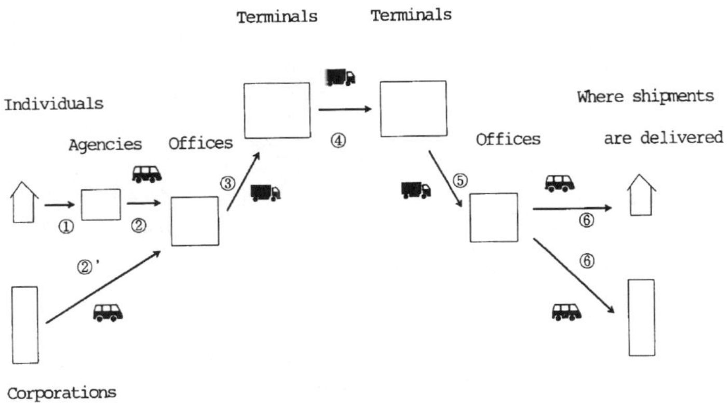

① Brought in (individual consignments accepted)

② Collected ②' Collected (corporate shipments accepted)

③ Transported between offices (includes sorting)

④ Transported between terminals

⑤ Transported between offices

⑥ Delivered(includes sorting)

Figure 3. Flow of Consignments in Parcel Delivery Service

2.1.1. Operation of Parcel Delivery Service

Parcel delivery service operation comprises four sections: acceptance, sorting, long distance transport, and delivery. For a clue to understanding where economy of scale peculiar to the individual market is at work, let us first clarify operational differences between parcel deliveries for individuals and those for enterprises in the four sections (figure 3).

Acceptance. To begin with, parcel delivery firms naturally accept shipment orders in various ways, and there exists a great difference between individual orders and those placed by enterprises:items consigned by individuals are basically accepted via agencies, while those from corporations are taken by transport company personnel who collect parcels directly. In both cases, articles accepted are forwarded to terminals through shipping offices.

Sorting. At freight terminals, high-speed automatic sorting machines separate articles for delivery to the respective shipping offices that cover geographical areas for which consignments are destined. Parcels routed to the same region and gathered in lots need not go through the sorting machine. Basically, though, shipments consigned by individuals and enterprises alike are processed in the same manner since most of them must pass through the sorting machine.

Long-Distance Transport. Sorted items are transferred from terminal to terminal by large van. As a matter of course, all parcels, whether consigned by individuals or corporations, are shipped together.

Delivery. After arrival at destination terminals, consignments are reloaded and forwarded to shipping offices, from where they are delivered by small van to residential or corporate addressees. This form of delivery takes place irrespective of whether commercial or individual in nature.

2.1.2. Acceptance Operation

It is generally acknowledged that, as in postal service, economy of scale works in the delivery phase. But as described in the preceding paragraph, there is no operational difference between the handling of shipments of an individual nature and those consigned by corporations in the delivery process. Accordingly, the assumption that economy of scale takes place in delivery fails to explain the advancing oligopoly seen in the individual as opposed to the corporate market. Inasmuch as individual and corporate shipments are treated differently only at the stage of acceptance, it is inferred that economy of scale peculiar to the individual market works essentially at that phase of their operation. Let us examine this.

2.2. Demand-Side Factors—Service Awareness and Agency Access Costs

The preceding section treated that economy of scale in the individual market characteristically works at the acceptance stage. As a matter of course, the accep-

Table 3. Criteria for Individual User Choice of a Small Package Delivery Firm	
1. A shipping agency is nearby	(28.4%)
2. Speedy Delivery	(25.1%)
3. No accidents such as loss or damage during shipment	(13.2%)
4. Delivery according to schedule	(11.7%)
5. The company is well known	(5.7%)
6. Less Costly	(4.2%)
7. Consigning parcels is easy	(3.6%)
Source: IPTP (1994)	

tance of consignment orders is directly related to the demand factor. This being the case, we all now explore the nature of shipping demand to determine what motivates it to produce economy of scale.

2.2.1. Costs to Individuals Who Use Parcel Delivery Service

A survey of individual users of small package carrier services conducted by IPTP revealed that the first criterion for choosing an express firm cited by the majority of pollees was the close proximity of one of its agencies (see table 3). From the standpoint of consumer costs, the nearness of an agency shows that it requires less cash outlay on the part of customers when they have easy access to a shipping and receiving station. Responses like "speedy delivery," a reputation for "no accidents such as loss or damage during shipment," "delivery according to schedule," and "the company is well known" indicate that information onto quality of service provided by the company is ready available and that the expense incurred by consumers when obtaining the facts is low. Also, since a service industry like parcel transport does not constitute a tangible product, customers find it hard to know in advance whether the content and quality of service will prove to be satisfactory. Corporations sometimes make arrangements with specific express firms regarding the nature of services rendered, but it is virtually impossible for individuals to do this since they generally consign fewer parcel per order and far less frequently. It stands as important, therefore, that individual shippers have easy access to information on parcel delivery services so as to minimize customer expense for finding out (serviceawareness cost).

2.2.2. Advertising and Publicity and Agency Policy

Inasmuch as parcel delivery shipping tariffs, as recommended by the government, are regularly observed, there has been virtually no price competition in the individual market. Conversely there has been fierce rivalry among express carriers in reducing ancillary costs to the consumer. Specifically, parcel delivery firms have conducted advertising and publicity activities to slash service awareness costs to prospective shippers and have actuated policies with respect to agency accessibility, again to lower the expense incured by individual users in this regard. The following paragraphs briefly describe how Yamato Transport and Nippon Express have waged their advertising and publicity campaigns, and the manner in which they have implemented their policies with respect to establishing agencies.

Advertising and Publicity. Yamato Transport began its express parcel delivery service in 1976. According to the "Seventy-year History of Yamato Transport," at the outset "their central theme was how to collect each consignment and numerically increase them." In March of that year the company launched a drive whose goal was to handle 50,000 parcels a month, its first systematic business campaign. The effort called for intensive sales directed toward housing complexes and retailers, advertising and publicity, the strengthening of operations to include the hiring and training of salesmen/drivers, and internal PR such as soliciting ideas for catch phrases. During the following year, 1977, the company intensified its publicity work and its commercials began to appear on TV. Since the use of television for advertising purposes was unprecedented for an express firm, it became a widespread topic of conversation. A few years later the song accompanying Yamato's TV commercials grew quite popular, which caused the company's name to evolve into a nationwide household word.

Nippon Express, on the other hand, initiated its parcel delivery service in 1977. In 1981, the company revised the name for the service and undertook deliveries on a full scale basis. In the following year, 1982, the firm launched a publicity campaign calling for TV commercials.

Yamato Transport and Nippon Express, both powerful in the individual market, waged publicity drives soon after starting their parcel delivery service. This implies that the ease with which enterprises make consumers aware of their services is of the utmost significance.

Agency Policies. Once again quoting from the "Seventy-year History of Yamato Transport," "the establishment of agencies was an idea obtained from discussions made from the demand-side viewpoint, and it mainly concerned ways to stimulate latent needs for shipping among many and varied potential clients." As early as 1976, when undertaking its parcel delivery service, Yamato Transport established all of 450 agencies and increased the number of agencies later thereby building a strong network for accepting orders. From 1980 to 1984 the firm was especially active in this, and the number of Yamato agencies grew tenfold during those five years, from 12,000 outlets to an amazing 130,000 (table 4). When considering it was a period when other transport companies were rushing to enter the parcel delivery trade, clearly Yamato gained an advantage over the mounting competition by swiftly expanding its order-accepting network of agencies, thereby reducing consumer access costs and making its services more attractive than those of rivals. By March 1993 Yamato Transport could point to having fully 276,023 agencies, the industry's largest, followed by Nippon Express, which at that time maintained 214,000 (table 5).

2.2.3. Factors Affecting Economies of Scale

Apparently, when individuals want to ship via parcel express, they choose a

Table 4. Growth in the Number of Yamato Transport Agencies

Fiscal Year	Number of Agencies
1976	450
1977	1,000
1978	3,500
1979	7,000
1980	12,289
1981	22,093
1982	44,449
1983	88,949
1984	129,563
1985	156,523
1986	178,540
1987	199,478
1988	224,593
1989	233,175
1990	246,731
1991	261,157
1992	276,023

Source: Yamato Transport Publicity Department

Table 5. Transition in the Number of Major Parcel Delivery Sevices Companies' Agencies

Unit: Number of Agencies

Year	Yamato Transport	Nippon Express	Footwork Express	Seino Transport.	Fukuyama Transporting	MPT
1984	129,560	134,239	61,800	13,800	9,000	——
1986	178,540	168,712	76,066	23,623	11,500	63,000
1988	224,593	207,924	85,000	25,100	12,000	78,000
1990	246,731	213,524	85,000	25,000	12,000	82,709
1992	276,023	214,000	85,000	19,261	12,000	81,153

Note: The Ministry of Posts and Telecommunications began establishing agencies in November 1985.

Source: Cargo News.

carrier by taking into account the total cost outlay involved, which includes not only the actual transport charges but also the cost of going to the agency and finding out about the quality and contents of its services. In order to lower the ancillary costs incurred by consumers, parcel delivery firms must improve and maintain a very large number of outlets and conduct extensive publicity activities. This, then, represents an economy of scale factor which operates at the acceptance stage of the individual market of parcel delivery service.

3. Measuring Economies of Scale in the Individual Market

Generally, measuring economies of scale for a particular type of industry requires a means of estimating production costs. As treated in the preceding section, in a service industry like parcel delivery, demand factors cannot be ignored. This standing as the criterion, we shall now undertake to construct an hypothetical instance of competition between two parcel delivery firms catering to individuals, using Yamato Transport and Nippon Express as the models. Based on statistical data, the effects generated by economy of scale may be determined by gauging the elasticity of demand. In doing this, economy of scale at the acceptance stage is examined by including service awareness and agency accessibility in the demand function and assessing their degree of elasticity.

3.1. Building a Model

We shall now build an hypothetical situation comprising two companies engaged in the parcel delivery trade aimed at individual clients, again, with Yamato Transport and Nippon Express as the models. In the example, each corporation renders its service so that supply, as based on the average cost formation principle,[2] will meet customer requirements based on each firm's demand function. It is also assumed that no price-slashing competition exists between the two enterprises; rather, their rivalry has taken the form of increasing the number of agencies they maintain.

3.1.1. Demand Function

Attempting to build the demand function for a certain parcel delivery service company requires knowing how individuals choose transport firms. In the preceding section, we stated that individuals decide on delivery companies on the basis of total costs, not merely the invoiced amount for shipping but also the time and effort spent to find out about the service and for getting to the nearest agency. This

---

2 With the enforcement of the Trucking Business Act in 1990, the tariff plan for parcel delivery services changed from approval to the reporting system. In line with this revision, the Ministry of Transport instituted its 'Criteria for Acceptance of Reports on Tariffs for Parcel Delivery Service' as a replacement for its former 'Criteria for Approval of Tariffs for Parcel Delivery Service.' Under the new scheme, whenever a parcel delivery corporation's report failed to satisfy the criteria, the firm was required to submit an explanation to the Minister of Transport together with a cost statement within ninety days. Considering the fact that few applications for tariffs exceeding the criteria have been received so far, it can be said that under the current plan parcel delivery companies cannot set their prices without restraint, even though they are allowed to establish their shipping rates, and that they list their charges on the assumption that they conform to the criteria for acceptance of reports imposed by the Ministry. In this regard, the criteria for acceptance of reports play the same role as criteria for approval of parcel delivery tariffs. Because the Ministry instituted its criteria on the basis of total costs, including a reasonable profit, it is assumed that each parcel carrier has determined its rates based on the average cost price formation principle.

being the case, we assume that demand is determined based on price (P), awareness of service as provided by the company (A), the number of agencies (N), and macroeconomic income (Y). Relations among them may be expressed by the demand formula:

$$Q_D = f(P, A, N, Y).$$

3.1.2. Cost Functions

As mentioned earlier, in an industry like parcel deliveries, service is rendered when demand occurs. Thus, in order to meet demand that fluctuates according to time of day and season, parcel delvery firms must equip themselves to enable transporting the volume of consignments anticipated at peak times or seasons. This means that a substantial amount of facilities may pass unused during slack periods. Consequently the average cost of parcel delivery is not always determined primarily on quantity of supply. Here, we asuume that the average cost (AC) of parcel deliveries for individuals is determined based on a combination of capital (K), labor (L), and the quantity of supply (Q_S), with the demand function established as:

$$AC = g(Q_S, K, L).$$

3.1.3. Competition in Setting Up Agencies

Competitive price-slashing in the individual market of parcel delivery service is virtually nonexistent. But fierce competition can be observed in opening more agencies to accommodate the trade. If we assume that our two transport companies determine their agency policies for the current fiscal year according to the trend in the number of agencies maintained by their rival, the following formula may be added to our model:

$$N = h(N_R).$$

In the above, N indicates the number of agencies, while N_R shows the number of agencies owned by the rival company.

3.2. Measurement Based on Statistical Data

3.2.1. Measurement

In the foregoing paragraphs, three formulas were presented:

$$Q_D = f(P, A, N, Y),$$

$$AC = g(Q_S, K, L), \text{ and}$$

$$N = h(N_R).$$

Among the three, the second formula may be reconstructed as:

$$Q_S = g'(AC, K, L).$$

We may surmise that, while various discounts, including for volume shipments, are made in the corporate market of parcel delivery, the established tariffs are observed in the individual market, and we can hypothesize that they have been set on the basis of the average cost price formation principle (see note 1). Accordingly each parcel delivery firm supplies service to the extent that P equals AC, with the above formula again revised as:

$$Q_S = g'(P, K, L).$$

The above formula explains supply according to the trio of variables: price, capital, labor. Accordingly, the three respective formulas become:

$$Q_D = f(P, A, N, Y),$$

$$Q_S = g'(P, K, L), \text{ and}$$

$$N = h(N_R).$$

It is presupposed in this model that parcel delivery firms determine Q and P so that supply meets demand on the basis of the first and second formulas. Thus, we may add the following conditional expression:

$$Q_D = Q_S.$$

Let us now measure elasticity as grounded on actual statistical data. A log-linear model is presented as a functional paradigm, and natural logarithms of each variable are incorporated. The merit in using natural logarithms is that parameters of the variables themselves show elasticity.[3]

Consequently, a model for service rendered by a firm engaged in the individual market of the parcel delivery trade may be rewritten as:

$$\ln Q_d = \alpha_0 + \alpha_1 \ln P + \alpha_2 \ln A + \alpha_3 \ln N + \alpha_4 \ln Y; \quad (1)$$

$$\ln Q_s = \beta_0 + \beta_1 \ln P + \beta_2 \ln K + \beta_3 \ln L; \quad (2)$$

$$\ln N = \gamma_0 + \gamma_1 \ln N_R; \quad (3)$$

$$\text{Conditional expression: } \ln Q_d = \ln Q_s. \quad (4)$$

Here, $Q = Q_d = Q_s$ (number of parcels), P (price), and N (the number of corporate

3 $\ln Q_d = \alpha_0 + \alpha_1 \ln P + \alpha_2 \ln A + \alpha_3 \ln \mathrm{N} + \alpha_4 \ln Y$;
$\ln Q_s = \beta_0 + \beta_1 \ln P + \beta_2 \ln K + \beta_3 \ln L$.
The parameters in the above model as shown in this analysis contain the following meanings for α_1 to α_4:

α_1 = price elasticity of demand;
α_2 = service awareness elasticity of demand;
α_3 = agency elasticity of demand; and
α_4 = income elasticity of demand.

agencies) are regarded as endogenous variables. The reason for making N (the rival firm's number of outlets) an exogenous variable is that we assume the company in question responds to the number of rival outlets when regarding it as a given condition. We also assume that, in order to obtain the primary approximate value, the rival company does not respond to such a move by the enterprise in question.

For Yamato Transport and Nippon Express, respectively, estimation is based on the foregoing simultaneous equations (1) through (3) plus the conditional expression (4) using time series data. In this context, particular attention is drawn to the parameter of service awareness and that of the number of agencies per firm (elasticity of service awareness and of agencies). If its value exceeds 1, demand increases more than one percent when the company raises the awareness of its service or boosts the number of its agencies by one percent. This, then, will show that increasing return to scale works. It also indicates that raising public awareness of corporate services and/or adding more agencies is rewarding and that economy of scale lies in those factors. However, should agency elasticity fall below 1, increasing the number of outlets by one percent will produce less than one percent expansion in the volume of parcels handled. This in turn will show that agency scale remains in realm of diminishing returns, hence economy of scale is not effective.

Using two-stage least squares (2SLS) presents a solid means of estimation. In simultaneous equation models, it becomes necessary to meet both order and rank conditions. In the model presented, however, all three equations are identifiable as they become over-identified.

3.2.2. Contents of Data

Time series data from 1984 to 1992 are used, and their contents are as shown below.

Number of Parcels Shipped (Q). In view of the impossibility to securing data regarding the number of parcels consigned by individuals to Yamato Transport and Nippon Express, we have substituted the total number handled by each firm, which includes packages consigned by corporations as well, on the assumption that the ratio of shipments by individuals versus those by companies for each express carrier remained constant during the period 1984 to 1992.

Price (P). As a means to give continuity to price data, rates for shipping parcels of ten kilograms within the same geographical area are used, and those substantiated by the consumer price index for parcels are used as tariffs.

Service Awareness (A). Since data on service awareness is extremely limited, we have substituted the advertising expenditures of Yamato Transport and Nippon Express. The respective firms' outlay for this is not reliable in terms of their absolute amount, however. But this data is used because there is no other way to secure precise information on their expense for publicity, also because in this analysis it is enough merely to know the relative amounts spent for advertising in each fiscal year rather than the absolute totals incurred. We substantiate advertising costs by dividing them by the price index for companies with respect to disbursement for advertising.

Income (Y). Statistics obtained by substantiating national income with GNP deflators are used.

Number of Agencies (N). The numbers of express firm agencies (N) and of those maintained by its rival (N_R) at the close of the fiscal year are used.

Capital (K). Here again, as data is limited, we have substituted the respective load capacities of shipping firms in tons based on the number of large, medium, and standard size, small and mini vans they own and operate. Extra-large vehicles, such as semis, have been excluded since it is not likely they be used for parcel delivery services.

Labor (L). Parcel delivery constitutes Yamato Transport's principle line of business, and sales from this account for more than 80 percent of the firm's aggregate returns, For this reason, the total number of male employees is used as an indicator of labor. Nippon Express, on the other hand, as a comprehensive distribution company engages in a wide range of business, including the operation of railway agencies (about 9% of its overall sales), trucking (44%), marine transport (9%), ware housing (5%), and air cargo (14%). Its parcel delivery trade merely represents part of its trucking operation. Consequently the indicator of labor for Nippon Express is obtained by multiplying the number of outdoor service employees and that of male clerks by the ratio of trucking business sales to the firm's total sales.

3.2.3. Estimation Results

The results of our estimation appear below. Each estimated parameter value indicates elasticity, and parenthesized figures show the "t values." Triple, double, and single asterisks denote that the figures so marked become meaningful through "t tests" at significance levels of one, five and ten percent, respectively.[4]

---

4 Significance level, coefficient of determination, the Durbin-Watson:

When posing an hypothesis H_0: $\theta = \theta_0$, and an alternative H_1: $\theta= \theta_0$, the hypothesis H_0 may be tested to prove that the alternative H_1 holds true. In this case, H_0 has its meaning in rejection and is called a null hypothesis, and the critical region size is known as the significant level.

The coefficient of determination R^2 and coefficients of determination adjusted for degree of freedom, which are indicators of appropriateness of fit of formulas in the method of least squares (OLS), lose their meaning in the two-stage least squares method (2SLS) wherein explanatory variables and residual sums are not orthogonal to each other. Therefore, R^2 is not listed here.

Estimation Formulas
Yamato Transport:

$$\underset{(-0.62)}{\ln Q_D = -28.90} - \underset{(-0.06)}{0.08 \ln P} + \underset{(0.65)}{0.05 \ln A} + \underset{(2.70)}{1.28{*} \ln N} + \underset{(0.54)}{0.97 \ln Y}; \tag{1}$$

$$\ln Q_S = \underset{(2.53)}{10.74{*}} - \underset{(-0.95)}{0.88 \ln P} + \underset{(1.05)}{1.12 \ln K} + \underset{(0.39)}{0.34 \ln L}; \tag{2}$$

$$\ln N = \underset{(-3.04)}{-4.92{*}{*}} + \underset{(10.61)}{1.41{*}{*}{*} \ln N_R}. \tag{3}$$

Nippon Express:

$$\underset{(-1.88)}{\ln Q_D = -77.10} - \underset{(-0.79)}{0.98 \ln P} + \underset{(0.09)}{0.03 \ln A} + \underset{(2.97)}{2.07{*}{*} \ln N} + \underset{(1.37)}{2.32 \ln Y}; \tag{1}$$

$$\ln Q_S = \underset{(3.05)}{184.54{*}{*}} - \underset{(3.11)}{8.47{*}{*} \ln P} - \underset{(-2.31)}{21.27{*} \ln K} - \underset{(-0.06)}{0.41 \ln L}; \tag{2}$$

$$\ln N = \underset{(5.88)}{4.10{*}{*}{*}} + \underset{(11.54)}{0.66{*}{*}{*} \ln N_R}. \tag{3}$$

3.2.4. Consideration of Parameters

Owing to severe restrictions on data, this estimation cannot produce a bold conclusion. It does, however, give highly significant and suggestive values.

Attention is drawn to formulas (1) and (3) for both express firms. In the former, for both companies, all parameters of the demand function meet code conditions. But significant results are obtained only in the agency parameter for both. Yamato Transport's value stands at 1.28(significant at the level of 10 percent), while that for Nippon Express is 2.07 (significant at 5 percent), with both exceeding 1. It can be said, therefore, that during the surveyed period, return to scale for both companies related to the gradual expansion of their respective agency networks. Judging solely from the results concerning agencies, it can be said that economy of scale is at work at their acceptance stages since both firms clearly have enjoyed advantages by enlarging their agency networks, thereby reducing consumer access cost.

Formula (3) show how the companies responded to each other's agency policy. Yamato Transport's parameter value is 1.41 (significant at the 1 percent level, while that of Nippon Express is 0.66 (also significant at 1 percent). From this, we can infer that the agency policies of the two firms are substantially correlated and that severe competition in structuring agency networks has existed between them. We can also conclude that Yamato transport, which placed greater emphasis on the individual market, has increased its number of agencies faster than Nippon Express. Thus, Nippon Express did not enlarge its network as much as Yamato did.

In this assessment, attention focused mainly on access and service awareness costs which are regarded as factors in economy of sale. However, in conclusion, while relatively significant values were obtained for the agency parameter, one closely associated with access costs, no significant results were obtained for the service awareness parameter.

The unsatisfactory results for the service awareness parameter can be ascribed to (1) the unavailability of sufficient information, as advertising expenditures were used as a substitute for data on service awareness, and exact statistics regarding the amounts spent by both firms for advertising their parcel delivery services were not obtainable; and (2) because the effect of service awareness is observed only through agencies, that of awareness was absorbed as the effect of the agencies in this measurement.

4. Conclusion

Concerning the individual parcel delivery services market, the data presented indicate that Yamato Transport is estimated to control an approximately 65 percent share of the market. From the standpoint of the individual consumer, however, it would seem that the structure of this market has been transformed from a competitive one to a Yamato Transport-monopolistic one.

On the other hand, concerning the corporate market, in which parcels are sent from corporations to individuals, for example, if we imagine the mail order business companies to be representative users, the structure of the market has not become oligopolized as much as has the individual market.

Thus, when comparing the degree of the oligopoly present between the individual and corporate markets, it is presumed that while the economy of scale in the delivery section is not as large as the market structure monopoly, that in the acceptance section is as extensive as this monopoly. This implies that in the individual parcel delivery service market, demand-side cost factors, such as accessibility and service awareness, are far more important than are supply-side cost factors.

References

Crew, M.A., and P.R. Kleindorfer. 1992. *Regulation and the Nature of Postal and Delivery Services*. Boston: Kluwer Academic Publishers.

Institute for Posts and Telecommunications Policy. 1990. *A Report of Studies and Serveys Regarding the Market Structure of Parcel Delivery Service and Behaviors in the Use of Parcel Delivery Service*. Tokyo: Ministry of Posts and Telecommunications.

Institute for Posts and Telecommunications Policy. 1994. *A Report of Surveys and Studies on the Analysis of the Parcel Delivery Service Market*. Tokyo: Ministry of Posts and Telecommunications.

Yamato Transport Company, Ltd. 1991. *The Seventy Year History of Yamato Transport Company, Ltd.* Tokyo: Yamato Transport Co., Ltd.

15

REPLACEMENT OF LETTER MAIL BY ELECTRONIC COMMUNICATIONS TO THE YEAR 2010

Heikki Nikali

1. Introduction

It has been assumed for a long time that electronic communications will replace letter mail. In addition to the telephone, other electronic communication media spread so rapidly in Finland in the 1980s that they are bound to have influenced trends in the traditional letter mail. It was difficult to observe any actual replacement of one by the other, however, as the volume of letters also increased remarkably at the same time. Reasons for this have been the boom in the economy, the moderate pricing policy of the Finland Post on postal services, and the ease with which new technology could equally well be used to produce written messages, for instance the advances made in photocopying techniques.

The telecommunications network in Finland and its service quality are among the best and least expensive in the world. Approximately 80% of the network has been digitalized. The aim is to complete this digitalization by 1996. There were a total of 54 telephone lines per 100 inhabitants in Finland in 1992, the fifth highest figure in the world, while the country occupies an even more prominent position[1] in terms of mobile phones, of which there are currently approximately 10 per 100 inhabitants.

Telephone call costs have declined considerably during the last 15 years. The real prices of trunk calls within Finland has declined by 1993 to less than a sixth of those in 1977. The prices are still declining due to opening up of the trunk calls market at the beginning of 1994. Also the real prices of local, mobile, and foreign calls have declined during the same time. Finland was the sixth cheapest country in the world for domestic business phone calls in 1992 and the second cheapest for international calls.[2] Business call costs in Finland were approximately 30 - 40%

---

1 *Financial Times*.
2 OECD Tariff Comparison Model.

below the average for the other OECD countries.

Finland needs good communication connections, as it is a large country with a small population. Japan and Finland have almost the same land area, but where Japan has more than 120 million inhabitants Finland has only 5 million. The difference in population is thus 25-fold.

Finland can be regarded as one of the pioneers in terms of the opening up of its postal and telecommunications services to competition. All the telecommunications and postal services are in Finland free for competition. In fact, corresponding competition conditions and circumstances can be found only in Britain, New Zealand, Australia, Japan, and Sweden. This liberalization and the possession of the most advanced and least expensive tele services in the world create an almost unregulated framework within which the letter mail could be replaced by electronic communications means.

2. Problem Definition

The aim of this study is to estimate the extent to which the expansion in electronic communications has reduced the volume of letters and to evaluate by models this trend up to the year 2010.

The study is based on cross-sectional material, i.e., data on the demand for postal services in Finland by province, and attempts to explain these differences in demand by reference to regional patterns in the numbers of electronic communication devices. As the economic resources of companies tend to be different in different provinces and dependent on their size and number, the provincial demand data has been related to the total turnover of companies in the province per head of population. This implies that if there are only a few companies in a province, or if these are small relative to the number of inhabitants, low volume of business letters may not necessarily be caused by an abundance of electronic communication devices but equally well to the general lack of entrepreneurship in respect to population. The adjustment of the demand by reference to the turnover of companies ensures that all parts of the country occupy an equal position in the study.

The current study focuses on the first- and second-class domestic letter mail, excluding bulk mail. The letter mail is divided into four content categories on the basis of the types of electronic communications assumed to have been and to be replaced. The selection of the latter being based on the technical applicability of given means for replacing letters in a certain content category. The categories and their electronic alternatives are:

Bills, replaceable by data communications;

Notices, i.e., documents, orders, offers, advertisements sent by first- or second-class post, and receipts, replaceable mainly by telefax;

Messages, i.e., personal letters, cards and invitations, replaceable mainly by electronic mail; and

Magazines, books, and goods sent by first- or second-class letter post, which are not expected to be replaced by electronic communications means.

Information on the demand for letter mail services was obtained from material used in the study (Nikali 1993) regarding the nature and contents of the letters made in 1993. The current material does not include the Åland Islands as they were not covered by the previous research.

The data on electronic communications means were calculated from material obtained in a study (Lyytikäinen 1993) regarding the use of postal services and telecommunications by companies and the public sector in 1992.

3. Methods

Equations have been estimated by least squares regression. The replaceability equations are of the form

$$q = \alpha + \beta * y,$$

where q = demand for letter mail by province;
y = numbers of tele services users instead of letters in respective province; and
α and β = parameters to be estimated.

Replaceabilities were calculated on the basis of the ranges of variation observed in the use of tele services between the provinces. The coefficients are mean values for these ranges. As tele services are expected to be more widespread in future than today, their effect on letter mail will not necessarily be as linear as can be concluded from these models.

The diffusion in tele services can be estimated using the following logistic curve:

$$q_t = \frac{Q}{1 + e^{\alpha + \beta t}},$$

where q_t = number of users in the year t;
Q = saturation level;
α and β = parameters to be estimated; and
t = time.

The saturation level denotes the total number of users, which must be evaluated before applying the formula. Parameters α and β in the diffusion model can be estimated from

$$\ln \frac{Q - q_t}{q_t} = \alpha + \beta t.$$

The assumption in diffusion models (Kangas 1991) is that new services will spread at a rate which complies with an S curve as a function of time, so that each service has a saturation level of its own. Expansion is fairly slow in the beginning, but becomes rapid at its most active phase until it comes close to the saturation point, after which it declines again towards a saturation threshold, which will not be exceeded.

4. Replaceability Models

4.1. Classification of Letter Mail by Content

The numbers of first- and second-class letters and their distribution by content in 1993 are given below. It should be noted, however, that the sum of the percentages is not 100, as more than 30% of the letters could be recorded in more than one content category, e.g., bills accompanied by notices. The sum of the percentage column indicates that each letter was classified into approximately 1.51 content categories.

Table 1

Content category	Proportion %	Number million items
Bills	34.2	252
Notices	73.1	538
Messages	36.0	265
Magazines, books, goods	7.7	57
Total	151.0	736

The replacement of letters by electronic communications is dependent on the economic resources available to potential senders and recipients to purchase the required equipment. These devices should be utilized to such an extent that the investments required for them are profitable. A further requirement from the sender's point of view is that the recipient should actually be contactable by this means. It is evident that written correspondence between organizations, i.e., companies, authorities, local councils, and associations, is most likely to be the first to be affected by this.

Table 2. Distribution of First- and Second-Class Letters by Sender-Recipient Categories in 1993

Sender	Recipient	Proportion in 1993 %
Organisation	Organisation	43
Organisation	Private person	44
Private person	Organisation	4
Private person	Private person	9
TOTAL		100

Communications between organizations constitute more than 40% of the total volume of letters. Electronic communication devices have decreased so much in price in recent times and are now so easy to use that they are becoming increasingly common even in private households. This increases opportunities of senders to contact their recipients. At the moment, letters sent by organizations either to other organizations or to households constitute almost 90% of the total letter mail, and the increased use of tele services in households was taken into account in the calculation of the replaceability models.

4.2. Replaceability Models

4.2.1. Replacement of Bills by Data Communications

Bills constitute 34% of all first- and second-class letters in Finland, with fairly little variation between the provinces, only from 30% to 38%. These figures would vary considerably more, i.e., from 32% to 51%, if all the provinces possessed the same total company turnover relative to population. There were major differences between the provinces in the frequency of possession of data transfer facilities, the range of variation in 1992 being 7 - 38%. There was a high coefficient of correlation, -0.92%, between the use of data transfers and the proportion of bills relative to turnover/inhabitant.

The following model was obtained for the replacement of bills with data communications:

$$q = \underset{(28,0)}{53.4} - \underset{(-7,1)}{0,58} * y,$$

$$r = 0.85,$$

where q = proportion of bills among first- and second-class letters in Finland, and y = frequency of data transfer facilities in business and public administration offices.

The model based on cross-sectional material explains a high proportion of the variance, r = 85%, and the coefficients are highly significant, as shown by the t values given in brackets below the parameters. The model is shown in figure 1.

The replaceability model indicates that a 10% increase in data transfer facilities would reduce volume of bills in the letter post by 6%. In view of the fact that a total of 252 million bills were sent by post in 1993, a 10% increase in the possession of modems would reduce this number by approximately 15 million, i.e., each new data connection would reduce it by approximately 500 items a year. Conversely, a total of 130-140 million more bills would be sent by post if no data transfer facilities existed. This means that *approximately one third of the bills sent by post have already been replaced by data transfer.*

The use of data transfer facilities has expanded rapidly. Where only 8.3% of business and public administration offices had access to such facilities in 1987 (Väyrynen 1988), the figure five years later was as much as 22.6%. There were a total of 280,000 data modems in use in Finland in 1993, and the assumed saturation threshold of 1,000,000 is likely to be achieved only after 2010. The calculated diffusion model is the following:

$$q_t = \frac{1,000,000}{1 + e^{586.0 - 0.294 * t}},$$

$$r = 0.99,$$

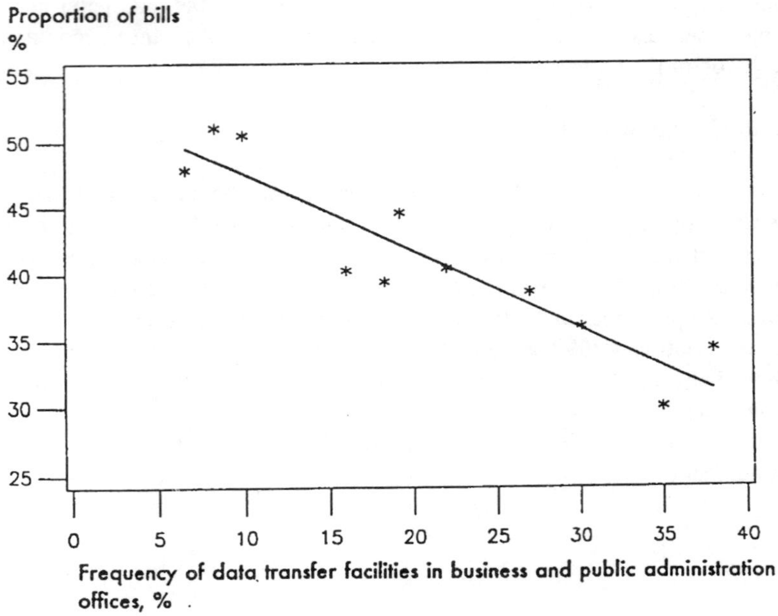

Figure 1. Proportion of the Bills in All First- and Second-Class Letters in Accordance with the Frequency of Data Transfer Facilities and the Model Calculated Accordingly

where q_t = number of data modems;
t = years 1971-2010; and
t values for the coefficients are 44.5 and -44.2.[3]

The model achieves a high explanation of variance, 99%, and the t values of the coefficients are also good.

The replaceability and diffusion models indicates that an average of 7.1% of bills will be replaced by other means of communication during the period 1994-2000. The annual change anticipated for the following decade being -2.7%, while the cumulative change will be -40% from 1993 to 2000 and -55% by the year 2010. As no allowance is made here for any overall increase in volume of bills, the decline in the volume of bills posted can be regarded entirely as a replacement effect caused by the spread of data communications.

4.2.2. Replacement of Notices by Telefax

Notices denote here letters, whose contents consist of documents, orders, offers, advertisements or receipts, as mentioned in Section 2.

3 The t values for α and β are in theory identical as can be shown.

Notices constitute 73% of all first- and second-class letters in Finland, often accompanying bills, for example. As bills were regarded as the primary content in such cases, where they were also notice or message. For this reason the data, of which demand on notices was calculated by provinces, bills were excluded.

The following model was obtained to indicate the replacement of notices by the use of telefax:

$$q = \underset{(31,7)}{88.6} - \underset{(-7,5)}{0.56} * y,$$

$$r = 0.86,$$

where q = proportion of notices among first- and second-class letters and y = frequency of telefax facilities in business and public administration offices.

The model has a high r value, i.e., 86%, and its coefficients according to the t test are highly significant. The correlation between the variables q and y is -0.93.

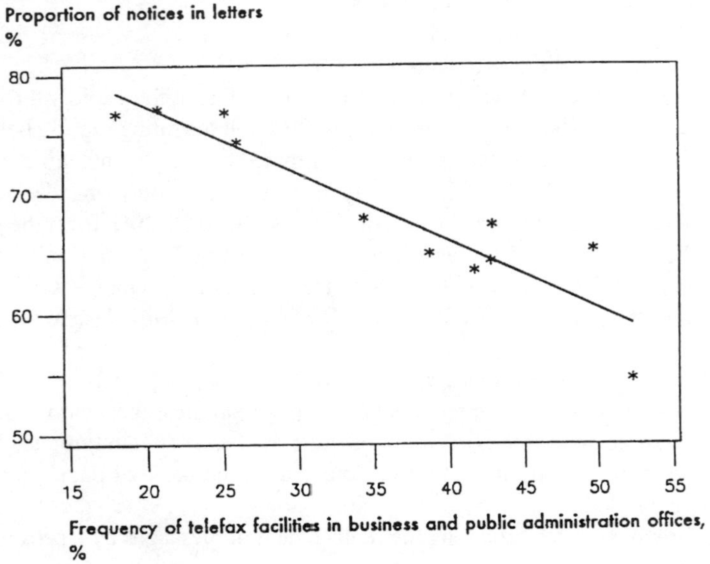

Figure 2. Proportion of Notices in All First- and Second-Class Letters in According to the Frequency of Telefax Facilities and the Model Calculated According

The model is shown in figure 2.

The replaceability model indicates that a 10% increase in the number of telefax machines will reduce the number of notices sent by letter mail by 6%. There were approximately 180,000 telefax machines in Finland in 1993, and in view of the fact that 538 million notices were sent by post in the same year, a 10% increase in the frequency of such machines would reduce volume of notices by approximately 30 million, i.e., each new machine would bring an average reduction of approximately 1700 notices a year. Conversely, it should be noted that approximately 300 million notices a year more would be posted if no telefax machines were available. This means that *telefax machines have already replaced approximately one third of all notices which would otherwise have been sent by post.* The outcome is the same as the one obtained for the replacement of bills by data communications.

A total of 43% of all business and public administration offices in Finland currently have a telefax machine. The figure was five years earlier only 12%. The saturation threshold assumed in the model is 400,000 machines. There were 180,000 machines in the country in 1993. It is likely that number of the machines in use comes close to this threshold around the year 2005. The following diffusion model was calculated:

$$q_t = \frac{400{,}000}{1 + e\,961.5 - 0.482 * t},$$

$$r = 0.99,$$

where q_t = number of telefax machines;
t = years 1980-2010; and
t values for the coefficients are 31.0 and -30.9.

The replacement of notices by telefax messages will continue rapidly throughout this decade. It will reach its peak in the mid-1990s but declining rapidly before the turn of the century. Thus, it can be roughly estimated that telefax machines will not remarkably reduce volume of letters any further in the following decade. The volume of notices sent by letter mail will have declined by 30% from the current level by the year 2000 but by less than 40% by the year 2010, assuming that no overall increase takes place in volume of notices. The average change will be -5.2% per year over the period 1994-2000 and -1.0% in the following decade.

4.2.3. Replacement of Messages by Electronic Mail

Messages, denoting here letters containing personal messages, cards, and invitations, constitute 36% of the first- and second-class letters sent in Finland. As with notices, the replaceability model was calculated on the basis of data from which bills were excluded.

The following model indicating the replacement of messages by electronic mail was obtained

$$\underset{(19{,}6)}{q = 55.6} - \underset{(-4{,}0)}{0.49} * y,$$

$$r = 0.64,$$

where q = proportion of messages among first- and second-class letters and y = frequency of electronic mail among business and public administration staff.

The model achieves a fairly high explanation of variance, 64%, and its coefficients according to the t test are highly significant. However, the inverse correlation between volume of messages and the occurrence of electronic mail is not as close as the one between bills and data transfer or notices and telefax. However, it should be noted that a sufficiently high correlation coefficient was obtained, -0.80.

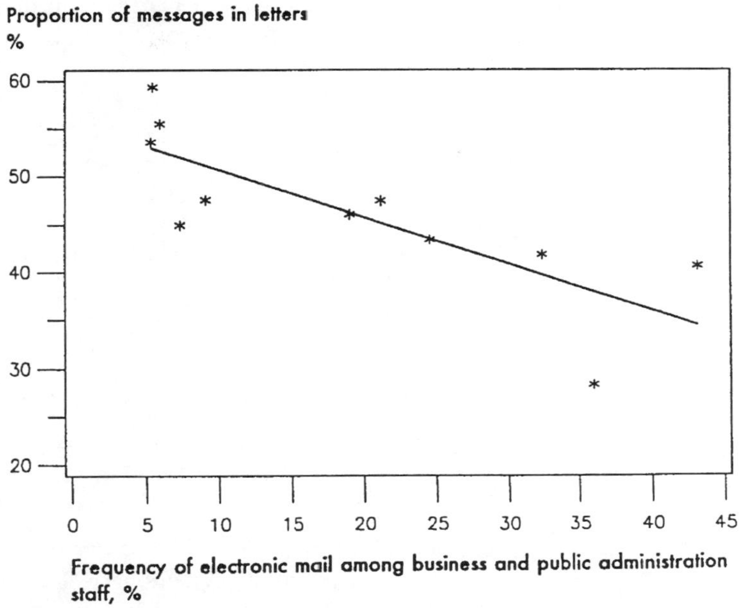

Figure 3. Proportion of Messages in all First- and Second-Class Letters According to the Frequency of Electronic Mail and the Model Calculated Accordingly

The model is shown in figure 3.

The replaceability model indicates that a 10% increase in the frequency of electronic mail will reduce the number of messages posted by 5%. Since approximately 400,000 persons had access to electronic mail in Finland in 1993 and a total of 265 million letters in the message category were sent in the same year. 10% increase in the use of electronic mail would increase the number of users by 40,000 and reduce volume of messages sent by letter mail by 13 million. Each new user of electronic mail would reduce volume of letters by an average of approximately 300 a year. Alternatively, if electronic mail did not exist, approximately 130 million more messages would be sent by post than is the case today. A rough conclusion is that *electronic mail has already replaced approximately one third of all messages sent by post*. The outcome is the same as for the replacement of bills and notices by data transfer and telefax.

Of all types of telecommunication examined here, electronic mail has increased most rapidly in recent years, as it has only existed for a relatively short time. Only 2% of business and public administration staff in Finland had access to it in 1987. The figure was five years later as much as 27%. There are approximately 465,000 users of electronic mail in the country at the present time (1994). It is likely that the assumed saturation threshold of 1.5 million users will be achieved by the year 2010. The idea behind this is that a person may belong to two user categories, one at home and one in the work. The following model was calculated for the diffusion of electronic mail:

$$q_t = \frac{1{,}500{,}000}{1 + e^{1571.1 - 0.789 * t}},$$

$$r = 0.97,$$

where q_t = number of users;
t = years 1983-2010; and
t values for the coefficients are 15.0 and -15.0.

Replacement will take place most rapidly at the beginning of the period under this review, but will gradually slow down after that. The volume of messages sent by post will have declined by one third from the current level by the turn of the century and to one half by the year 2010. The average annual change will be -6.1% in 1994-2000 and -2.6% a year in 2001-2010.

5. Demand for Letter Mail to the Year 2010

The evaluations of the replaceability models in Section 4 do not take the trend in the overall volume of mail into consideration at all. According to the demand models, trends in the first- and second-class letter mail go along with the volume of the gross national product (Nikali 1992). Predicted trends for 1994-2010 are indicated in table 3 with reference to three levels of average annual change in gross national product: 0%, +1.7%, and +3.0% a year. It was assumed these to remain constant over the whole period. As the real price of the letter mail also influences demand, the figures for 1993 are used throughout in these calculations.

Evaluation of the drop in letter volumes occasioned by the spread of electronic communications involves comparing the reduction in respect to the situation in 1993. A vision was set out as to how the situation would be changed in the letter mail if electronic devices suddenly became far more popular than they are at present.

The columns in which the GNP does not change represent a pure replacement effect. Replacement is expected to be rapid throughout the current decade, reaching its maximum in 1995 but declining steadily after that. One third of the volume of letters sent in 1993 will have been replaced by electronic communications by the year 2000, i.e., approximately 5.5% per year, and more than 40% by the year 2010.

As all the models indicate that electronic communications means have already replaced one third of the letters in each respective category, the same must also apply to the total volume of first- and second-class letters sent in Finland. Note that the part of the letter mail (magazines, books, and goods) which is not replaceable by electronic communications is less than 8% of total volume of the mail. The Finland Post would have had 350-400 million more letters to deliver in 1993 if these had not been replaced earlier by electronic communications means.

Increase in the gross national product would have to be on average 5.5 - 6.0% a year in 1994-2000 in order to compensate for the loss of total letter volumes caused

Table 3. Predicted Volumes of First- and Second-Class Letters in 1994-2010, Given Different Trends in GNP

Year	GNP change 0.0 %/y			GNP change +1.7 %/y			GNP change +3.0%/y		
	Number million items	change/y %	Cumulat. changes from 93 %	Number million items	change/y %	Cumulat. changes from 93 %	Number million items	change/y %	Cumulat. changes from 93 %
1991	748			748			748		
1992	751	+0.4		751	+0.4		751	+0.4	
1993	736	-2.0		736	-2.0		736	-2.0	
1994	693	-5.8	-6	705	-4.2	-4	714	-3.0	-3
1995	644	-7.1	-12	666	-5.5	-9	683	-4.3	-7
1996	602	-6.6	-18	633	-5.0	-14	657	-3.8	-11
1997	569	-5.5	-23	608	-3.9	-17	640	-2.6	-13
1998	540	-5.1	-27	587	-3.5	-20	626	-2.2	-15
1999	515	-4.6	-30	570	-3.0	-23	615	-1.7	-16
2000	495	-3.9	-33	557	-2.3	-24	609	-1.1	-17
2001	481	-2.9	-35	550	-1.2	-25	609	0.0	-17
2002	468	-2.6	-36	545	-0.9	-26	611	+0.3	-17
2003	458	-2.3	-38	542	-0.6	-26	615	+0.7	-16
2004	448	-2.3	-39	540	-0.3	-27	621	+0.9	-16
2005	442	-2.0	-40	541	+0.1	-27	630	+1.4	-14
2006	435	-1.5	-41	542	+0.3	-26	639	+1.6	-13
2007	430	-1.4	-42	545	+0.5	-26	651	+1.8	-12
2008	426	-1.1	-42	549	+0.6	-25	664	+1.9	-10
2009	423	-1.0	-43	554	+1.0	-25	679	+2.3	-8
2010	422	-0.7	-43	562	+1.4	-24	679	+2.7	-5
Average annual change									
1994-2000		-5.5 %			-3.9 %			-2.7 %	
1994-2010		-3.2 %			-1.6 %			-0.3 %	

by this replacement effect. Even in this case, the total letter volume would not increase but remain at the 1993 level. The corresponding average annual rise in GNP in the first decade of the next century would have to be 1.5 - 2.0%.

Since the beginning of the current decade, Finland has been undergoing the most severe depression of this century, which produced a 13% drop in its GNP over the period 1991-1993. A 2% increase is forecasted for 1994. An annual rise of 5 - 6% may be achieved in the following few years, though this is not likely to be maintained throughout the rest of the current decade.

If the GNP rises by approximately 1.7% a year in 1994-2010, letter volumes will be approximately 25% smaller in the year 2010 than today. Under these conditions, no increase in volume would take place until the middle of the next decade.

If the average increase is 3.0% a year, however, the letter volumes will begin to

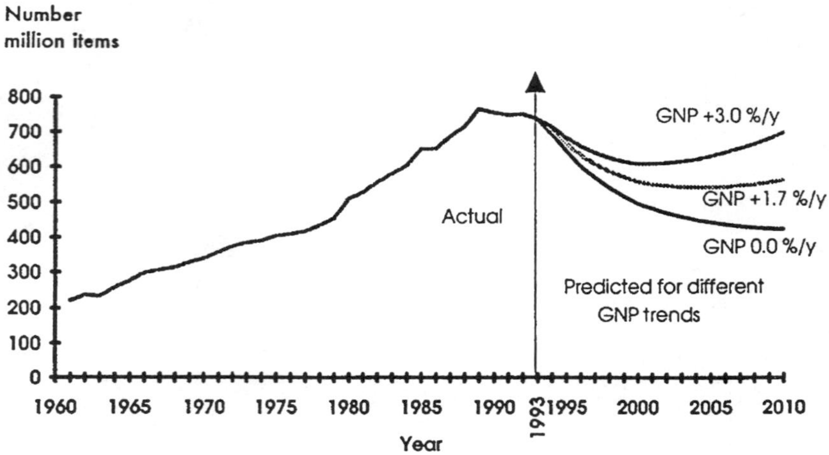

Figure 4. Actual Trends in the Volumes of First- and Second-Class Letters in 1961-1993 and Anticipated Trends for 1994-2010 Corresponding to Three GNP Predictions

increase at the turn of the century. In any case, the total volume will remain some 5% below the figure recorded for 1993.

Trends in the letter volumes corresponding to the three GNP predictions (change 0% per year, +1.7% per year or +3.0% per year) are shown in figure 4, which indicates actual trends in the volumes of first- and second-class letters in 1961-1993 and predictions up to the year 2010.

The most detrimental electronic communication device with regard to the future of the letter mail seems to be the telefax machine, the influence of which is predicted to be almost as great as that of data communications and electronic mail together. The dangers posed by it are further compounded by the fact that the diffusion of telefax machines will come close to its saturation threshold more rapidly than will electronic mail or the modem. Furthermore, the telefax its replacement effect will be mainly focused on the current decade.

It must be borne in mind when applying the results, however, that they show only tendencies. The calculated models indicate largely simplified effects of electronic communications on the letter mail. The models have taken the influence of only one factor into consideration, whereas actual trends will be dependent many other factors as well.

The prospects for the traditional letter mail may not even be as favorable as figured out above. Further innovations in electronic communications are almost certain to be introduced and used in the next decade which may change the prospects radically. Technology tends to adopt increasingly versatile, easy-to-use, and inexpensive forms. The present the study is based on the replacement effects of those communications means which are already in widespread use.

To illustrate, a survey of the frequency of personal computers in households in Finland carried out by IDC Finland Oy and Finnish Gallup Market Research

(Aaltonen 1994) indicates that 23% of households currently have access to a computer and 7% to a modem. According to IDC evaluations, more than one out of every three households in Finland will have a computer by 1996 and the number of modems will double. The conclusion which they reached was that "households create a basis for the development and supply of increasingly advanced applications and services," thanks to the extensive distribution of computers and high standards of user habits. Clearly, there is potential inherent in such applications for further erosion of letter mail volumes.

References

Aaltonen, Tapio. 1994. "Every Fifth Household Has a Computer." Finnish Teleservices staff publication *Serveri* (April).

Kangas, Pertti. 1991. "Diffusion Models of Tele Services." PT/Research Division, Research Publications (January 10).

Lyytikäinen, Lea. 1993. "Study on Postal and Telecom Traffic of Companies and the Public Sector in 1992." PT/Research Division, Research Publications (December 31).

Nikali, Heikki, 1992. "Study on Demand on Letter Mail in 1971-1991, Final Report." PT/Research Division, Research Publications (October 5).

Nikali, Heikki. 1993. "Study on Nature and Contents of the Letters in 1993." PT/Research Division, Research Publications (May 11).

Väyrynen, Esko. 1988. "Study on Postal and Telecom Traffic of Companies and the Public Sector in 1987." PTH/TO/ttt, PM 20 (August 22).

16

REGULATION OF UNREGULATED FIRMS: THE POSTAL SERVICE AND UPS

E. Rand Costich
W. Gail Willette[1]

Introduction[2]

Actions taken by a regulatory body toward a regulated entity affect unregulated firms in the industry. The Postal Rate Commission (PRC), which regulates rates and fees charged for postal services, can indirectly regulate private companies that compete with the United States Postal Service. The primary example considered in this paper is the relationship between the Postal Service and United Parcel Service (UPS), a private firm that delivers packages nationwide. Regulatory actions taken by the PRC can affect the nature of this relationship. However, as the number of private firms increases, the ability of a regulator like the PRC to affect their prices diminishes.

In a duopoly market, the pricing options of the unregulated firm can be severely constrained by the restrictions imposed on the regulated firm's prices. Indeed, if a regulator sets the actual price charged by the regulated firm, the unregulated duopolist's profit-maximizing price is uniquely determined by its reaction function. This statement is no doubt unremarkable to economists, but our experience suggests that regulators are not consciously aware of the power that they exert over unregulated firms. During the 1980s the PRC effectively set prices for UPS. Yet the PRC never received nor sought evidence of UPS's reaction function. Only in a 1993 case did a witness explicitly mention reaction functions. But, by that time, the PRC's power over UPS had eroded due to the entry of another firm, Roadway Package Systems.

In October 1992, the Postal Service proposed to the PRC the offering of Bulk

1 The authors wish to express their appreciation to Roger Sherman for many helpful comments and suggestions on an earlier draft and for presenting this paper in their stead. Comments of conference participants are also gratefully acknowledged. Any remaining errors are solely those of the authors.

2 The views expressed in this paper are those of the authors and do not necessarily represent the opinions of the Postal Rate Commission or its Office of Consumer Advocate.

Small Parcel Service (BSPS) as a new class of mail designed to meet the needs of the bulk small parcel mailer. BSPS had the potential to affect in a major way the nationwide parcel delivery market. In order to understand that potential, it is necessary to comprehend the nature of the current market and the relationship among the various competitors.

The nationwide parcel delivery market was served exclusively by the Postal Service until UPS expanded its regional delivery network. Over the last twenty years, the parcel market has been served predominantly by UPS and the Postal Service. Figure 1 compares Postal Service total Fourth Class volumes with UPS volumes for the period 1970 to 1991. As figure 1 dramatically illustrates, over this period UPS eroded the Postal Service's market share of the parcel business. During this period of time, UPS was arguing before the PRC that the Postal Service was understating its processing and delivery costs for parcels.[3]

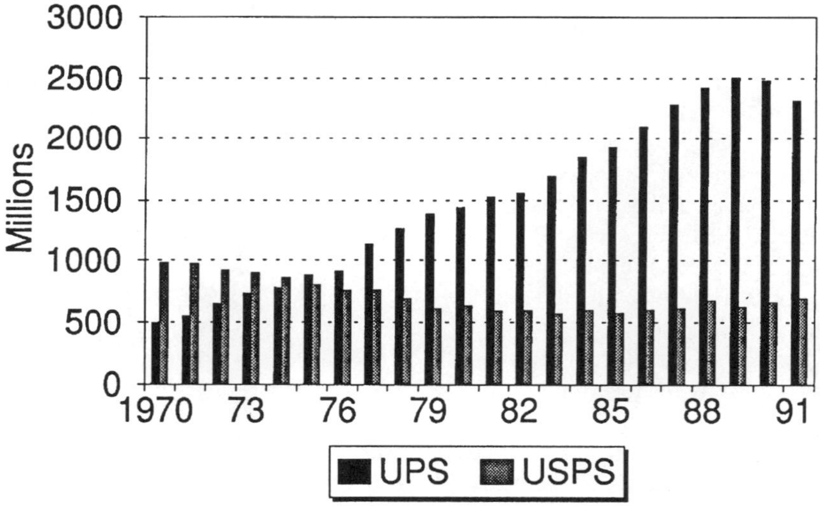

Figure 1. USPS and UPS Volumes, 1970 to 1991

In 1989 Roadway Package Systems became a national carrier, as a result of extending its four-year-old regional service. In 1992, UPS appears to have had the largest market share, with the remaining shared by the Postal Service, Roadway, and smaller regional carriers. Figure 2 shows a recent estimate of relative market share.

The Postal Service's BSPS proposal would have produced a major revision of the traditional parcel services offered by the Postal Service within its fourth class of mail. The extremely low rates (relative to existing rates) were expected to induce

3 See, e.g., PRC Opinion, Docket No. R90-1, January 4, 1991 at V-335-336.

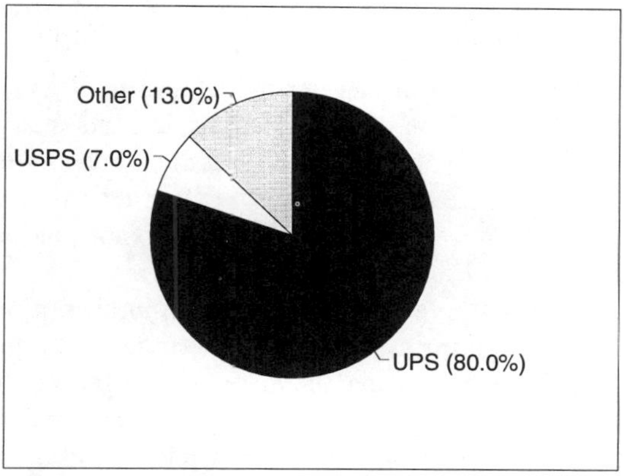

Figure 2. Parcel Market Share Estimate, June 1992

Source: Catalog Age, June 1992

88 million parcels in existing zone-rated parcel post to shift to BSPS. The Postal Service also expected to capture about 88 million additional parcels from UPS.[4] Rates charged by the Postal Service must, by law, cover costs. In supporting the cost basis for its proposed rate structure, the Postal Service likened the proposed small parcel service to existing special-rate fourth-class service (book rate). Using special-rate fourth class was justified by the Postal Service on the basis of BSPS' having proposed fees that were dependent on weight and size (cube) only, independent of distance. Parcel post rates, by contrast vary with distance.

UPS responded that the current Postal Service parcel post rates constituted unfair competition in that they did not recover costs.[5] Unfair competition exists whenever a regulated business applies revenues earned from a protected monopoly service to subsidize all or a portion of a competitive good or service. The PRC applies a three-part test to prevent unfair competition: (1) setting the rate above cost, (2) considering competitor's complaints that rates be far enough above cost to be fair, and (3) considering adverse impact on competitors.[6]

Some Economic Considerations

The market for parcel processing and delivery contains relatively few sellers. The Postal Service and UPS are the major market participants. Roadway Package Systems has recently expanded its service area. Over the last two decades, the small

4 PRC Opinion, Docket No. MC93-1, August 25, 1993, at 24.
5 See PRC Docket No. C93-2, Parcel Post Rate Complaint.
6 PRC Opinion, Docket No. MC93-1, August 25, 1993, at 142

parcel market has exhibited the characteristics of a duopoly, with the Postal Service and UPS dominating the small parcel market, giving rise to the duopoly. However, expansion of Roadway may be turning the market into an oligopoly.

It is important to note that the actions of all participants in a given market are influenced (to a greater or lesser degree) by actions of other participants. In a market where one participant is a regulated entity, this implies that the actions of the regulatory agency have a direct impact on the regulated entity and an indirect impact on its competitors.

In a competitive market, there are typically a large number of firms, and barriers to entry are minimal. New firms may enter whenever there is the prospect of profits to be extracted. Similarly, firms leave the market when prospects for rent (profit) are unattractive. In certain circumstances, however, the basic assumptions required to support a competitive market do not obtain. Factors limiting competition may include barriers to entry, requirements for fixed assets that render competition difficult or impossible, and legal or regulatory proscriptions.

One aim of a regulatory agency, such as the PRC, is to ensure that, in the absence of competitive market forces, monopolists, duopolists, or oligopolists behave in a socially beneficial manner. With respect to the small parcel market, the PRC is in a sense regulating UPS as well as the Postal Service when it sets rates for services such as BSPS.[7]

Empirical data analysis is a cornerstone for identifying market type in preparation for applying the economic theory. The Postal Service lacked actual cost and revenue information for BSPS, however, because the service was new. Historical behavior may be discerned from observed data in order to identify the specific form of market dynamics outlined above. One way to determine whether the introduction of BSPS would have a positive effect on the small parcel delivery market would be to estimate the reaction function of UPS with respect to the Postal Service. The reaction function of each firm in a duopoly market depends upon the behavioral assumptions that each firm makes about the other. In the case of UPS and the Postal Service, figure 1 suggests UPS was successfully battling the Postal Service for market share over the years. However, the data underlying figure 1 are insufficient to estimate reaction functions.

A complementary form of analysis, which may be called heuristic, is also valuable in circumstances such as those surrounding the BSPS case. Whenever specific data are not available, observable behavior gives clues that can identify the type of market. Identification of market type in this case is largely a "pattern recognition" exercise. That is, if the behavior patterns of the market participants match the behavior predicted by a specific market identification theory, it is

7 There is a body of literature espousing the view that regulation is actually sought by firms as a means of cartelizing an industry. However, cartelization does not necessarily imply profit-maximization. A regulator with accurate information is still *capable* of setting welfare-maximizing prices.

probably legitimate to infer that the market is operating according to the premises of that theory.

Historical Perspectives

Historically, the parcel delivery market has exhibited the characteristics of a monopoly, duopoly, and oligopoly. During the period prior to UPS's offering a nationwide service, the Postal Service dominated as a monopoly, since it had the only nationwide delivery service. This period was characterized by a unilaterally controlled rate and service structure, determined first by the Post Office Department and, after 1970, by the Postal Service, within the regulatory frameworks associated with each. As a nonprofit monopoly server, there would have been little incentive for the Postal Service to discriminate among the parcel markets. Specifically, there would have been little incentive for the Postal Service to identify high-cost and low-cost parcels.[8] This could certainly have been the case prior to 1970. This arrangement would encourage the introduction of a competitive service, since handling only the low-cost parcels at the prevailing uniform rate could be very profitable.

During the second period, extending from UPS's introduction of nationwide service in the 1970s until about 1990, parcel delivery is best characterized as a duopoly market. The Postal Service and UPS jointly controlled the market. During this period the PRC would have had the most power over the direction the market took. The market type appears as a kind of Stackelberg leader-follower.[9] The Postal Service set rates and service standards through its formal regulatory procedures. UPS, armed with knowledge of what the Postal Service was doing, then countered with rates and service standards designed to increase its market share and maximize profits. This may look like simple Cournot behavior,[10] but UPS had an incentive to maintain the Postal Service as a viable competitor, thus maintaining national regulation of the small parcel market. In other words, UPS would want to consider the effect of its prices on future Postal Service behavior.

UPS carefully pursued prices and markets where profit opportunities existed. Thus, it discriminated among broad classes of postal customers. The primary

8 There is a body of literature, identified with Niskanen, asserting that nonprofit organizations are sales-maximizers. Cross-subsidization between high-cost and low-cost parcels, i.e., cost averaging, could be attractive to a sales maximizer.

9 Although the Postal Service announced prices first, we do not consider it a leader. Its historical pricing policy has been to set parcel post rates as little above cost as possible. The existence of UPS served as rationalization for this policy, but the ultimate goal seems to have been sales maximization. The observed pricing policy is consistent with Niskanen's description of a "budget constrained" organization; i.e., one that expands output until revenues just cover costs.

10 A Cournot duopolist takes its rival's price as fixed; i.e., ignores the rival's reaction function. A Stackelberg follower is a Cournot duopolist. A Stackelberg leader, on the other hand, estimates its rival's reaction function and includes it in its profit calculus. See James Friedman (1983, 109).

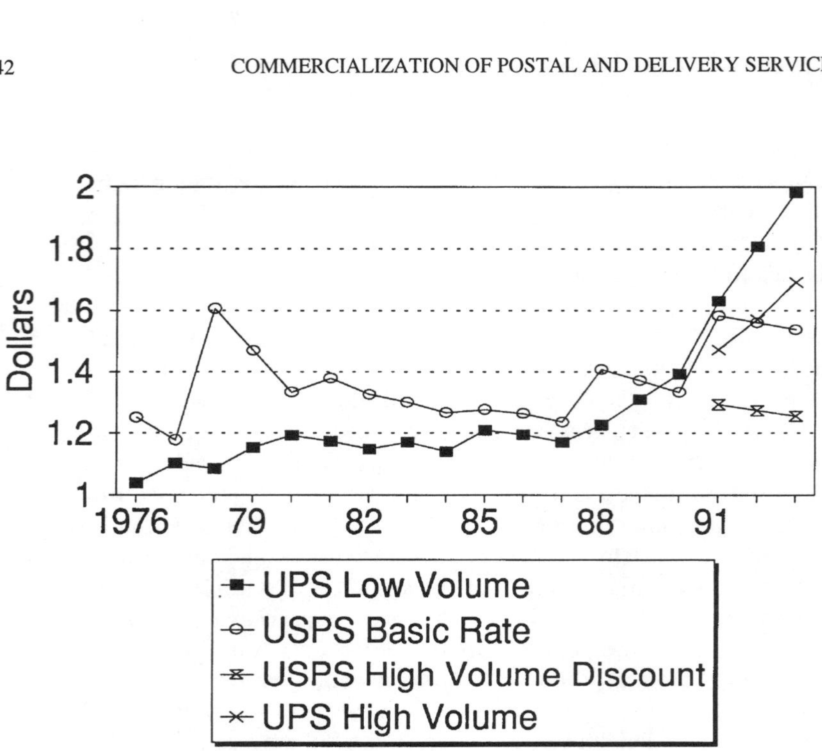

Figure 3. Four-Pound Parcel to Zone 4

discriminating factors were convenience and quality of service. UPS provided a high quality of service to business shippers but did not pursue household shippers. Figure 3 shows a comparison of deflated Postal Service and UPS rates over the period 1976 to 1993 for a four pound package to zone 4, a distance of 300 to 600 miles.[11] As can be seen from this figure, the rates charged by UPS were lower than those of the Postal Service until 1990. Discounts introduced by the Postal Service and a surcharge introduced by UPS in 1991 are also illustrated in figure 3.

In or about 1990, soon after Roadway Package Systems established itself as a nationwide carrier, the parcel delivery market entered an apparent new phase of oligopoly. The impact of the PRC on the market diminished with the arrival of Roadway. Whereas UPS historically could take its pricing cues solely from the Postal Service, i.e., from the PRC, and maintain the objective of maximizing profits on the basis of rates (while increasing market share on the basis of service superiority), the market structure fundamentally changed in response to entry by Roadway. Roadway could engage in a finer degree of discrimination than UPS had, by offering varying discounts off published rates to specific shippers based on cost of service.[12] No longer would a simple distinction between high-cost (households)

11 Because of service differences (UPS is generally considered to provide the higher quality of service) prices are not perfectly comparable.

12 Roadway's published rates have been identical to UPS's.

and low-cost (businesses) parcels suffice as a pricing policy for UPS.

Likewise the PRC now needed to permit a finer degree of price discrimination by the Postal Service. That is to say, the PRC needed to allow the Postal Service to distinguish among customers who need different services (impose different costs) and can be won with different service/price combinations. To be sure, the PRC could set prices for all Postal Service parcels below the lowest rate charged by private competitors. But even if the cost structure of the Postal Service were such that parcel post would still cover its costs under such a pricing regime, efficiency considerations would militate in favor of acknowledging cost differences among shippers. And with private firms recognizing more and more cost differences among shippers, it would be extremely difficult to justify continued cost averaging by the Postal Service. On the other hand, if the cost structure and customer base of the Postal Service were similar to those of competitors, the PRC would have to let the Postal Service discriminate or face serious diversion of volume to competitors. Thus, the more rivalry among competitors, the less influence the PRC can exert.[13]

For the first time, UPS had to be concerned with a different type of competitor—one that could change rates and service standards for individual shippers and discriminate more finely than had UPS. Figure 3 suggests that up until about 1989 UPS used parcel post rates as an umbrella for its own published rates. However, around 1991, when the Postal Service introduced significant bulk discounts, UPS's published rates began to climb relative to Postal Service rates. One might infer that UPS began pricing irrationally. Not only was the Postal Service offering discounts, but Roadway Package Systems had begun undercutting UPS for delivery of packages to commercial recipients (as opposed to deliveries to residences).The UPS rates graphed in figure 3 are published rates. However, UPS now offers discounts to individual shippers. Thus, UPS can, and probably does, engage in a much finer degree of discrimination, based on cost of providing service, than is apparent from the two published rates displayed in figure 3.

The fact that UPS did not publicly acknowledge a cost difference between shippers to residences and shippers to businesses prior to the entry of Roadway suggests that UPS may have engaged in cross-subsidization as an entry-deterring policy. That is, by publishing a single rate and refusing to negotiate with shippers, UPS could conceal from potential competitors the existence of highly profitable niches. However, Roadway found a niche and began skimming cream from UPS.

BSPS is an example of innovation inspired by competitive pressure and based on market information. Having lost over the years most of its market share to UPS, in offering a new low-cost parcel service, the Postal Service was looking toward regaining market share using the same discriminating strategy followed by Road-

13 A corollary to this conclusion is that if private rivals continued to take their pricing cues from the PRC, the small parcel delivery market would remain cartelized. However, it is well known that as the number of rivals increases, the incentives for one to cheat on its fellows (a prisoners' dilemma problem) also increases.

way and UPS.

With respect to BSPS, the issue of cross-subsidy arose. Would BSPS be subsidized by protected services? The PRC essentially avoided this issue by structuring BSPS as a set of discounts in parcel post based on mailer worksharing. By recommending discounts smaller than the cost savings associated with worksharing, the PRC could be certain it was not creating new cross-subsidies.

On February 1, 1994, the Governors of the Postal Service rejected the BSPS discounts recommended by the PRC. Even if the Governors had accepted the PRC's recommendation, however, the issue of allowing the Postal Service to discriminate between high-cost and low-cost shippers would remain for future resolution. The introduction of BSPS looked like a way for the Postal Service to begin to take back market share from UPS. Diversion of pieces from the Postal Service's existing parcel post to the new BSPS, however, would most likely have required the Postal Service to raise other parcel post rates. In addition, diverted pieces would most likely have the highest price-to-cost ratios, so their diversion into lower-priced BSPS would probably lower the overall average price-to-cost ratio for parcel post. This would have made the existing implicit cross-subsidy explicit, without curing it. BSPS rates would have been above cost, but rates for remaining parcel post would not.

The issue of high-cost low-cost discrimination would have been much easier to resolve if the recommended discounts had been adopted so that actual cost data for the purported low-cost shippers could have been collected. However, accurate cost data provide only half of the information needed to estimate the effect of a separate BSPS service on overall postal finances. One still needs to estimate the amount of "cannibalization" of existing postal products that would occur and how much volume could be taken from UPS. Only if the "profit" on volume taken from UPS outweighed the net revenue sacrificed to cannibalization would it make financial sense for the Postal Service to explicitly acknowledge low-cost shippers in its rate schedules without raising rates for high-cost parcels.

But how much volume can be taken from UPS? If UPS behaves as a Stackelberg duopolist, as suggested above , then any estimate of volume to be taken from UPS by BSPS must recognize UPS's reaction function. However, the market research that supported the Postal Service's original BSPS request did not account for the possibility that UPS would make rate concessions to potential BSPS customers.

Conclusions

We have indicated in this paper that rational pricing decisions by the Postal Service require explicit recognition of the likely reaction of competitors to the Service's price changes. In a market such as the small parcel market, this means accounting for the behavior of a few large competitors. The naive approach to market research taken by the Postal Service in developing BSPS precluded any reliable estimate of the volume shifts that would have occurred had BSPS been implemented. Not only did the Service include in its market surveys respondents who knew that their responses could affect prices charged both by the Postal Service and UPS (thus building in an incentive for strategic behavior by respondents), but the Service never asked respondents for estimates of BSPS volumes conditioned on various possible UPS or Roadway prices.

Suppose the Postal Service had surveyed shippers in a way that discouraged strategic responses (a big if) and explicitly sought respondents' reactions to various UPS-USPS price pairs (or Roadway-UPS-USPS price triplets). Not only would it have been possible to estimate a meaningful demand curve for small parcel shipping service, but it might have been possible to predict the effect of Postal Service price changes on UPS (or Roadway) prices. The demonstration of such an effect would also have revealed the degree of indirect regulation imposed on UPS (and Roadway) by the Postal Rate Commission. A strong indirect regulation effect would in turn demonstrate the possible failure of BSPS to attract significant volumes from UPS (or Roadway). If (1) competitors' costs are at or below the Postal Service's BSPS costs and (2) BSPS rates are above BSPS costs, competitors could profitably match BSPS rates. In this situation, benefits to BSPS customers would come at the expense of high-cost parcel post shippers and competitors' shareholders. This is the result that would occur in the presence of vigorous competition, suggesting that rational regulation of one member of an oligopolistic industry can preserve a quasi-competitive outcome for the entire industry.

References

Friedman, James. 1983. *Oligopoly Theory*. New York: Cambridge University Press.

Postal Rate Commission. August 25, 1993. *Opinion and Recommended Decision*. Docket No. MC93-1.

Postal Rate Commission. December 23, 1992. *Parcel Post Rate Complaint*. Docket No. C93-2.

Postal Rate Commission. January 4, 1991. *Opinion and Recommended Decision*. Docket No. R90-1.

17

ALTERNATIVE SCENARIOS FOR THE REFORM OF POSTAL SERVICES: Optimal Pricing and Welfare[1]

Helmuth Cremer
Marc De Rycke
André Grimaud

1. Introduction

Over the next decade one can expect dramatic changes in the structure and organization of the postal sector in Europe. The European integration process has launched an ongoing discussion concerning the harmonization and reorganization of the national postal services. One of the key features of most of the proposed reforms is a call for more competition. While the national public mail services (NPS) will (most likely) continue to exist, the scope of their legal monopoly would be considerably reduced. Private firms would be allowed to compete in most of the markets for which the public firms are currently granted a monopoly.

Two particular reform scenarios have recently been suggested. In both cases, the national mail services would maintain some monopoly position over a so-called *reserved sector*. In the first scenario (scenario L) this reserved sector includes one or several *products*, in particular the "standard" letter. The monopoly then covers all services related to these products (from collection to distribution). All other products are open to competition. The second scenario (scenario D) defines the reserved sector by activity: the national postal service would retain its monopoly for the *distribution* of all types of mail. Collection, transportation and sorting are then open to competition. The national post services would be allowed to compete

---

1 The views expressed in this paper are those of the authors and do not necessarily reflect the views of La Poste. We would like to thank the participants at the *Conference on Postal and Delivery Services* (Stockholm, Sweden) and especially our discussant, John Panzar, for valuable comments and suggestions. Thanks also to Catherine Gallet, Marc Ivaldi, Regis Renault, Bruno Rosselini, Jacques Salais, Joëlle Toledano, and seminar participants at La Poste for their insightful remarks.

in these markets and they would have to provide their competitors with access to their distribution network.

Under both scenarios the national post service would face a universal service constraint: it may not, for instance, refuse to deliver a letter to a remote location. In addition, pricing has to be geographically uniform: consumers in remote locations with low population densities, for instance, pay the same prices as consumers in urban areas, even though they are more costly to serve. Roughly speaking, mail services would also be expected to break-even. More specifically the reserved sector is supposed to generate enough revenue for the firm to finance the potential deficit generated by the universal service constraint.

The paper uses a stylized model of a postal network to study the implications of each of the two scenarios. There are only two activities: distribution and a composite activity consisting of collection, transportation, and sorting. There are two products, the letter and another product, and two types of consumer: low-cost (e.g., urban) and high-cost (e.g., rural). Private entrants (if any) form a competitive fringe. They face no universal service obligation so that cream-skimming is possible.

First, we consider each of the two scenarios separately (Sections 3 and 4). The formal model provides a simple description of the market structure that obtains. It shows that the organization of the market crucially affects the feasible outcomes; in particular, it determines which pricing policies are feasible for the NPS. Each scenario imposes specific constraints on the NPS. Some of these constraints are of institutional nature, others are imposed by the market mechanism itself and reflect the behavior of consumers, as well as the impact of competition. This description is interesting in itself, as it allows us to understand the precise implications of each scenario. It is also a necessary ingredient for the study of optimal pricing policies, which constitutes a natural next step. We derive optimal Ramsey-Boiteux type prices in each setting. In the second scenario, this raises the issue of the optimal access price charged to competitors who use the postal network for the distribution of their products. In either case, competition (and cream-skimming) has a crucial impact. Depending on the relative weights given to the surplus of low-cost and high-cost consumers, different types of solution can arise. Under uniform pricing, optimality calls, in general, for cross-subsidies between activities and/or products.

Finally, we compare the solutions achieved under the alternative scenarios (Section 5). Even if one abstracts from increasing returns to scale in the distribution and from any form of economies of scope, it turns out that scenario D implies, in general, a higher level of welfare. This result is not due to increasing returns to scale in the distribution or to any form of economies of scope. It arises, in essence, because the restrictions imposed on the pricing policy appear to be more severe in scenario L. To see this, note that the scenario D grants in fact more instruments to the NPS (or its regulator). In addition to choosing its own prices, it can set the access fee and thus affect the competitors' prices. If the fee is set above the marginal cost of access, it also provides a source of revenue which can be used to finance the universal service. In scenario L, on the other hand, there is no counterpart to this instrument.

2. The Model

We consider a stylized model of a postal network. There are only two activities: distribution, on the one hand, and a composite activity consisting of collection, transportation, and sorting, on the other hand. There are two products which are indexed by $j = 1,2$. One can, for instance, think of good 1 as the standard letter and of good 2 as some other product (or a composite good). There are two types of consumers, of equal number, indexed by $h = r,u$. The cost of satisfying one unit of demand of either product is higher for r (e.g., rural) customers than for u (e.g., urban) customers.

Two types of firms are (potentially) active in the market:

- A national postal service (NPS), indexed by m, which is a welfare-maximizing public firm.
- Private firms, indexed by c, which form a competitive fringe.

Let q_{jh} be the consumption of good j by consumers of type h, while q^i_{jh} is quantity of good j supplied by firm i to type h customers. Throughout the paper, superscripts are used to refer to the value of a variable for a particular type of firm. Market clearing requires $q_{jh} = q^m_{jh} + q^c_{jh}$. Utility functions are given by

$$U_h = S_h(q_{1h}, q_{2h}) - p_{1h}q_{1h} - p_{2h}q_{2h}, \quad h = r,u, \tag{1}$$

where p_{jh} is the price of q_{jh}. Consumers patronize the cheapest firm, so that $p_{jh} = \min\,[p^m_{jh}; p^c_{jh}]$. For future reference, note that the first-order conditions for utility maximization imply

$$\frac{\partial S_h}{\partial q_{jh}} = p_{jh}\,. \tag{2}$$

To keep the expressions tractable, we make the additional simplifying assumption that S_h is additively separable so that $\partial^2 S_h/\partial q_{1h}\,\partial q_{2h} = 0$. As a consequence, a consumer's demand for good j depends only on p_j and is independent of the price of the other good.

All firms have the same cost structure:

- The per unit cost associated with activity 1 (collecting, sorting, and transportation) is consumer- and product-specific, but independent of quantity (linear technology). It is denoted by c_{jh}, with $c_{jr} > c_{ju}$.
- The per unit cost of distributing mail (activity 2) is denoted by k. For simplicity, it is assumed independent of j (consumer type), h (product), and quantity. Our results would not change if a consumer- or product-specific cost of distribution were introduced.[2]
- There is no fixed cost.[3]
- The product- and consumer-specific total per unit cost is thus given by $c_{jh} + k$.

The objective function of the NPS is

$$W = \alpha U_r + U_u, \quad \text{with } \alpha \geq 1. \tag{3}$$

In words, it maximizes a weighted sum of utilities.[4] If $\alpha = 1$, W is a simple utilitarian welfare function which, given quasi-linear preferences, is equivalent to total surplus. On the other hand, $\alpha > 1$ implies that a higher weight is put on the (high-cost) consumers of type r. The parameter α can be interpreted as reflecting the intensity of redistributional concerns between consumer types. If $\alpha = 1$, the NPS is concerned with efficiency only, and there is no justification to, say, subsidizing the high-cost consumers at the expense of low-cost consumers. With $\alpha > 1$, the objective also reflect equity considerations, and the pricing policy will be (in part) used as an instrument for redistribution. The NPS faces three constraints.

- Budget constraint, $\pi^m = 0$: prices must be set so that total revenues cover total costs.[5]
- Uniform pricing constraint, $p_{jr}^m = p_{ju}^m = p_j^m$: prices must be the same for all consumers.
- Universal service constraint: it must satisfy the demand of all types of consumers given p_j^m. In other words, it cannot refuse to serve high-cost consumers.[6]

Two different scenarios for the organization of the market will be considered

1. **Scenario L**: The NPS has the legal monopoly (reserved service) for good 1, while good 2 is open to competition. Note that the universal service constraint is imposed on the NPS for both goods and not just for the reserved service.

---

2 The cost differential between consumer types is already captured by activity 1. Introducing further asymmetries would complicate notation without affecting any of the results.

3 The introduction of a positive fixed cost into our setting is a straightforward exercise. It would make our model more realistic and consistent with the conclusion reached by a number of authors, that the postal sector is a natural monopoly (e.g., Estrin and de Meza (1991), Panzar (1991), and Merewitz and Zurpan (1993)). However, it would not affect any of our conclusions. To keep the model as simple as possible, we have therefore decided to neglect this aspect.

4 To concentrate on issues of pricing and competition, we assume away any agency problem between the NPS and its regulator. An adequate treatment of this problem would go beyond the scope of this paper. However, it constitutes a natural extension of our model which we shall investigate in the future.

5 Our results would not change if profits were only required to be non-negative $\pi^m \geq 0$). This would complicate the model because profits would have to be included in the objective function. Not surprisingly, however, it is then a straightforward exercise to show that the budget constraint is necessarily binding at the optimum.

6 The importance of institutional constraints (such as universal service and uniform pricing) has often been emphasized in the literature on postal service (see e.g., Crew and Kleindorfer (1992)). In particular it has been shown that such constraints exist in many countries (Albon 1991), in spite of significant differences in cost between consumer types (Comen et al. 1993).

2. **Scenario D**: The NPS retains the legal monopoly of the distribution network. The other activity is open to competition in which the NPS is allowed to participate.[7] The private competitors must use the NPS's network for the distribution of their mail. The NPS charges an access price of a_j (per unit of product), and it has to provide access to its network to anyone who is willing to pay the access charge.

3. Scenario L

This scenario allows us to study the implications of the reform propositions contained in the *Green Paper on the Development of the Single Market for Postal Services*. In this document, the Commission of the European Communities advocates the limitation of the public operators' reserved sectors to a small number of products.[8] In addition, it recommends average cost pricing.

We shall show that the optimal tarification rule may indeed call for average cost pricing. However, this result arises only if the objective function of the NPS weights the two types of consumers equally. Note that the uniform pricing constraint then implies that the NPS is not able to attract the low-cost consumers in the competitive sector. This market segment will be served by private firms at marginal cost. Hence, consumers of type r end up paying a high price for good 2 in spite of (and in a sense because of) the uniform pricing constraint which is imposed on the NPS.

On the other hand, if the objective function puts a high weight on consumers of type r (large value of α) it will find it optimal to match the price of the private firms in the competitive sector. It then incurs substantial losses on good 2 which have to be compensated by a high price in the monopoly sector. Hence, there are cross-subsidies from the reserved sector towards the competitive sector.

Finally, for intermediate values of α, the NPS sells good 2 at a price which is below the cost of type r consumers (but not as low as the marginal cost of type u consumers). In this case, there is again a need for cross-subsidies between goods but of course to a lesser extend than when it matches the private firm's price. Our formal model provides a more precise description of the different outcomes.

Let us start the formal analysis by determining the equilibrium prices and profits of the private firms. Good 1 being reserved to the NPS, the private firm can only be active in the market for good 2. Perfect competition in the fringe together with the linearity of technologies imply that equilibrium profits are zero ($\pi^c = 0$) and that prices are given by

$$p_{2h}^c = c_{2h} + k, \quad h = r,u. \tag{4}$$

7 The universal service constraint implies that it is in fact required to participate.

8 Commission of the European Communities (1992). See also Cotton and Betteridge (1993) for a discussion of the Green Paper's recommendations.

Expression (4) says that prices in the competitive fringe equal marginal cost. Since costs differ between consumer types, prices will also differ, and one has of course $p_{2r}^c > p_{2u}^c$. Note that no uniform pricing or universal service constraint is imposed on private firms.

The NPS, on the other hand, is allowed to be active on the two markets. Its pricing policy consists in setting p_1^m and p_2^m: prices are restricted to be uniform across consumer types, but they may of course differ between goods. We assume that the NPS is not allowed to set its price of good 2 so low that private firms could no longer be active in either market segment. Formally, if $p_2^m < p_{2u}^c$ the NPS would undercut the private firms in both segments of the market, and we thus impose $p_2^m \geq p_{2u}^c$ as a constraint in the NPS' pricing problem.

Furthermore, we can assume without loss of generality that p_2^m not (strictly) exceed $c_{2r} + k$, that is the marginal cost of serving a high cost consumers. It can be readily verified that $p_2^m > c_{2r} + k = p_{2r}^c$ is, in terms of social welfare, equivalent to $p_2^m = c_{2r} + k$. In the first case, all consumers buy from the private firms. In the second case, consumers of type r are indifferent between the patronizing the NPS or a private firm. Hence, in both situations, consumers pay the same price, and the NPS realizes zero profits in the market for good 2.[9]

The optimal pricing problem of the NPS can now be stated as follows:

Problem 1

$$\max_{p_1^m, p_2^m} \alpha[S_r(q_{1r}, q_{2r}) - p_1^m q_{1r} - p_2^m q_{2r}] + S_u(q_{1u}, q_{2u}) - p_1^m q_{1u} - p_{2u}^c q_{2u} \tag{5a}$$

such that

$$(p_1^m - c_{1r} - k)q_{1r} + (p_2^m - c_{2r} - k)q_{2r} + (p_1^m - c_{1u} - k)q_{1u} = 0, \tag{5b}$$

$$p_2^m \geq p_{2u}^c. \tag{5c}$$

Condition (5b) is the budget constraint. Each of the terms measures the benefits (or losses) from serving a particular segment of the markets. No term is included for the demand of good 2 by consumers of type u, since the NPS necessarily realizes zero profits on this segment: demand is positive only if the price equals the cost.

The setup of this problem requires some additional comments. First, the objective function (5a) is written as if all the demand of good 2 by type u consumers is satisfied by the private firms. This is necessarily true if (5c) is not binding. On the other hand, if the constraint is binding, the NPS will have a positive market share, but since prices are the same for both types of firms, the specification of the

9 Either because its market share is zero, or because its price is just equal to the cost.

objective function remains valid. Similarly, the specification of the problem assumes that all r type consumers buy from the NPS. If $p_2^m = c_{2r} + k = p_{2r}^c$, some consumers patronize the private firms, but once again the objective function remains valid in that case.

Assume for the time being that (5c) is *not* binding at the optimal solution. Further, let λ_1 denote the Lagrangian expression corresponding to Problem 1, while λ is the multiplier associated with the budget constraint (5b). Differentiating λ_1 with respect to the decision variables and using (2) to simplify yields the following first-order conditions

$$\frac{\partial \lambda_1}{\partial p_1^m} = \alpha(-q_{1r}) - q_{1u} + \lambda\left[\frac{\partial q_{1r}}{\partial p_1^m}(p_1^m - c_{1r} - k) + \frac{\partial q_{1u}}{p_1^m}(p_1^m - c_{1u} - k) + q_{1r} + q_{ju}\right] = 0, \tag{6a}$$

$$\frac{\partial \lambda_1}{\partial p_2^m} = \alpha(-q_{2r}) + \lambda\left[\frac{\partial q_{2r}}{\partial p_2^m}(p_2^m - c_{2r} - k) + q_{2r}\right] = 0. \tag{6b}$$

The interpretation of these conditions is, in general, quite complicated, as a number of cases can arise. To reduce the number of cases to be considered, we will concentrate our formal analysis for the remainder of this section on a special case. We shall assume that consumers are identical in all aspects, except for their location. Formally, we thus assume $S_r(q_1, q_2) = S_u(q_1, q_2)$ for all (q_1, q_2). Since both types of consumer pay the same price for good 1, one then has $q_{1r} = q_{1u}$.[10] For this special, but quite meaningful case, clearcut results can be obtained. They provide a lot of insight, and they are the key to understanding the results for the more general cases which we shall briefly sketch below.

The following lemma is useful for the formal study of this case. It is obtained by rearranging (6a) and (6b).

Lemma 1. Assume $S_r(q_1, q_2) = S_u(q_1, q_2)$ for all (q_1, q_2). If (5c) is not binding, optimal prices satisfy the following conditions

$$\frac{p_1^m - \frac{c_{1r} + c_{1u}}{2} - k}{p_1^m} = \frac{\lambda - \frac{1+\alpha}{2}}{\lambda}\frac{1}{\varepsilon_1}, \tag{7a}$$

10 Recall that the demand for good 1 does not depend on the price of the other good.

$$\frac{p_2^m - c_{2r} - k}{p_2^m} = \frac{\lambda - \alpha}{\lambda} \frac{1}{\varepsilon_{2r}}, \tag{7b}$$

where ε_{jh} is the absolute value of the elasticity of q_{jh} with respect to p_{jh}, with $\varepsilon_1 = \varepsilon_{1r} = \varepsilon_{1u}$, the elasticity of demand for good 1 (which is the same for both types of consumers).

We are now in a position to study the properties of the optimal pricing policy. First, we can state the following proposition which is proved in Appendix A.

Proposition 1. If $S_r(q_1, q_2) = S_u(q_1, q_2)$ for all (q_1, q_2), then the optimal prices satisfy

$$p_1^m \geq \frac{c_{1r} + c_{1u}}{2} + k, \tag{8a}$$

$$p_2^m \leq c_{2r} + k. \tag{8b}$$

Furthermore one has

(i) If $\alpha = 1$, conditions (8a) and (8b) hold with equality, so that prices for both goods equal their average cost.

(ii) If $\alpha > 1$, conditions (8a) and (8b) hold with strict inequality. Hence, the price for good 1 exceeds its average cost, while the price for good 2 is below its average cost.

It can be noted in passing that Proposition 1 is not based on any assumptions as to whether or not (5c) is binding. As is made clear in the proof, it applies to both cases.

The results in Proposition 1 show that if $\alpha > 1$ there is a subsidy from good 1 towards good 2. This is rather intuitive. The NPS supplies good 2 only to consumers of type r, who have a higher weight in its objective function, while good 1, is supplied to both types of consumers. What's more, the NPS has the legal monopoly for good 1, and the consumers of type u have no alternative to buying from the NPS. Hence, it is possible to "tax" them by charging a price which exceeds their cost. Subsidizing good 2 thus allows to favor those individuals who have a higher weight in the welfare function. On the other hand, if $\alpha = 1$ all individuals are weighted equally and there is no reason for performing redistribution through cross-subsidies.

Note that (7b) indicates that p_2^m tends to decrease as α increases. If $\alpha = 1$, p_2^m equals the cost of r type consumers and one automatically has $p_2^m > p_{2u}^c$ so that (5c) is not binding. If $\alpha > 1$, p_2^m is set below the cost of r type consumers but as long as

α is not too large (5c) remains non-binding so that prices are indeed given by (7a) and (7b). However, as α becomes sufficiently large, it cannot be ruled out that (5c) becomes binding. We shall now take a closer look at this case.

First, recall that Proposition 1 continues to apply so that the results discussed so far remain valid.[11] Second, one can observe that once p_2^m is set equal to p_{2u}^c the price for good 1 is determined by the budget constraint alone. There is no degree of freedom left, and, hence, there is no room for any further maximization here. This is in fact true even if our above symmetry assumption is dropped, that is even if preferences are allowed to differ between categories. Substituting $p_2^m = p_2^c = c_{2u} + k$ into the budget constraint establishes the following proposition:

Proposition 2. If (5c) is binding at the solution to Problem 1, the price for good 1 is given by

$$p_1^m = (c_{1r} + k)\frac{q_{1r}}{q_{1r} + q_{1u}} + (c_{1u} + k)\frac{q_{1u}}{q_{1r} + q_{1u}} + (c_{2r} - c_{2u})\frac{q_{2r}}{q_{1r} + q_{1u}}. \tag{9a}$$

If, in addition one has $S_r(q_1, q_2) = S_u(q_1, q_2)$ for all (q_1, q_2), then (9a) reduces to

$$p_1^m = \frac{c_{1r} + c_{1u}}{2} + k + (c_{2r} - c_{2u})\frac{q_{2r}}{q_{1r} + q_{1u}}. \tag{9b}$$

Intuitively, these expressions can be easily understood. In the market for good 2, the NPS now simply matches the price that private firms charge for consumers of type u. Recall that this price equals their marginal cost. Unlike the private firms, the NPS serves all consumers at this low price. Hence, each unit of good 2 sold to high cost consumers brings about a loss of $(c_{2r} - c_{2u})$. The total loss in market 2 is then equal to $(c_{2r} - c_{2u})q_{2r}$ and to balance the budget an equivalent surplus must be realized in the reserved market. The last term in expressions (9a) and (9b) corresponds to the per unit surcharge which has to be imposed on good 1 to cover the losses on good 2. The price is then determined by adding this surcharge to the average cost of good 1. If all types of consumers have the same demand, the average cost is a simple arithmetic mean of the cost levels in each group; see (9b). If demands are different, the group-specific costs have to be weighted by the respective levels of demand.

With the exception of Proposition 2, most of this section has concentrated on the case where consumers only differ in locations, but are otherwise identical. To conclude the analysis of this scenario, we shall now briefly comment on the general

11 Except, of course, that (7a) and (7b) no longer apply.

case, where consumers are not restricted to have identical preferences. A detailed presentation of the results that obtain in this case is only of limited interest. It is quite tiresome (since a large number of cases can arise) and not much additional insight can be gained. Therefore, we shall limit ourself to a brief sketch of the main results. First, it can be shown that all our results (and in particular Proposition 1) continue to hold as long as the different types of individuals consume the two goods in similar proportions. Specifically, a sufficient conditions for Proposition 1 to hold is that the *relative* consumption levels q_{1u}/q_{2u} and q_{1r}/q_{2r} are "not too different."[12] In fact, the only case where the results could be reverse is when q_{1r}/q_{2r} is much larger than q_{1u}/q_{2u}, that is when consumers of type r devote a much larger proportion of their (postal) budget to good 1 than consumers of type u. This is very intuitive. Proposition 1 shows that a subsidy from good 1 (for which the NPS serve all consumers) to good 2 (for which the NPS serves only r type consumers) may be an effective way to perform redistribution towards the consumers who have a high weight in its objective function. Now, if consumers of type r spend most of their budged on good 1, while consumers of type u mainly buy good 2, such an attempt to redistribute may of course turn out to be counterproductive.

4. Scenario D

Under this scenario, the NPS retains the legal monopoly of the distribution network. The other activity is open to competition (for both products). The private competitors must use the NPS's network for the distribution of the two types of mail. The determination of the optimal pricing policy now raises the question of what should be the access price charged to the private firms who use the distribution network of the NPS. Through the access fee, the NPS (or its regulator) can affect the competitors prices. In addition, a fee which is set above the marginal cost of access provides revenue to the NPS which contributes towards the financing of universal service.[13]

As in the previous scenario, the parameter α plays a crucial role in determining the type of solution that arises. If $\alpha = 1$ (all consumers are weighted equally), optimality calls for marginal cost pricing. There are no cross-subsidies of any kind (neither between products, nor between categories of consumers), and the access fee is set at marginal cost of distribution. The NPS charges a uniform but high price which equals the cost of r type consumers. There is cream-skimming: low cost consumers are served by private firms at their own marginal cost. This solution is first-best efficient.[14] However, it results in a situation where uniform pricing is in

12 Differences in *absolute* demand level, on the other hand are of no relevance.

13 The implications of imposing an access fee to competitors using the postal network has been studied by Panzar (1993) and Dobbs and Richards (1993). A general treatment of the problem of access pricing is provided by Laffont and Tirole (1993, ch. 5; and 1994).

fact an empty constraint. The NPS offers the same price to everyone, but a more attractive alternative is available to low-cost consumers.

A large value of α on the other hand will once again result in the NPS matching the competitors prices. However, the market price may now be above the cost of u type consumers, since the access fees can be used to increase the competitors prices. Interestingly, this solution involves cross-subsidies between groups (from u to r), but not necessarily between products.

Finally, an intermediate value of α also results in cross-subsidies between groups, though at a lower level. Consumers of type r pay a price which is below their cost, but which is higher than the price that u type consumers pay to private firms.

Our formal analysis starts once again with the determination of the private firms' equilibrium prices and profits. Perfect competition in the fringe, the linearity of technologies, and the fact that the per unit access fee is constant imply that equilibrium profits are zero ($\pi^c = 0$) and that prices are given by

$$p_{jh}^c = c_{jh} + a_j. \tag{10}$$

Expression (10) says that prices in the competitive fringe equal marginal cost, which includes the access price paid to the network operator.

We can now turn to the optimal pricing problem of the NPS. In addition to fixing its own uniform prices p_1^m and p_2^m, it sets the constant access prices for the two products, a_1 and a_2. Per equation (10), these access charges determine the prices of its competitors. To simplify notation, we shall use p_j^c's as decision variables (instead of a_j's), keeping in mind that access prices are then determined by (10), so that $a_j = p_{jh}^c - c_{jh}$.

Consider the demand of consumer h in the market for good j. Since the consumers buy from the cheapest firm, the following three cases can arise:

i. $p_j^m > p_{jh}^c$: the price of the NPS is larger than the price that competitors charge for consumers of type h. Accordingly, they do not demand the NPS's product, and one has $q_{jh}^c = q_{jh}$ and $q_{jh}^m = 0$.

ii. $p_j^m = p_{jh}^c$: Consumers are now indifferent between the two firms so that both m and c can have a positive market share. Formally one has: $q_{jh}^m + q_{jh}^c = q_{jh}$ with $q_{jh}^m \geq 0$ and $q_{jh}^c \geq 0$.

iii. $p_j^m < p_{jh}^c$: now the NPS satisfies the entire demand in the considered market

---

14 This is in contrast to the results obtained under scenario L, where the solution is *never* first-best efficient.

segment, so that $q^c_{jh} = 0$ and $q^m_{jh} = q_{jh}$.

Without loss of generality, we can set up the pricing problem by assuming that cases (i) or (ii) prevail for type u consumers while case (iii) prevails for type r. It can easily be seen that the remaining combinations of cases are either impossible or equivalent to one of the considered combinations. In addition, notations are simplified if one assumes that in case (ii) all consumers (of type u) buy from the private firms, so that $q^m_{ju} = 0$. This is of no relevance for the results: consumers are indifferent between the two types of firms and neither firms profits are affected by the allocation of consumers between m and c. To see that the NPS's profits are unaffected, note that $p^m_j = p^c_{jh}$ together with (10) imply

$$p^m_j - c_{ju} - k = a_j - k. \tag{11}$$

Hence, the NPS's per unit profits if it serves a consumer (LHS of (11)) are the same as the net access fee it collects if the consumer is served by the competitor (RHS of (11)). Finally, note that since case (iii) prevails for type r, p^c_{jr} needs not to be explicitly introduced. As no confusion can arise, we shall drop the second subscript and use p^c_j instead of p^c_{ju}, however, keeping in mind that this price applies only to consumers of type u.

We are now in a position to formally state the problem of the NPS:

Problem 2

$$\max_{p^m_1, p^m_2, p^c_1, p^c_2} \alpha[S_r(q_{1r}, q_{2r}) - p^m_1 q_{1r} - p^m_2 q_{2r}] + S_u(q_{1u}, q_{2u}) - p^c_1 q_{1u} - p^c_2 q_{2u} \tag{12a}$$

such that

$$(p^m_1 - c_{1r} - k)q_{1r} + (p^m_2 - c_{2r} - k)q_{2r} + (p^c_1 - c_{1u} - k)q_{1u} + (p^c_2 - c_{2u} - k)q_{2u} = 0, \tag{12b}$$

$$p^m_j \geq p^c_j \quad j = 1{,}2. \tag{12c}$$

Condition (12b) is the budget constraint of the NPS. The first two terms measure the direct profits (or losses) from sales to its own consumers, while the remaining terms correspond to the total access charges collected from the competitors (see equation (11)). The objective function (12a) is a valid specification of (3) only if cases (i) or (ii) do prevail for type u. Conditions (12c) ensure that this is indeed true.

Let Λ denote the Lagrangian expression corresponding to Problem 2, while λ and γ_j are the multipliers associated with constraints (12b) and (12c) respectively. Differentiating Λ with respect to the decision variable and using (2) to simplify yields the following first-order conditions

$$\frac{\partial \Lambda}{\partial p_j^m} = \alpha(-q_{jr}) + \lambda\left[\frac{\partial q_{jr}}{\partial p_j^m}(p_j^m - c_{jr} - k) + q_{jr}\right] + \gamma_j = 0 \quad j = 1,2, \tag{13a}$$

$$\frac{\partial \lambda}{\partial p_j^c} = -q_{ju} + \lambda\left[\frac{\partial q_{ju}}{\partial p_j^c}(p_j^c - c_{ju} - k) + q_{ju}\right] - \gamma_j = 0 \quad j = 1,2. \tag{13b}$$

It can be readily verified that $\lambda > 0$. On the other hand, γ_j's may be positive or zero, depending on which case prevails at the optimum. Specifically, $\gamma_j = 0$ implies $p_j^m > p_j^c$ so that case (i) arises for good j, while $\gamma_j > 0$ implies case (ii).

We are now in a position to characterize the solution to Problem 2. We first assume that $\alpha = 1$ (utilitarian welfare function), which is an interesting benchmark case, and then study the solution for $\alpha > 1$.

4.1. Utilitarian Welfare Function

The following proposition is easily established by substituting $\alpha = 1$ into the first-order conditions (13a)-(13b) and then solving while making use of (12b) and (10).

Proposition 3. If $\alpha = 1$ one has

(i) The solution to Problem 2 (for $j = 1,2$) is given by: $p_j^m = c_{jr} + k$ and $p_j^c = c_{ju} + k$, so that $a_j = k$.

(ii) The corresponding values for the Lagrange multipliers are $\lambda = 1$ and $\gamma_j = 0$.

This result is very intuitive. If $\alpha = 1$, all consumers receive the same weight, and there is no concern for redistribution. The optimum (first-best outcome) is then achieved through marginal cost pricing, provided that this is a feasible solution. In our setting, marginal cost pricing is indeed feasible though in a somewhat indirect way. The NPC charges a price which equals the marginal cost of r type consumers. While this price is offered to all consumers, only the high-cost consumers will patronize the NPS. The private firms offer consumers of type u a price which equals their own marginal cost (but do not accept to serve high-cost consumers at that price). The access price is set equal to the marginal cost of access, k, to ensure that the marginal cost of a private firm reflect the true (social) marginal cost.

Interestingly, it thus turns out that in this case cream-skimming by private firms is in fact socially optimal, as it allows to achieve marginal cost pricing for all consumers, in spite of the fact that the NPS faces a uniform pricing constraint.

4.2. Welfare Functions With Unequal Weights

Different types of solution can now arise depending on whether or not the constraints (12c) are binding. We will concentrate on symmetric outcomes for which one has either $\gamma_1 = \gamma_2 = 0$ or $\gamma_1 > 0$ and $\gamma_2 > 0$. Our analysis could easily be extended to the asymmetric cases, but not much additional insight would be gained from such an exercise.

The previous section has shown that $\alpha = 1$ results in $\gamma_j = 0$. By continuity, one can expect this to be also the case if $\alpha > 1$, but not too large. One can conjecture that the redistributional concern implies some subsidization of *r* type customers at the expense of type *u* consumers, with the former paying a price below (their type specific) marginal cost while the latter are charged above marginal cost. However, if α is small, the redistributional concern will not be strong enough to make an equalization of prices optimal. On the other hand, if α is sufficiently large, redistributional concern may call for an equalization of prices.[15]

We now turn to the formal analysis of these cases.

4.2.1. Case 1: $\gamma_1 = \gamma_2 = 0$

Using the first-order conditions (13a)-(13b) and expressions (12b) and (10), one can easily establish the following proposition.

Proposition 4. Assume $\alpha > 1$. If the solution to Problem 2 implies $\gamma_1 = \gamma_2 = 0$, we have:

(i) Optimal prices satisfy the following conditions for $j = 1,2$

$$\frac{p_j^m - c_{jr} - k}{p_j^m} = \frac{\lambda - \alpha}{\lambda} \frac{1}{\varepsilon_{jr}}, \tag{14a}$$

$$\frac{p_j^c - c_{ju} - k}{p_j^c} = \frac{\lambda - 1}{\lambda} \frac{1}{\varepsilon_{ju}}, \tag{14b}$$

where ε_{jh} is the absolute value of the elasticity of q_{jh} with respect to p_{jh}.

(ii) The multiplier of the budget constraint satisfies $\alpha > \lambda > 1$.

(iii) The access price is given by

15 If α is very large, it might even be desirable to charge higher prices to type *u* than to type *r*. However, such a situation is not feasible in our setting: *u* type consumers have always the option to patronize the NPS and thus pay the same price as the *r* type individuals.

$$a_j = k + \frac{\lambda - 1}{\lambda} \frac{p_j^c}{\varepsilon_{ju}} > k. \tag{15}$$

Proposition 4 confirms our conjecture. With $\alpha > 1$, there is subsidization between consumer types: r consumers pay a price that is lower than their cost, while u consumers pay more than their cost. The price subsidy to r consumers is financed by setting the access price above the marginal cost of access (see (15)). Hence, the access price is, in fact, used to levy a tax on consumers of type u; the proceeds of this tax are then used to subsidize the high-cost consumers.

4.2.2. Case 2: $\gamma_1 > 0$ *and* $\gamma_2 > 0$

The solution described in the previous section is only meaningful if it implies $p_j^m > p_j^c$. Expression (14a) indicates that p_j^m tends to decrease as α increases: The more weight the welfare function puts on the utility of type r, the higher the subsidy to these consumers. Now, if α is large enough, (14a) and (14b) result in $p_j^m < p_j^c$: Redistributive consideration are so important that it becomes optimal for the high-cost consumers to pay a lower price than the low-cost consumers. However, within our setting, such an outcome is *not* feasible: $p_j^m < p_j^c$ will simply imply that consumers of type u buy from the NPS.[16] The best *feasible* policy is then to equalize prices between consumer types. Formally, this implies that constraints (12c) are binding so that $\gamma_j > 0$.

This, in essence, reduces the degrees of freedom available in the maximization problem. If there were only one product, the solution could be derived from the budget constraint alone: Prices would have to be set at average cost (over all consumer types). With two products, as in our setting, there continues to be one degree of freedom: The NPS can use cross-subsidies between goods. The pricing problem is then similar to a standard optimal commodity taxation problem with heterogenous individual (Diamond (1975), Mirrlees (1975); see Atkinson and Stiglitz (1981, ch. 12) for a survey).

The following lemma is useful for the formal study of this case. It is obtained by combining (13a) and (13b) and by defining $p_j = p_j^m = p_j^c$.

Lemma 2. Assume $\alpha > 1$. If the solution to Problem 2 implies $\gamma_j > 0$, $j = 1,2$, optimal prices satisfy the following condition:

16 Recall that the NPS faces a universal service constraint. Hence, it cannot refuse to serve these consumers.

$$\frac{\frac{\partial q_{jr}}{p_j}(p_j - c_{jr} - k) + \frac{\partial q_{ju}}{\partial p_j}(p_j - c_{ju} - k)}{2\bar{q}_j} = -\left[1 - \frac{1}{2\lambda}\left(\frac{\alpha q_{jr}}{\bar{q}_j} + \frac{q_{ju}}{\bar{q}_j}\right)\right], \qquad (16)$$

where $\bar{q}_j = (q_{jr} + q_{ju})/2)$ is the average consumption of good j.

To understand the intuition behind this expression, it is helpful to first consider a special case. Let us thus assume for the time being that consumers are identical in all respects except for location. Formally, we then have $S_r(q_1, q_2) = S_u(q_1, q_2)$ for all (q_1, q_2). With $p_j = p_j^m = p_j^c$ one then has $q_{jr} = q_{ju} = \bar{q}_j$ so that the LHS of (16) is independent of j. Using the budget constraint (12b), one then shows the following proposition:

Proposition 5. Assume $\alpha > 1$ and $S_r(q_1, q_2) = S_u(q_1, q_2)$ for all (q_1, q_2). If the solution to Problem 2 implies $\gamma_j > 0$, $j = 1,2$, it is optimal to set prices at average cost (per product):

$$p_j^m = p_j^c = p_j = \frac{c_{jr} + c_{ju}}{2} + k. \qquad (17)$$

The corresponding access price is given by

$$a_j = \frac{c_{jr} - c_{ju}}{2} + k. \qquad (18)$$

Intuitively, these results can be understood as follows. If consumers have identical preferences, their consumption patterns are similar. Hence, the two goods are consumed in the same proportion by all consumers, and it is clear that a cross-subsidy between good cannot achieve any redistribution (beyond that already achieved by equalizing prices for each good between consumers). Cross-subsidies would be a useful tool for redistribution only if say good 1 would be consumed in higher proportion by consumers of type r. In that case, a subsidy from good 2 toward good 1 would benefit consumers of type r and, hence, achieve some redistribution.[17] The optimal price structure is then determined by balancing the redistributional benefits against the efficiency losses brought about by such distortions. If proportions are

17 This result can be formally derived from expression (16). If goods are consumed in different proportions by consumer types, the LHS of this expression depends on j. Specifically, if consumers r buy good 1 in higher proportions one will have

$$(\alpha q_{1r}/\bar{q}_1 + q_{1u}/\bar{q}_1) > (\alpha q_{2r}/\bar{q}_2 + q_{2u}/\bar{q}_2).$$

Using (16), it can be shown that this implies (under some additional conditions) that the price of good 1 should be below its average cost.

equal, no such redistributional benefits are possible, and the optimum simply calls for average cost pricing (no cross subsidies).

5. Scenario L versus Scenario D

So far, the two scenarios have been studied separately. For each of them, the *feasible* pricing policies have been characterized first. Then, *optimal* scenario-specific pricing rules have been derived. To conclude, we shall now compare the two scenarios. Specifically, we want to determine which form of market organization results in a higher level of welfare.

Based on the results obtained in the previous sections, an intuitive answer to this question can easily be provided. While each setting involves its specific constraints, the restrictions imposed on the pricing policy certainly appear to be more severe in the scenario L. To see this, note that the scenario D grants in fact more instruments to the NPS. In addition to choosing its own prices, it can set the access fee and thus affect the competitors prices. Since private firms specialize in low-cost consumers, the access fee is, in fact, equivalent to a (commodity) tax imposed on these consumers.[18] Its proceeds can be used to subsidize the high-cost consumers (which have a high weight in the welfare function). In scenario L, on the other hand, there is no counterpart to this instrument. The NPS has no leverage on the competitors prices, and redistribution (if called for) can be performed through its own pricing policy only.

This line of argument suggests that one can expect scenario D to perform better, at least in a large number of cases. At closer scrutiny, it becomes clear though that this informal argument is not sufficient to draw a definitive conclusion. Under scenario D, the NPS faces competition in both markets, while it can freely set its price for one of the goods in the alternative setting. One may thus wonder if the additional instrument (the access fee) is sufficient to make up for this additional handicap. The following proposition provides an answer to this question.

Proposition 6. The set of feasible outcomes under scenario L is a strict subset of the set of feasible outcomes under scenario D. Hence, any allocation that can be achieved under scenario L can also be achieved under scenario D. In addition, there exist allocations which are feasible under scenario D but are not feasible under scenario L.

The formal proof is given in the appendix. It is simple but rather tiresome. Intuitively, it can most easily be understood from the following sketch: We consider a pricing policy which is feasible under scenario L and show that the corresponding allocation is also feasible under scenario D. The equivalent pricing

18 On this interpretation see Laffont and Tirole (1993), who show (in a different setting) that access can have the same impact as a commodity tax.

policy under scenario D is constructed as follows.

- The NPS continues to set the same prices one both products.
- It sets an access price for good 1 of $a_1 = p^{m_1} - c_{1u}$ which results in $p^{c_1} = p^{m_1}$. Hence, consumer of type u are indifferent between all firms, and the NPS realizes the same per unit profit whether it sells the good directly or whether the good is sold by the competitor (so that it receives the access fee).
- The access price for good 2 is set to k so that consumers u continue to buy good 2 at marginal cost.

Overall, we then find that all consumers pay the same prices under D as under L, and that the NPS realizes the same revenue. It may loose some of its costumers u for good 1, but the access charge that is then collected exactly makes up for the loss in revenue. Note that to replicate an L-scenario allocation under scenario D, it is in general necessary to set access prices which differ between goods. The proposition thus rests on the assumption that such a differentiation in access prices is technically feasible. Clearly, the degree of realism of this assumption depends on the technologies which are employed, on the nature of the products, and on the exact stage at which access occurs.[19]

We are now in a position to compare the levels of welfare achieved under the alternative scenarios. It follows immediately from Proposition 6 that the level of welfare under scenario D is at least as high as the level of welfare under scenario L.[20] To determine if it is *strictly* greater, it is then sufficient to check whether or not the optimal prices under D are also feasible under L. Considering the optimal pricing policies under D for the various cases which are stated in Propositions 3-5, it is readily verified that neither of these policies would be feasible under L. First, recall that under scenario L one necessarily has $p_{2u}^c = c_{2u} + k$ (see Problem 1): Consumers of type u pay their own marginal cost for the good which is open to competition. This condition is violated by the prices given in Propositions 4 and 5. It is satisfied, by the solution presented in Proposition 3 (case of $\alpha = 1$). However, in that case, one also has non-uniform (marginal-cost) pricing for good 1 which is not feasible under scenario L.

We can thus conclude that in all the considered cases, scenario D *strictly* dominates scenario L. This conclusion arises because the NPS (or its regulator) has a broader range of instruments under scenario D. Recall that it is obtained in a setting which abstracts from increasing returns to scale in the distribution. It is quite clear though that including such a (more realistic) cost structure into our model could only strengthen this conclusion.

---

19 We thank John Panzar for bringing this point to our attention. In other network industries (such as telecommunications), it is often argued that differential access fees are difficult to implement on technical grounds. However, this appears to be less of a problem in postal services.

20 Provided of course that the prices are set optimally.

A final qualification is related to the issue of differential access fees. It can be readily verified that if access fees are restricted to be uniform, the strict dominance of scenario D can no longer be established without imposing further restrictions on demands and/or technologies. Nevertheless it can be shown that scenario D continues to be superior for a large class of specification and, in particular, for all the symmetric cases considered in the previous sections.

Appendix

A. Proof of Proposition

If $\alpha = 1$, it is readily verified that the prices given in (8a) and (8b) together with $\lambda = 1$ are the unique solution to the system of equations formed by (7a), (7b), and (5b). In addition, this solution necessarily satisfies constraint (5c).

On the other hand, $\alpha > 1$ implies $(1 + \alpha)/2 < \alpha$ so that

$$\frac{\lambda - (1+\alpha)/2}{\lambda} > \frac{\lambda - \alpha}{\lambda}. \tag{A1}$$

In addition, the budget constraint implies that the left-hand-sides of (7a) and (7b) must be either both zero or of opposite sign. The same must then be true for the right-hand-sides of these expression. This together with (A1) implies

$$\frac{\lambda - (1+\alpha)/2}{\lambda} > 0 > \frac{\lambda - \alpha}{\lambda},$$

so that $\alpha > \lambda > (1 + \alpha)/2$. This establishes part (ii) for the case where (5c) is not binding. On the other hand, if (5c) is binding, one has $p_2^m = p_{2u}^c = c_{2u} + k$ so that (8a), (8b), and (ii) follow immediately.

B. Proof of Proposition 6

Formally, we proceed by comparing the set of feasible outcomes under scenario L to the set of feasible outcomes under scenario D. In both cases, an allocation is completely characterized by a vector of (type specific) prices: $(p_{1u}, p_{2u}, p_{1r}, p_{2r})$. These prices (unambiguously) determine quantities and, hence, welfare.

Let E_L and E_D be the set of feasible outcomes under scenario L and scenario D respectively. Formally, we define

- E_L as the set of price vectors $(p_{1u}, p_{2u}, p_{1r}, p_{2r})$ such that $p_{1u} = p_{1r} = p_1^m$, $p_{2u} = p_{2u}^c = c_{2u} + k$ and $p_{2r} = p_2^m$, where (p_1^m, p_2^m) satisfies the constraints (5b) and (5c) which are imposed in Problem 1.
- E_D as the set of price vectors $(p_{1u}, p_{2u}, p_{1r}, p_{2r})$ such that $p_{1u} = p_1^c$, $p_{2u} = p_2^c$, $p_{1r} = p_1^m$, and $p_{2r} = p_2^m$, where $(p_1^m, p_2^m, p_1^c, p_2^c)$ satisfies the constraints (12b) and (12c) which are imposed in Problem 2.

Consider $(\bar{p}_{1u}, \bar{p}_{2u}, \bar{p}_{1r}, \bar{p}_{2r}) \in E_L$, that is a price vector which is feasible under scenario L. Using the definition of E_L we can write this vector as $(\bar{p}_1^m, \bar{p}_{2u}^c, \bar{p}_1^m, \bar{p}_2^m)$, with $(\bar{p}_1^m, \bar{p}_2^m)$ satisfying (5b) and (5c). Then define $\tilde{p}_1^c = \bar{p}_1^m$, $\tilde{p}_2^c = \bar{p}_{2u}$, $\tilde{p}_1^m = \bar{p}_1^m$, and $\tilde{p}_2^m = \bar{p}_2^m$. Recalling that $(\bar{p}_1^m, \bar{p}_2^m)$, satisfies (5b) and making use of the fact that $\tilde{p}_2^c - c_{2u} - k = 0$, it immediately follows that $(\tilde{p}_1^c, \tilde{p}_2^c, \tilde{p}_1^m, \tilde{p}_2^m)$ satisfies (12b). In addition, (5c) together with $\tilde{p}_1^m = \bar{p}_1^m = \tilde{p}_1^c$ imply that $(\tilde{p}_1^c, \tilde{p}_2^c, \tilde{p}_1^m, \tilde{p}_2^m)$ also satisfies (12c), so that it satisfies all the constraints imposed in Problem 2. Hence, it follows from the definition of E_D that $(\bar{p}_{1u}, \bar{p}_{2u}, \bar{p}_{1r}, \bar{p}_{2r}) \in E_D$ so that the considered price vector is also feasible under scenario L.

To complete the proof it remains to be shown that the inclusion is strict. This is straightforward, since any vector in E_D which is such that $p_{1u} \neq p_{2u}$ cannot belong to E_L; see the definition of E_L.

References

Albon, R. 1991. "Postal Rate-making Procedures and Outcomes in Various Countries." In *Competition and Innovation in Postal Services,* edited by Michael A. Crew and Paul R. Kleindorfer. Boston: Kluwer Academic Publishers.

Atkinson, A.B., and J.E. Stiglitz. 1980. *Lectures on Public Economics.* New York: McGraw-Hill.

Comen, R.H., W.W. Ferguson and S.S. Xenakis. 1993. "Rural Delivery and the Universal Service: A Quantitative Investigation." In *Regulation and the Nature Of Postal and Delivery Services,* edited by Michael A. Crew and Paul R. Kleindorfer. Boston: Kluwer Academic Publishers.

Commission of the European Communities. 1992. "Green Paper on the Development of the Single Market for Postal Services." Publication Office of the EC, Luxembourg.

Cotton-Betteridge, J.A. 1993. "The Regulation of International Mail Services." In *Regulation and the Nature of Postal and Delivery Services,* edited by Michael A. Crew and Paul R. Kleindorfer. Boston: Kluwer Academic Publishers.

Crew, Michael A. and Paul R. Kleindorfer. 1992. *The Economics of Postal Services.* Boston: Kluwer Academic Publishers.

Diamond, P.A. 1975. "A Many-person Ramsey Tax Rule." *Journal of Public Economics* 4:335-342.

Dobbs, I.M., and P. Richards. 1993. "Policy Implications of Postal Network Access." In *Regulation and the Nature of Postal and Delivery Services,* edited by Michael A. Crew and Paul R. Kleindorfer. Boston: Kluwer Academic Publishers.

Estrin, S. and D. de Mezza 1991. "Delivering Letters: Should it be Decriminalized?" In *Competition and Innovation in Postal Services,* edited by Michael A. Crew and Paul R. Kleindorfer. Boston: Kluwer Academic Publishers.

Laffont, J.J. and J. Tirole. 1993. *A Theory of Incentives in Procurement and Regulation.* Cambridge, MA: MIT Press.

Laffont, J.J. and J. Tirole 1994. "Access Pricing and Competition." mimeo, IDEI, University of Toulouse.

Merewitz L., and M.A. Zupan. 1993. "Franchise Bidding, Contracting Out, and Worksharing in the Production of Postal Services: Can they Collect, Sort and Deliver." In *Regulation and the Nature of Postal and Delivery Services,* edited by Michael A. Crew and Paul R. Kleindorfer. Boston: Kluwer Academic Publishers.

Mirrlees, J.A. 1975. "Optimal Commodity Taxation in a Two-Class Economy." *Journal of Public Economics* 4:27-33.

Panzar, John C. 1991. Is Postal Service a Natural Monopoly?" In *Regulation and the Nature of Postal and Delivery Services,* edited by Michael A. Crew and Paul R. Kleindorfer. Boston: Kluwer Academic Publishers.

Panzar, John C., 1993. "Competition, Efficiency, and the Vertical Structure of Postal Services," In *Competition and Innovation in Postal Services,* edited by Michael A. Crew and Paul R. Kleindorfer. Boston: Kluwer Academic Publishers.

Sherman, R. 1991. "Competition in Postal Service," In *Competition and Innovation in Postal Services,* edited by Michael A. Crew and Paul R. Kleindorfer. Boston: Kluwer Academic Publishers.

18

AGGREGATE LETTER TRAFFIC DEMAND IN THE UNITED KINGDOM AND THE ECONOMY[1]

John Nankervis
Frank Rodriguez

1. Background and Content

The prospect of a dramatic fall in letter traffic levels has been a constant theme in the discussion of the mail market for several years. The development of electronic data interchange, fax, and a host of other electronically based means of communication have been seen as posing a fundamental and, ultimately, decisive threat to communication by letter. So far, however, the trend in letter volumes has remained upwards. As table 1 shows, average annual growth rates in domestic postal traffic through the 1980s were quite rapid in most developed countries. The highest rates of increase were found in France, the United Kingdom and the United States at over 4% per annum, and in none of these major economies did total volumes come close to remaining static, let alone showing signs of decline.

A number of characteristics of letter traffic are worth highlighting and are reviewed extensively, for example, in the European Commission's Green Paper (Commission of the European Communities 1992). The first of these is that mail levels per capita or per household tend to be highest in countries where economic activity per unit (measured by Gross Domestic Product) is highest. Secondly, the mix of traffic is changing over time and, also, as mail levels themselves vary across countries. The growth of direct mail is a clear example. Thirdly, mail originates primarily from the business sector, but it is destined largely for private individuals and households.

Knowledge about past movement in letter volumes and its use in producing projections for the future is relevant on a number of counts. In particular, it informs

1 The work reported in this paper has been undertaken for the U.K. Post Office and has benefitted from comments by colleagues within the organisation. The views expressed within the paper are those of the authors and are not necessarily held by the Post Office as a whole.

Table 1. Domestic Letter Post Traffic, 1980 to 1991

	Items in Billions 1991	Average Annual Growth Rate % 1980 to 1991
Australia	3.7	3.7
France	21.2	4.8
Italy	7.5	2.7
Japan	23.4	3.8
Netherlands*	5.5	3.1
Spain**	5.0	1.7
United Kingdom	15.4	4.5
United States	163.7	4.1
West Germany	16.1	1.8

*1989 and average 1980 to 1989

**1990 and average 1980 to 1990

Sources: Eurostat. 1993. *Communication Services Annual Statistics 1980 to 1991* (European Countries)

Union Postale Universelle. 1980 and 1991. *Statistique des Services Postaux* (Non European and Missing 1991 data)

Note: The definition of traffic used is the UPU's "Total 'Letter Post' Traffic" (Domestic Service) (Poste aux Lettres - Service Intérieur) and includes Letter Items, Postcards, Printed Matter and Small Packets.

plans on capacity and manpower levels and impacts on future profitability through higher volumes releasing the beneficial effects of economies of scale and scope in postal networks. At the same time, trend extrapolation is clearly not sufficient in itself to provide complete projections of letter traffic. The mail market is open not only to the influence of technological change but also to growing competition in an increasingly liberalised environment which together imply that previous relationships "explaining" letter volumes may not hold. Indeed, these may change radically. Nevertheless, attempts to model traffic levels from historical data can provide relevant information on some of the key drivers of volume change and act as a benchmark against which to assess the impact of such developments or apply judgement about their possible future influence.

There are two general approaches to statistical exercises of this type. The first, a bottom-up or micro approach, works at the level of disaggregated mail streams which may be defined either by product or by customer/market. Evidence given by the United States Postal Service at its periodic rate cases provides an example of product based analysis (USPS 1990), while marketing divisions within postal administrations generally may build up an overall picture of mail volumes, in part, by assessing expected demand from top customers. The second, a top-down or macro approach, tries to relate total letter traffic (or at most traffic in two or three streams) to a small set of economy or society-wide factors (Cuthbertson and Richards 1990), perhaps in a subsequent stage attempting to allocate this total to a number of key streams.

Both approaches have advantages and disadvantages and may be more or less appropriate depending on the objective in hand. They are complements rather than substitutes in analysing traffic. This paper follows a macro approach to the modelling of United Kingdom inland or domestic letter traffic and, indeed, is concerned only with the *total* volume of mail. After a brief review of trends in United Kingdom inland letter traffic, the paper discusses a number of potential factors influencing total volumes and reports, in a non-technical manner, estimates for the impact of those that are most important. It concludes with a short discussion of the possible effect of the changing environment on these trends. An Appendix contains material which is more technical and statistical in content.

2. Trends in United Kingdom Inland Letter Traffic

Annual growth rates in total United Kingdom inland letter traffic are shown in figure 1 for the period 1976 to 1992. The definition of traffic corresponds to the UPU's total "Letter Post" traffic measure (domestic service) and includes letter items, postcards, printed matter, and small packets. From quarter to quarter, the annual growth rates are volatile, but the smoothed version of the time series identifies clearly two main cycles. These had troughs in 1980-81 and 1991-92 and peaks in 1978-79 and 1985-88. The period overall was one of substantial growth in letter traffic volumes, averaging about 3½% per annum, with the second half of the 1980s being a time of particularly high rates of increase. As noted by table 1, the total number of inland items of mail reached 15.4 billion during the financial year 1991-92 as a whole. Within each year there is a strong seasonal pattern in quarterly traffic levels. The data used in the modelling exclude December figures when mail volumes rise sharply due to increases in social mail flows at Christmas. Even excluding this effect, however, the October-November period and the January

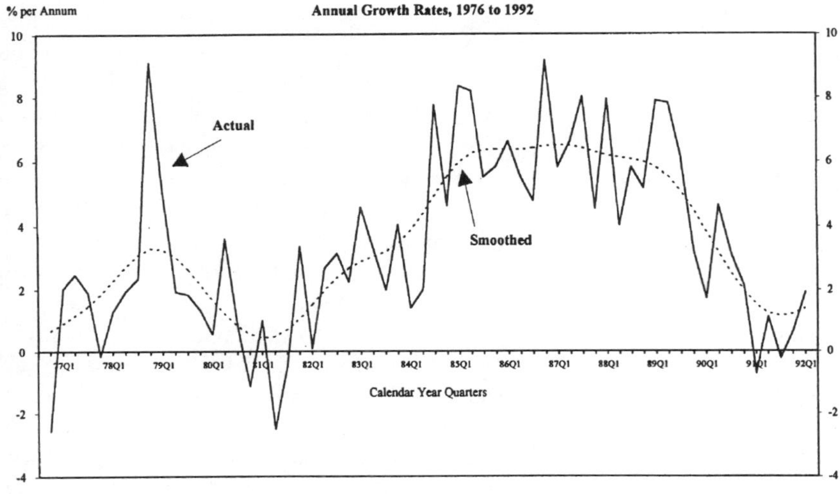

Figure 1. United Kingdom Total Inland Letter Traffic

to March quarter have higher traffic volumes than the rest of the year and, in particular, the Summer quarter (July to September).

The Green Paper, using data from the late 1980s, noted that about three quarters of United Kingdom letter traffic originates in the business sector, and the figure is similar today. At the same time, about two in three items are sent to private households. These figures have changed only modestly over time. There are two principal inland public services in the United Kingdom First Class, which is targeted for arrival the following day (day B), and Second Class (day D). Over time, the shares of these services have fluctuated from about 30 : 70, 1st Class : 2nd Class in the mid-1970s to 50:50 by the late 1980s and, more recently, the ratio has fallen back. These figures include in the 2nd Class group most of the non-public tariff mail, which has grown in importance during the period.

3. Factors Affecting Total Letter Demand in the United Kingdom

The macro approach used in the modelling of total United Kingdom inland letter traffic volumes stems from two commonplace observations:

- The preponderance of letter traffic *originates* from business, but it is *destined* largely for private individuals and households.
- Communication by paper has a range of substitutes which compete on a number of criteria, not least price.

These observations suggest a number of likely factors impacting on traffic volumes, in particular, some overall measures of business activity such as Gross Domestic Product or a derivative of this, demographic change, and the relative price of mail to telecommunications services.

The results from the modelling show a statistically significant role for each of these factors and the rest of the paper concentrates on them. Before moving on to these, however, two general points are worth noting. First, various other variables were included for analysis but found not to be of importance on United Kingdom data over the period 1976 to 1992 as a whole. These included letter prices relative to the general price level, business confidence indicators, and total numbers of businesses. Quality of service levels, which might be expected to have some impact, were not included due to an absence of adequate data over the estimation period as a whole. Secondly, there is no variable measuring internal activity to promote mail volumes, such as marketing or sales, again because of a lack of a suitable indicator. Strictly, therefore, the estimates below measure impacts of outside macro variables combined with Royal Mail activity.

The measure of overall economic activity used in the statistical analysis is *GDP(L)* or letter demand weighted GDP, first reported in Cuthbertson and Richards (1990). Different sectors of the economy generate different amounts of mail. In particular, in the United Kingdom proportionately much more traffic originates from business and financial services than that sector contributes to economy-wide value added. The converse is true for manufacturing and construction industries. The measure uses this information on the origins of letter traffic from businesses

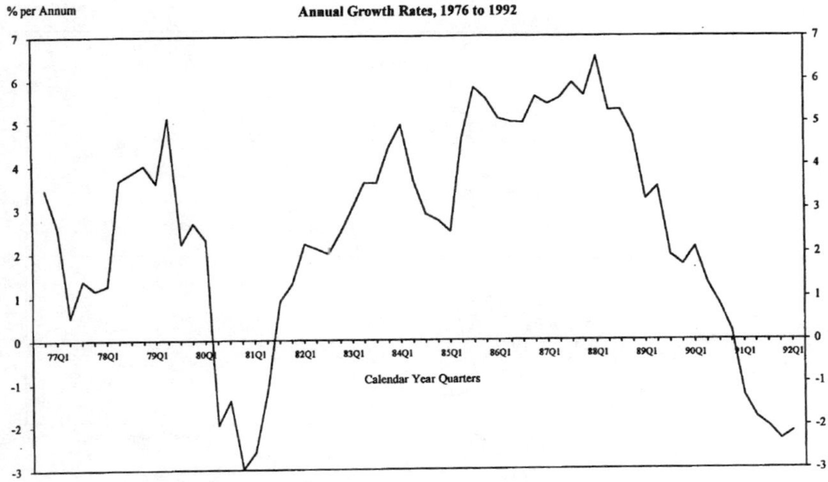

Figure 2. United Kingdom Gross Domestic Product (Letter Demand Weighted)

as a whole to weight together the output performance of each individual sector.

The *GDP(L)* measure incorporates the effect not only of the average rate of growth in the economy but also the impact from changes in industrial structure over time. If a particular sector has a higher propensity to generate mail and that sector grows more quickly than average then, because of that industry's higher weighting, *GDP(L)* increases more rapidly than GDP. By contrast, the reverse would hold if a sector grew more slowly than the average. This reweighting of different sectors to take account of their contribution to letter demand means that *GDP(L)* provides an estimate of the rate of growth of the United Kingdom economy viewed from the position of the overall mail market and taking into account the effect on the market of changes in industrial structure.

The growth of *GDP(L)* in the United Kingdom is shown in figure 2. For virtually the whole of this period and particularly during the 1980s, *GDP(L)* grew more rapidly than GDP. The most letter intensive sector in the United Kingdom is business and financial services. This was also the fastest growing industry during that period, buoyed by a number of factors including financial deregulation, the contracting out, or outsourcing, of service type activity from other sectors, and the selling of various financial products with high income elasticities of demand. Conversely, United Kingdom manufacturing output, in relative terms one of the least important sectors for letter demand, consistently grew at below the average of GDP except for a short-lived boom at the end of the 1980s. Note that the business cycle mapped by the *GDP(L)* series is similar to that for letter traffic with troughs in 1980-81 and 1991-92 and peaks in 1978-79 and the late 1980s. This point is emphasised in figure 3 which shows the levels of total United Kingdom inland letter traffic together with those for *GDP(L)* over this period, both indexed at 1985 = 100. *GDP(L)* grew more slowly than letter traffic, particularly from the mid-1980s

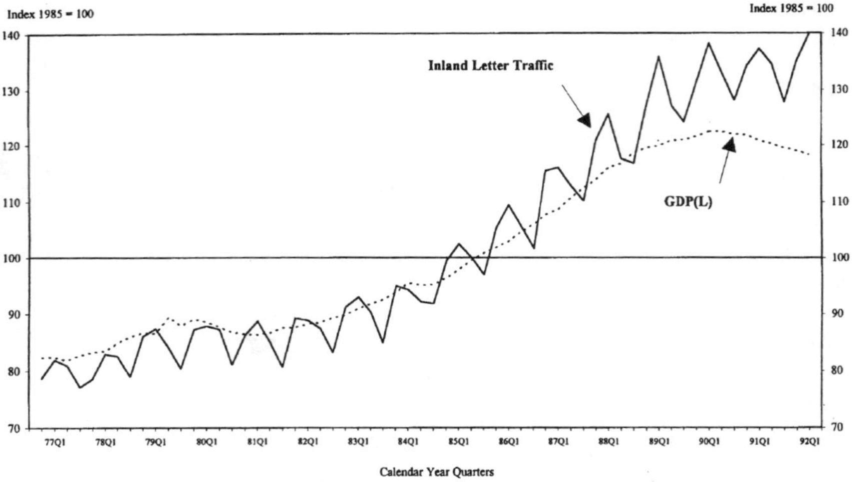

Figure 3. United Kingdom Inland Letter Traffic and GDP (Letter Demand Weighted)

onwards. The chart also highlights the seasonal pattern of letter traffic discussed earlier.

The demographic variable reported in figure 4 is the growth in the number of *households* which, for data reasons, were estimated and cover Great Britain only (United Kingdom excluding Northern Ireland and of the order of 2% to 3% of households). Throughout this period, average household size in the Great Britain/United Kingdom fell resulting in a stronger growth in household numbers than in total population. Many types of mail are directed at households as a unit rather

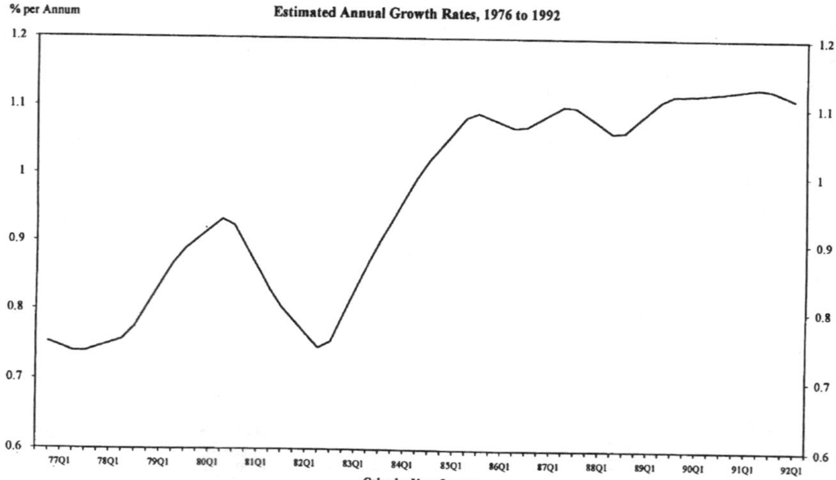

Figure 4. Great Britain Number of Households

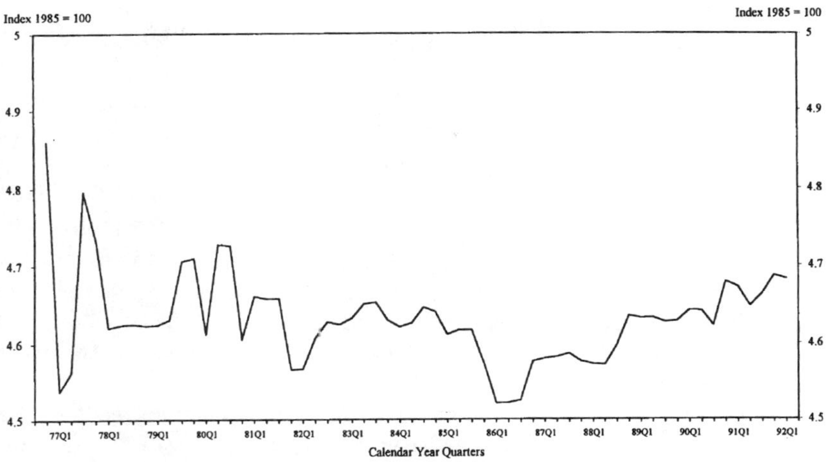

Figure 5. Ratio of United Kingdom Average Letter Price to Average Telephone Price

than individuals. The statistical analysis leading to the results reported later did not reject the hypothesis that the number of households provides the principal demographic link to letter traffic rather than an alternative demographic variable such as total population or adult population. A combination of falling household size and a changing pattern in the age distribution of the population led to a rise in the growth of household numbers in Great Britain during the 1980s, although only to a peak just above 1% per annum.

The third main variable in the econometric analysis is the ratio of average letter prices to average *telephone prices*, indexed at 1985 = 100, shown in figure 5. Ideally, this series would include a general price index to business users of electronic substitutes, most obviously telecommunications. No such series is available in the United Kingdom over the time period. Instead, the telephone price component of the main consumer price index in the United Kingdom (the Retail Prices Index) has been applied. This probably trends in a similar fashion to a series for business over the period, with the possible exception of the last few years when there was a rebalancing of tariffs in favour of the business customer and against private households. Letter prices actually fell relative to telephone prices through much of the period although almost of the significant changes occurred in the 1970s. More recently, however, telephone prices have dropped relative to those of letters.

4. Model and Estimates

The model, for which results are reported below, is of the following general form, where only those variables found to be statistically significant are included in the equation:

$$Q = f(Y, H, P),$$

where Q = Total volume of inland letter traffic;
Y = Letter demand weighted Gross Domestic Product *(GDP(L))*;
H = Total number of households; and
P = Ratio of average letter prices to average telephone prices.

In order to capture both short-term effects and long-term effects from these variables on total letter traffic, an error correction model was constructed. In its general form, the growth rate of total traffic is expressed as a function of the growth rate in *GDP(L)*, the growth rate in the number of households, the deviation of letter traffic from its long-run average or equilibrium relationship to these variables, particularly *GDP(L)*, and the relative price of mail to that of telephone services. Since quarterly data were used, the most general version of the model allowed for values of variables in up to four previous quarters to influence the current growth rate in total traffic.

Examination of the time series properties of the variables showed that there was evidence of a long-run relationship between total inland letter traffic, the number of households, and *GDP(L)*. The final model was derived through including this long-run relationship and deleting a set of insignificant variables, throughout ensuring that the model satisfied a set of diagnostic statistical tests. In this preferred model, the growth rate in total letter traffic *per household* in the current quarter is a function of the growth rate in *GDP(L)*, the relative price of mail to telecoms in the previous quarter, and the ratio of total inland letter traffic per household to *GDP(L)* in the same quarter of the previous year. The last term reflects the form of the long-run relationship in the final model. Alternative measures of demographic change were considered, but the number of households was found to be the most satisfactory. Technical details on the model, statistical results and data issues are contained in the Appendix.

A plot of the actual growth rate in total letter traffic per household and the fitted values given by the model is shown in figure 6. Note that the fitted model captures all the major cyclical movements in the observed series, clearly identifying both

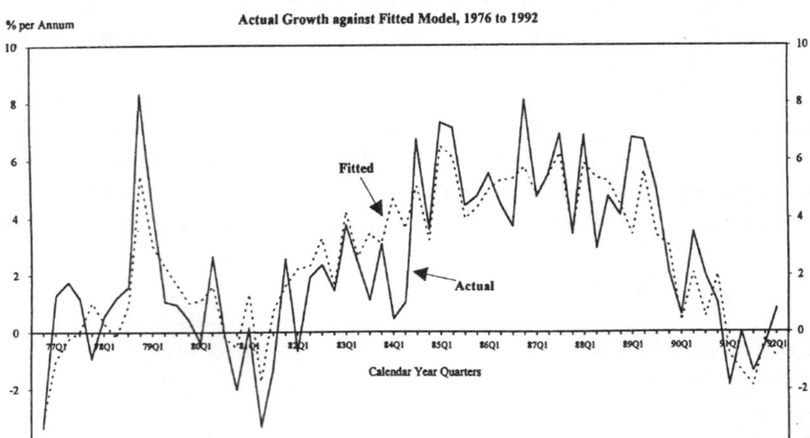

Figure 6. United Kingdom Total Inland Letter Traffic per Household

the boom of the second half of the 1980s and the downturns of the early 1980s and 1990s. The fit on individual quarters is poorer, as might be expected, given the very marked volatility in the annualised growth rate of letter traffic from quarter to quarter. However, there is no appreciable divergence between the two series for more than two to three quarters at any one time. Other work has been undertaken within the Post Office to improve the quality of short-term forecasting using Box-Jenkins and other similar modelling techniques.

The Appendix reports the coefficients of the preferred model together with various diagnostics on the properties of the statistical results. The most useful application of these results, however, is the set of elasticities these coefficients imply about the effects of changes in *GDP(L)*, household numbers and relative prices on total inland letter traffic levels during the estimation period. The penultimate specification of the model found that there was approximately a one-to-one relationship between percentage changes in *GDP(L)* and letter traffic per household over the long-run, and certainly one that was well within the statistical bounds for accepting a hypothesis of a unit elasticity between the two. This was then imposed at the final stage, and the main elasticities from this specification are reported in table 2. Averaged over the estimation period of 1976Q4 to 1992Q1, the unit long run elasticity between *GDP(L)* and inland traffic per household developed fairly quickly with most of the effect through within a year or so (elasticity of 0.86 by the end of year 1). Similarly, during this period, an 8% rise in average letter prices relative to telecoms prices is estimated to have been associated with a 1% fall in traffic volume per household over the long run, again with most of this effect through within a year.

Table 2. Impacts on United Kingdom Total Inland Letter Traffic Volumes per Household, 1976 to 1992

	Elasticities	
	GDP(L)	Average Letter Price Relative to Telecoms Price
a. Current quarter/next quarter	0.52	-.09
b. 1 Year	0.86	-.11
c. Long run	1.00	-.12

Note: The elasticities reported are averages estimated on quarterly data over the period 1976Q4 to 1992Q1. They show the average percentage effect on total traffic volumes per household of a 1% change in GDP(L) or of letter price relative to telecom price (by the end of the period identified in that row) during that period.

A unit long-run elasticity for *GDP(L)* with respect to total letter traffic per household implies that average growth each year in total United Kingdom inland traffic (ignoring lags) is given approximately by:

Total inland traffic growth =
GDP(L) growth + Household growth + Other impacts (e.g., from price, technological erosion, etc).

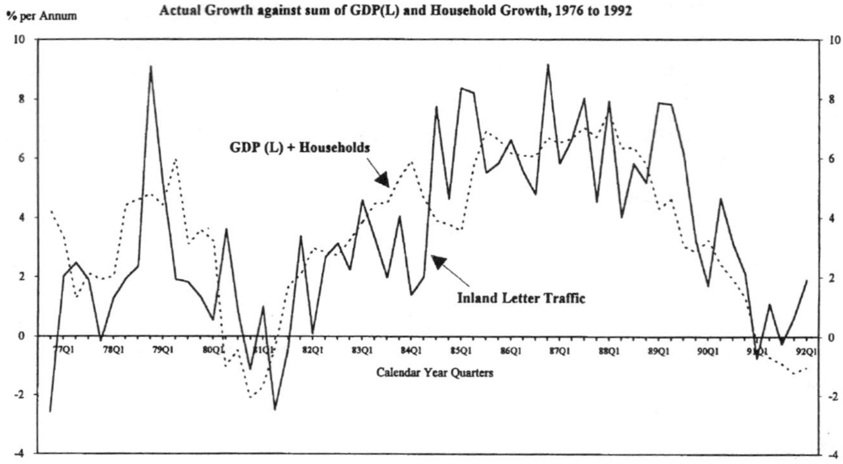

Figure 7. United Kingdom Total Inland Letter Traffic

Figure 7 shows total inland traffic growth against the sum of *GDP(L)* plus household growth only, omitting the final set of effects from prices and other factors. Quarter to quarter, the correspondence between the two is relatively poor. However, a smoothed version is shown in figure 8. The match at the start and finish is affected by the precise end points and the smoothing device chosen (here a weighted 15 - quarter moving average). After allowing for this, however, the similarity in the trends and cycles of the series between 1978 to 1990 is striking. Over time, long-run trends in letter traffic volumes in the United Kingdom have tracked the sum of economic growth (letter demand weighted) and demographic growth very closely.

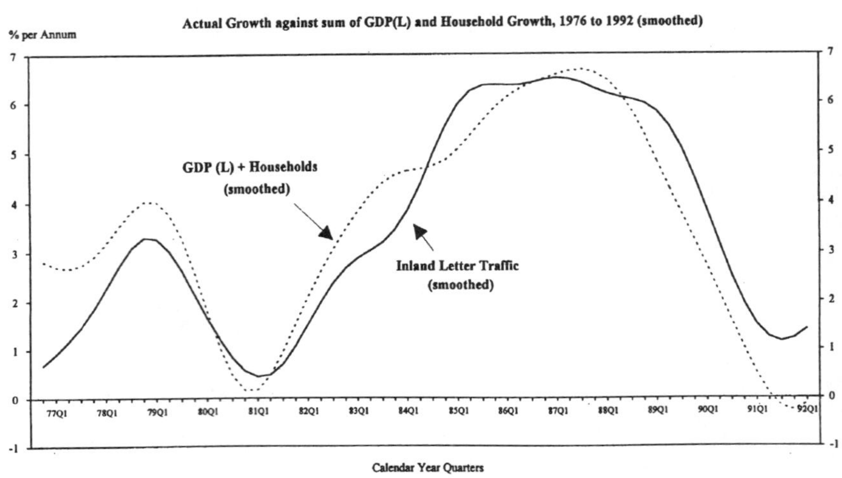

Figure 8. United Kingdom Total Inland Letter Traffic (Smoothed)

5. Total Letter Volumes in a Changing Environment

One of the main uses of statistical associations from the past is to benchmark future prospects. The question that arises is whether the simple rule of thumb for United Kingdom total letter volume growth from the last decade and half or so (that it equals approximately *GDP(L)* growth plus household growth) is likely to break down or will it instead continue to provide a useful guide to underlying trends in the years ahead. Information on this issue from the latter part of the modelling period is affected by the impact of the 1980s boom, but there is no indication that the *GDP(L)* elasticity was other than relatively stable into the start of the 1990s, while price effects may have become slightly weaker. There is little evidence here that technological erosion and the cheapening and greater availability of electronic substitutes had been impacting negatively on letter traffic levels at that time.

More significant changes, both in kind and scale, have occurred after the end of the modelling period (1992Q1). Electronic substitutes are becoming even cheaper and technological change continues to open up many new opportunities for alternatives to mail. The price leader in the United Kingdom on the price of telephone services is the regulated company, British Telecom. This is subject to a price cap of an "RPI-X" type where RPI is the Retail Prices Index and the X has been set at 7½% per annum through the current regulatory period. Unless there are much larger falls in United Kingdom real letter prices than have occurred historically, the rise in the ratio of average letter prices to telephone prices will be more rapid than in recent years. The price elasticity reported earlier may give some indication of the possible impact of this on traffic volumes although, if the scale of these changes does prove to be larger than over the last decade or so, then it may understate the size of this effect. Similarly, rising numbers of fax users, higher volumes of electronic mail and other developments in electronic communication both feed and are fed by lower usage costs, encouraging an increase in the absolute size of this elasticity, and add further to the potential for erosion of letter volumes. These developments suggest that, even if the United Kingdom were to grow rapidly again as in the late 1980s, total letter traffic growth would find it difficult to reach the historical benchmark of *GDP(L)* plus household growth.

Nevertheless, it may be premature to rule out any future growth in total United Kingdom mail volumes:

- Economic and demographic growth in the United Kingdom are likely to continue at a reasonable rate during the next few years, with the sum of *GDP(L)* and household growth perhaps centred in the range 3% to 4% per annum.
- Across countries, there is a strong association between GDP per household and the number of mail items per household, which, to some degree, is the international cross-sectional analogue to the time series position for an individual country such as the United Kingdom. United Kingdom mail levels are broadly at around the average of those in other countries on an equivalent basis, suggesting both scope and opportunity for mail levels to rise as GDP

grows.

- There is limited evidence to date that traffic levels have been falling below those consistent with past trends. There are measurement issues involved here including the lagged effects of the United Kingdom's economic recession and in estimating household numbers, where published data are poor and household formation may have been affected by the economic cycle.
- In terms of the origin and destination matrix of United Kingdom letter traffic, less than a third is in the "business to business" cell. This is the flow where most erosion is likely to occur although any impacts to date have not been enormous. More importantly, over two thirds of mail involves private households and for those the technology either to receive or send electronic substitutes (other than telephone messages) remains limited. That situation is likely to continue for some time.

The macro modelling approach followed in this paper has identified some links between total mail volumes and economic and demographic variables, including a simple rule of thumb for the long run association between them based on data from the period 1976 to 1992. It is often the case that the accuracy and relevance of statistically estimated relationships of the past tend to weaken the further into the future one projects them. Even so, it seems likely that economic and demographic factors will continue to exert an upward pull on the overall volume of mail at the same time as technological and relative price changes work in the opposite direction.

Technical Appendix. Model, Statistical Results and Data

A.1. Integration and Cointegration

As stated in section 4 of the paper, the models considered are of the form $Q = f(Y,H,P)$, where Q is total traffic, Y is $GDP(L)$, H is the number of households, and P is the ratio of average letter prices to average telephone prices. The models were estimated in terms of the logarithms of the variables which are denoted by lower case letters, e.g., $q_t = \log_e(Q_t)$. It can be seen from figure 3 (although it is not in logs) that q and y are trending series and h also has this property so that each series is non-stationary (the distribution of the series is changing over time, e.g., the mean or variance is not constant). Since the properties of estimators and test statistics in the models depend on the nature of this non-stationarity, the time series properties of the variables are considered first (see e.g., Banerjee, Dolado, Galbraith, and Hendry 1993)– the order of integration of the variables is tested for followed by a test for cointegration. All the following tests are calculated using data from 1976, quarter 4 to 1992, quarter 1.

The total traffic variable, q_t, although it excludes December figures, is highly seasonal and to test for integration, allowing for the possibility of seasonal integration, use was made of the so-called HEGY tests developed by Hylleberg, Engle, Granger, and Yoo (1990). The purpose of these tests was to determine whether the seasonal pattern remains sufficiently constant so that it can be modelled as a

Table A1. HEGY Tests for Seasonal Integration for q_t - The Logarithm of Total Traffic

π_1	π_2	π_3	π_4	$\pi_3 \cap \pi_4$
-1.56	-3.99[a]	-3.46[b]	-1.63	7.2[a]

Notes:

(1) For details of the test see Hylleberg et al (1990).

(2) [a] reject at the 5% level; [b] reject at the 10% level.

(3) The regression included an intercept, trend and seasonal dummies and was augmented with second, sixth and seventh order lags of $\Delta_4 q_t$ in order to obtain uncorrelated residuals.

(non-seasonal) integrated series with seasonal dummy variables or whether there is seasonal integration. The interpretation of these test statistics, which are reported in table A1, is somewhat complex, but the conclusion from them is that there is a non-seasonal unit root and that the seasonal dummy variables satisfactorily capture the seasonal movement in the series.

The other variables were also tested for integration using Dickey-Fuller tests for unit roots and the results are shown in table A2. The conclusion from these is that y_t and h_t are I(1) series where I(1) stands for integrated of order 1 (the first difference of the series is stationary). By contrast, p_t is an I(0) series (stationary).

Table A2. Dickey-Fuller (DF) and Augmented Dickey-Fuller (ADF) Tests for Unit Roots

	y_t	h_t	p_t
DF	-0.69	-1.79	-5.47[a]
ADF(1)	-0.96	-2.04	-5.57[a]
ADF(2)	-1.69	-1.37	-4.36[a]

Notes:

(1) For details of the test see Banerjee et al. (1993)

(2) For y_t and h_t the null hypothesis of a unit root is tested against trend-stationary alternatives and for p_t the alternative hypothesis is stationarity.

(3) [a] denotes that the calculated test statistic is less than the critical value and so the null hypothesis is rejected at the 5% level.

The tests above indicated that q, h and y are all I(1) variables. If any linear combination of the three I(1) variables is I(0), then the series are said to be cointegrated and the coefficients of this linear combination provide estimates of the long-run (equilibrium) relationship between the variables. Given that the variables are cointegrated, an error correction model can be formed which expresses the growth in total traffic as a function of the (short run) growth in income and households, the level of prices, and the deviations from the long-run (equilibrium) relationship. Only if all variables in the model are stationary is it possible to make reliable inferences from the coefficients and test statistics produced in the modelling process. Cointegration among the three I(1) variables was tested for using Johansen's procedure. From the results in table A3, the hypothesis that there is at most

Table A3. Johansen Maximum Eigenvalue Test Statistics

H_0: Maximum number of Cointegrating vectors	Test Statistic
0	26.00[a]
1	4.58
2	0.172

Notes:
(1) For details of the test see Banerjee et al. (1993)
(2) [a] denotes that null hypothesis is rejected at 5% level.
(3) Maximum lag in VAR = 2.

one cointegrating vector is not rejected (that is, one linear combination of the three I(1) variables is I(0)). Consequently, it is possible to build an error correction model that incorporates this cointegrating vector.

A.2. Estimates

Initially a model was considered which had up to 4 lags in each of the variables:

$$q_t = \alpha_0 + \sum_{i=1}^{3} \alpha_i s_{it} + \sum_{i=1}^{4} \beta_i q_{t-i} + \sum_{i=0}^{4} \gamma_i y_{t-i} + \sum_{i=0}^{4} \delta_i p_{t-i} + \sum_{i=0}^{4} \lambda_i h_{t-i} + \varepsilon_t$$

where s_{it}, $i = 1,2,3$ are quarterly seasonal dummy variables.

The model was estimated over the period 1976Q4 to 1990Q1 so that 8 observations were available for *ex ante* forecasts. By eliminating insignificant regressors, the models reported in table A4 were obtained. The dependent variable in each of the models is the annual growth rate in total traffic per household, i.e., $\Delta_4(q_t - h_t) = (q_t - h_t) - (q_{t-4} - h_{t-4})$. The final "preferred" model is Model II. The difference between Model I and Model II is that Model II has imposed upon it a long run unit income elasticity– the coefficients of $(q_{t-4} - h_{t-4})$ and y_{t-4} are set to be exactly opposite values. This restriction was easily accepted and allowed the model to be written in the following parsimonious error correction form:

$$\Delta_4(q_t - h_t) = \theta_1 \Delta_4 y_t + \theta_2(q_{t-4} - h_{t-4} - y_{t-4}) + \theta_3 p_{t-1} + \text{constant and seasonals.}$$

The cointegrating relationship is given by the term $(q_{t-4} - h_{t-4} - y_{t-4})$. The above model is described in words in the main paper and is Model II and Model III in table A4.

All the diagnostic tests reported in table A4 are satisfactory; on the basis of the calculated Lagrange multiplier test statistics, Z_1, we do not reject the null hypotheses of no autocorrelation against the alternatives of up to fourth order autocorrelation. Tests for up to fourth order autocorrelation were considered since quarterly data was used in our models. On the basis of the statistics Z_2, Z_3, and Z_4 we do not reject the null hypotheses of no misspecification, normally distributed errors and no predictive failure. Model III, the final "preferred" model, is Model II estimated

Table A4. Estimates and Test Statistics (Dependent Variable is $\Delta_4(q_t - h_t)$)

Variable	MODEL I		MODEL II		MODEL III	
Constant	-7.27	(-6.52)	-7.41	(-7.06)	-7.32	(-7.23)
s_1	0.012	(1.94)	0.013	(2.00)	0.014	(2.38)
s_2	-0.022	(-3.06)	-0.023	(-3.30)	-0.019	(-3.06)
s_3	-0.054	(-5.08)	-0.055	(-5.61)	-0.052	(-5.74)
$\Delta_4 y_t$	0.561	(5.02)	0.574	(5.39)	0.524	(6.07)
y_{t-4}	0.722	(6.55)				
$q_{t-4} - h_{t-4}$	-0.713	(-6.11)				
$q_{t-4} - h_{t-4} - y_{t-4}$			-0.731	(-6.81)	-0.713	(-6.98)
p_{t-1}	-0.087	(-2.04)	-0.091	(-2.43)	-0.086	(-2.42)
R^2	0.73		0.73		0.73	
Regression s.e.	0.0160		0.0159		0.0155	
DW	1.67		1.65		1.64	
	$Z_1(4,42) = 0.67$		$Z_1(4,43) = 0.65$		$Z_1(4,50) = 0.42$	
	$Z_2(1,45) = 1.82$		$Z_2(1,46) = 1.89$		$Z_2(1,54) = 2.06$	
	$Z_3(2) = 0.46$		$Z_3(2) = 0.65$		$Z_3(2) = 0.91$	
	$Z_4(8,46) = 0.50$		$Z_4(8,47) = 0.67$			
Estimation Period	1976/4 - 1990/1		1976/4 - 1990/1		1976/4 - 1992/1	

Notes:

(1) The values in parentheses after the estimates are *t* ratios.

(2) $Z_1(4,df)$ is a Lagrange multiplier test for fourth-order autocorrelation distributed approximately F(4,df) under the null hypothesis of no autocorrelation. $Z_2(1,df)$ is Ramsey's RESET test of functional form misspecification distributed approximately F(1,df) under the null of no misspecification. $Z_3(2)$ is a test for normality distributed approximately chi-squared (2) under the null of normal errors. $Z_4(p,df)$ is Chow's predictive failure test distributed approximately F(p,df) under the null of no predictive failure.

using all the observations. The model was also estimated recursively and plots reveal that the coefficients in Model III exhibited reasonable stability over the estimation period.

A.3. Data Issues

The data used in the modelling were collected from both internal sources (U.K. Post Office) and external sources (Government agencies). These are outlined below. Wherever possible, data were assembled which were not seasonally adjusted but this did not prove feasible for all variables. The data on letter traffic (Q_t) and price (P_t) are not seasonally adjusted; the households series (H_t) is interpolated from annual data while *GDP(L)* (Y_t) is seasonally adjusted. The issue of the use of mixed data is discussed below.

Q_t: Letter traffic data are total United Kingdom inland volumes on a traffic per working day basis (excluding December) from internal sources (U.K. Post Office).

Y_t: The *GDP(L)* series is calculated from seasonally adjusted national income accounts *GDP(O)* data weighted by each sector's contribution to letter demand. It would have been desirable to have used unadjusted data for the *GDP(L)* series but these are not released by the Central Statistical Office. The results of the HEGY tests reported in table A1 on total traffic imply that seasonality in that series is relatively stable and hence any distortion due to the use of mixed data is likely to be relatively minor.

H_t: Data on household numbers are published irregularly in the United Kingdom. The series used in the modelling was constructed on an annual basis using Office of Population Censuses and Surveys mid-year population estimates and a smoothed series on average household size from the General Household Survey. This series was then interpolated to obtain quarterly estimates.

P_t: The ratio of average letter prices to average telephone prices was constructed as follows. The average letter price is the volume weighted average of First and Second Class service basic weight step prices. As noted in the main paper, the average telephone price was taken from the component series of the Retail Prices Index, published by the Central Statistical Office.

References

Banerjee, A., J. Dolado, J.W. Galbraith, and D. Hendry. 1993. *Co-Integration, Error-Correction, and The Econometric Analysis of Non-Stationary Data.* Oxford University Press.

Commission of the European Communities. 1992. *Green Paper on the Development of the Single Market for Postal Services.*

Cuthbertson, K., and P. Richards. 1990. "An Econometric Study of the Demand for First and Second Class Inland Letter Services" *Review of Economics and Statistics* 72: 640 - 648.

Eurostat. 1993. *Communication Services Annual Statistics, 1980 to 1991.*

Hylleberg, S., C.W.J. Granger, R.F. Engle, and B.S. Yoo. 1990. "Seasonal Integration and Co-Integration." *Journal of Econometrics* 44: 215-238.

Union Postale Universelle. 1980 and 1991. *Statistique des Services Postaux.*

United States Postal Service. 1990. Docket No R90-1. USPS-T-2. *Direct Testimony of George S. Tolley.*